Koryŏsa

Koryŏsa

THE HISTORY OF KORYŎ, ANNALS OF THE KINGS, 918–1095

BOOK II

*Edited by Howard Kahm, John B. Duncan,
Park Jongki, Lee Joung Hoon,
and Edward J. Shultz*

University of Hawai'i Press
Honolulu

This translation was funded by the Academy of Korean Studies through the Korean Studies Promotion Program (AKS-2016-KCL-1230001). Publication of this translation was generously supported by a grant from the Asian Research Foundation.

© 2024 University of Hawaiʻi Press
All rights reserved
Printed in the United States of America

First printing, 2024

Library of Congress Cataloging-in-Publication Data

Names: Kahm, Howard, editor. | Duncan, John B., editor. | Yi, Chŏng-hun, editor. | Pak, Chong-gi, editor. | Shultz, Edward J., editor.
Title: Koryŏsa : the history of Koryŏ, annals of the kings, 918–1095 / edited by Howard Kahm, John B. Duncan, Park Jongki, Lee Joung Hoon, and Edward J. Shultz.
Other titles: Koryŏsa. Sega. Kwŏn che–1–10. English | History of Koryŏ, annals of the kings, 918–1095
Description: Honolulu : University of Hawaiʻi Press, [2024] | Includes index.
Identifiers: LCCN 2023045375 (print) | LCCN 2023045376 (ebook) | ISBN 9780824895211 (hardcover) | ISBN 9780824897154 (kindle edition) | ISBN 9780824897130 (pdf) | ISBN 9780824897147 (epub)
Subjects: LCSH: Korea—History—Koryŏ period, 935–1392.
Classification: LCC DS912.2 .K6797 2024 (print) | LCC DS912.2 (ebook) | DDC 951.9/01—dc23/eng/20231220
LC record available at https://lccn.loc.gov/2023045375
LC ebook record available at https://lccn.loc.gov/2023045376

University of Hawaiʻi Press books are printed on acid-free paper and meet the guidelines for permanence and durability of the Council on Library Resources.

Designed by Nord Compo

CONTENTS – BOOK II

KORYŎSA: THE HISTORY OF KORYŎ   1

   ANNALS OF THE KINGS
Vol. 6	Chŏngjong (1034–1046)	5
Vol. 7	Munjong (1046–1056)	66
Vol. 8	Munjong (1057–1071)	134
Vol. 9	Munjong (1072–1083)	200
	Sunjong (1083)	256
Vol. 10	Sŏnjong (1083–1094)	260
	Hŏnjong (1094–1095)	314

Appendix: Weights and Measures   325
Contributors   327
Index   331

Koryŏsa
THE HISTORY OF KORYŎ

ANNALS OF THE KINGS

(*Sega* 世家)

VOLUME 6

Compiled by Chŏng Inji, Chŏnghŏn grand master, minister of works, director of the Hall of Worthies, deputy director of the Royal Lectures Office and State Records Office, headmaster of the Royal Confucian Academy.

CHŎNGJONG

Chŏngjong 靖宗, reigned 1034–1046

Chŏngjong, the Great King of Expansive Filiality (*honghyo* 弘孝), Deep Peace (*anŭi* 安懿), Peaceful Provision (*kanghŏn* 康獻), and Holder of Benevolence (*yonghye* 容惠), was named Hyŏng 亨 at birth, and his adult name was Sinjo 申照. He was the younger brother of Tŏkchong and was born on *muin* (18th day)[1] in the seventh month of the ninth year of King Hyŏnjong's reign (1018). Intelligent and precocious as a child, he was given the titles of Director of the Imperial Secretariat and Lord of P'yŏngyang at the age of five.

On *kyemyo* (17th day) in the ninth month of the third year of King Tŏkchong's reign (1034), Chŏngjong acceded to the throne in Chunggwang Hall in accordance with the late king's regal will.

---

1. The actual date is uncertain. The Hyŏnjong annals report the birth as having taken place on *chŏngch'uk,* the 17th day.

Accession Year of Chŏngjong (1034)

Tenth Month, Winter

Chŏngsa (1st day). The king performed the rite for Distributing the Calendar (*kosak* 告朔)[2] at the Imperial Ancestral Shrine.

Kyŏngo (14th day). King Tŏkchong was laid to rest at Suk Tomb.

The king sent his royal aides to the Western Capital for two days to dispense food and drink at the Assembly of the Eight Prohibitions to be held there.

Eleventh Month

Kyŏngin (4th day). The king went to Sinbong Pavilion to receive the congratulations of central and local officials. He proclaimed a general amnesty.

Song merchants, eastern and western [Jurchen] tribesmen 西蕃, and the country of T'amna presented offerings of their native products.

Kyŏngja (14th day). The king held the Assembly of the Eight Prohibitions. He first went to Sinbong Pavilion and gave food and drink to his officials. In the evening, he went to Pŏbwang monastery. On the following day, the king again bestowed food and drink at the Grand Assembly[3] and watched a music performance. Congratulatory memorials were received from the officials of the Eastern Capital and the Western Capital, the military commissioner of the Eastern Frontier Circuit (*tongno pyŏngmasa* 東路兵馬使), the military commissioner of the Northern Frontier Circuit (*pungno pyŏngmasa* 北路兵馬使), the four regional military commands (*tohobu* 都護府), and the eight *moks*. The Song merchants, eastern and western [Jurchen] tribesmen, and envoys from the country of T'amna who had presented offerings of their native products were given seats to observe the ceremony. All of this became the custom thereafter.

---

2. In the twelfth month of every year, the emperor issued a calendar charting each month of the next year to the kings and feudal lords serving him. The calendar would then be given a place of honor in their ancestral shrines, and the first day of each subsequent month would be marked with the sacrifice of a live sheep and distribution of that month's calendar throughout the country.

3. This gathering was the culmination of the Assembly of the Eight Prohibitions.

Twelfth Month

Kisa (13th day). The king invested his younger brother Wang Sǒ with the titles of High Grand Preceptor (*su t'aesa* 守太師) and Director of the Imperial Secretariat, and his other younger brother Wang Ki with the title of High Grand Protector. He also appointed Hwang Churyang as director of the Rites Ministry and senior governmental advisor, Ch'oe Chean as director of the Civil Personnel Ministry, Yu Chisǒng 劉志誠 as director of the Public Works Ministry, Yi Chin 李珍 as director of the Revenue Ministry, Kwak Sin as director of the Palace Administration, Kim Yǒnggi as vice director of the Censorate, Kim Ch'ungch'an as left scholarly counselor-in-ordinary, and Yi Chakch'ung as right scholarly counselor-in-ordinary.

FIRST YEAR OF CHǑNGJONG (1035)

First Month, Spring

Pyǒngsul (1st day). The king canceled the New Year Congratulations.[4]
Imin (17th day). The king appointed Ch'oe Ch'ung as commissioner of the Palace Secretariat and director of the Ministry of Punishments.

Fifty-seven Eastern Jurchens, led by General Embracing Transformation Moira, were granted an audience with the court. The king gave them assorted goods in accordance with their rank and seniority.

Chǒngmi (22nd day). The king appointed Yu Ch'ang 庾昌 as executive of the Palace Administration, Yu Un as imperial diarist, Kim Chǒngjun 金廷俊 as palace censor, Chǒng Paegǒl as left reminder and drafter of imperial edicts and proclamations, Kim Hyǒn as right reminder and drafter of imperial edicts and proclamations, and P'ung Sunji 酆順之 as investigating censor.

---

4. The officials of the court usually offered New Year's greetings in a special ceremony on the first day of each year. In this situation, since King Tǒkchong had recently died, the decision was made to avoid an ostentatious display, in keeping with the Confucian tradition of mourning the dead for three years.

Sinhae (26th day). A prince was born in Yŏnhŭng Palace 延興宮. The king named him Hyŏng 詗.

Second Month

Kimyo (24th day). Twelve Western Jurchens, led by Chief Kaago 哥兒古, were granted an audience with the court.

Sinsa (26th day). Thirty-five Eastern Jurchens, led by General Supporting the State Kojimun, were granted an audience with the court.

Third Month

Ŭryu (1st day). The king appointed Yi Tan as vice director of the Chancellery with a concurrent assignment as Imperial Secretariat–Chancellery joint affairs manager, and Hwangbo Yuŭi as vice director of the Imperial Secretariat with a concurrent assignment as Imperial Secretariat–Chancellery joint affairs manager.

Pyŏngsul (2nd day). Kim Much'e 金無滯 and others passed the state examination.

Kyemyo (19th day). The king invested the lady of Yŏnhŭng Palace, Lady Han 韓 (d. 1036), with the title of Gracious Consort (*hyebi* 惠妃). On the following day, the king pardoned criminals sentenced to penal servitude or less.

Fourth Month, Summer

Kabin (1st day). The king himself hosted men and women of the state who were eighty or older at the Polo Field.

Chŏngsa (4th day). The Rites Ministry submitted a petition.

> Collecting firewood from the famed mountains of Kaegyŏng should be prohibited. Trees should be planted everywhere.

The king approved.

Fifth Month

Kapchin (21st day). The king prayed on the riverside for clear skies.

The Khitan commissioner of Naewŏn Fortress (*Naewŏnsŏngsa* 來遠城使) and acting right cavalier attendant-in-ordinary (*kŏmgyo u san'gi sangsi* 檢校右散騎常侍) An Sŏ 安署 sent an official dispatch to Hŭnghwa Garrison.

> It occurred to me that with Naewŏn Fortress's close proximity to Koryŏ, we have scrupulously given you information on anything worthy of notice. Your country is a tributary state, and it was the custom of our late emperor to warmly receive the envoys you sent year after year with tribute offerings. Yet there have been no tribute missions since the year we punished the rebels. With the traitors exterminated, tribute missions should have resumed. But instead of maintaining our traditional friendship, you built high stone walls to block the roads and erected wooded fences to hinder the passage of our troops. Do you not understand that no matter how rugged the terrain, there is always a way to conquer it?[5]
>
> Our emperor received his inheritance from his imperial ancestors and has so unified the states and domains in every direction under his rule that even the kings in the far south of China have paid their respects out of admiration for his righteousness. What's more, the monarchs in the lands to the west have also sent their sincere greetings in recognition of his virtue. Only the land across the Eastern Sea [Koryŏ] has not sent anyone to prostrate before the northern throne. If the emperor's thunderbolt of fury should suddenly flash, how safe and peaceful will your people be? Whether you disobey or not is up to you.

Sixth Month

Pyŏngjin (4th day). An earthquake occurred in Kaegyŏng.

Venus was visible during the day.

Kyehae (11th day). The king appointed the retired officials Hyŏng Yŏn'gi 邢研機 and Yi Chingjwa 李徵佐 as eminent right vice director of the State Affairs

---

5. The Khitan commissioner is alluding to the famous story of how King Hui 惠王 of Qin used five stone oxen to attack the state of Shu 蜀.

Department and vice director of the Military Affairs Ministry (*sangsŏ pyŏngbu sirang* 尚書兵部侍郎), respectively, to show that elders are respected.

Sinmi (19th day). Twenty-seven Eastern Jurchens, led by Oŏgo 烏於古, were granted an audience with the court.

This month, Yŏngdŏk Garrison sent an official response to the message from the Khitan-held Naewŏn Fortress.

> We have gratefully received your official message. It touched on many problems, which we should certainly address in detail, but let us save words and get to the main point immediately. You said that the ceremonial visits of our envoys to your imperial court had ceased since the time you punished the rebels and that our tribute offerings, after the traitors were eliminated, should have resumed. What we saw, however, was that the roads were blocked during the first stage of Tae Yŏllim's uprising and your subsequent mobilization of troops, so our envoys could not pass. But after that, the Imperial Secretariat drafter Kim Ka resumed our diplomatic missions to the Khitan Eastern Capital, and he was followed by the Revenue Ministry vice director Yi Suhwa, who went with a tribute offering of our native products. Upon the death of our former king, the commissioner of audience ceremonies Ch'ae Ch'unghyŏn 蔡忠顯 was sent by the new king to report his death. Then, when we heard of the late emperor's death, our State Affairs left office chief Yu Kyo 柳喬 rushed to attend the imperial funeral. When the reigning emperor ascended the throne, our supervising secretary Kim Haenggong went on horseback to offer congratulations. Ever since the subjugation of the Hŭngnyo kingdom, our envoys have continued their diplomatic missions, so how can you say, "There have been no tribute missions"? You also say, "You built high stone walls to block the roads and erected wooded fences to hinder the passage of our troops." But according to the lines in Fuxi's 伏羲 eight trigrams, constructing fortifications at rugged strategic locations is merely good practice. The state of Lu 魯 collapsed after removing the sentry posts along its borders, and this has served as a warning to the wise men of all ages. Thus, the construction of walls and barricades for defensive purposes has as its aim the protection of our borderland residents. It should not be construed as rebellion against imperial rule. So, even though you said that only the land across the Eastern Sea has not sent anyone to prostrate before the northern throne whereas six of

our tribute envoys have been detained while making their way to your imperial court, your army actually penetrated our frontier to build two fortresses, Sŏnhwa Garrison and Chŏngwŏn Garrison, and still holds them, forcing us to earnestly request their return.

Fortunately, at the start of a new epoch, our king has made restoration of imperial rule his touchstone for extending his grace in all directions and securing happiness for his people. At this hour, we wish to present a memorial to the throne to request the release of our traveling officials and the restoration of the land that is currently occupied by imperial troops. Before today, we could not see an open path to presenting such a request, and if our earnest wish is granted, we will not fail to resume our presentation of ceremonious greetings.

While we await his gracious command, we wonder how we can avoid further admonishments like your threat to the peace of our people "if the emperor's thunderbolt of fury should suddenly flash." We know that the reigning emperor extends his loving care to small nations and listens to the words of all the weak under Heaven, so we are confident that he will embrace this eastern land and grant his favor to it once again. Since we are faultless, why should he bear us any anger? Your letter of instructions can hardly be taken seriously.

Seventh Month, Autumn

Chŏnghae (6th day). The king appointed Kim Ch'ungch'an as director of military affairs, Yi Hoe as commissioner of state finance, Yi Yudo as palace censor, Kim Hyŏn as left reminder, Cho P'ae 趙覇 as right reminder, and Yi Konghyŏn 李公顯 and Ŭn Paek 殷伯 as investigating censors.

Kyesa (12th day). The Civil Personnel Ministry *sangsŏ ibu* 尚書吏部) submitted a petition.

> The former left vice director of state affairs Yi Kong committed a shameful crime, but since he has been pardoned on several occasions, we request that he be reinstated to his former office.

The king approved. However, Yi Kong was again dismissed soon after the Censorate deliberated on his crime.

Kabo (13th day). The king appointed Hwangbo Yŏng as commissioner of the Palace Secretariat and director of the Censorate. The king's birthday became the Day of Long Life (*changnyŏngjŏl* 長齡節).

Kyŏngsul (29th day). The king issued a decree.

> Since the mourning period for the late king has not yet ended, criminals sentenced to be beheaded should instead be flogged and exiled to an uninhabited island. Criminals sentenced to be strangled should be flogged and exiled to an inhabited island.

Eighth Month

Kyŏngsin (9th day). The king appointed Yi Chayŏn as supervising secretary and Kim Yŏnggi as an Imperial Secretariat drafter.

Kyehae (12th day). Venus was visible during the day.

Sinmi (20th day). An earthquake occurred in the capital and sounded like thunder.

Kapsul (23rd day). Forty-four Western Jurchens, led by Grand General Niubul, were granted an audience with the court.

Kyŏngjin (29th day). Fifty-two Eastern Jurchens, led by the Taewan Kaedahan 皆多漢, were granted an audience with the court.

Ninth Month

Muja (8th day). Twenty-three eastern [Jurchen] tribesmen, led by General Submitting to Virtue Oda 吳多, were granted an audience with the court.

Kyemyo (23th day). Earthquakes occurred in nineteen *chus*, including Kyŏngju.

This month, a long wall was constructed winding to the east of Songnyŏng 松嶺 in the Northwestern Circuit to defend the frontier against enemy attack.

Tenth Month, Winter

Sinyu (11th day). Six Eastern Jurchens with Ŏbullo 魚弗老 as their leader were granted an audience with the court.

Imsul (12th day). The king appointed Im Chonghan 林宗翰 as an investigating censor.

Pyŏngin (16th day). The Law and Regulation Council (*singmok togam* 式目都監) submitted a proposal.

> We should reclaim the official seals of state-sanctioned monks in ten *chus* and prefectures, including Hwangju.

Eleventh Month

Kyemi (13th day). Sixty-five Eastern Jurchens, led by Chief Arogan 阿盧幹, were granted an audience with the court.

Twelfth Month

Imja (2nd day). Thirty eastern [Jurchen] tribesmen, led by the Taewan Kodohwa 高陶化, were granted an audience with the court.

SECOND YEAR OF CHŎNGJONG (1036)

First Month, Spring

Kyŏngjin (1st day). The king canceled the New Year Congratulations.

Ŭryu (6th day). Eighty-three eastern [Jurchen] tribesmen, led by General Embracing Transformation Sara 沙羅, were granted an audience with the court.

Kabo (15th day). Those sentenced to penal servitude or less for public malfeasance and those sentenced to flogging or less for private malfeasance, as well as anyone who had to pay a fine, were all pardoned.

Second Month

Kyŏngsul (1st day). The Rites for the Earth Gods were performed.

Imja (3rd day). The king went to the main throne hall to hold court and bestow stipend certificates (*nokp'ae* 祿牌)[6] to the officials.

The king appointed Yu So as vice director of the Chancellery with a concurrent assignment as Imperial Secretariat–Chancellery joint affairs manager, Ch'oe Chean as left vice director of state affairs and commissioner of the Palace Secretariat, and Yi Chakch'ung as director of civil personnel and Hallim academician recipient of edicts.

The king issued a decree.

> Although Grand Marshal (*t'aewi* 太尉) Yi Ungbo retired from office as the left executive in the Department of Ministries due to old age, I dare not forget the meritorious services he rendered to the state. See that his descendants without official titles are given entry-level government posts.

Kabin (5th day). A leader of the eastern [Jurchen] tribesmen, Taesin 大信, and others came to the court with an offering of camels.

Kimi (10th day). A party of 135 eastern [Jurchen] tribesmen, led by General Comforting the Frontier Agol, were granted an audience with the court.

Kisa (20th day). Seventy-one eastern [Jurchen] tribesmen, led by General Kaero, came to the court with an offering of excellent horses.

Kyŏngo (21st day). The king appointed Yi Chujwa as right scholarly counselor-in-ordinary, Chin Hyŏnsŏk as director of the Imperial Regalia Court (*wiwikyŏng* 衛尉卿) and grand master of remonstrance, Wŏn T'aejin as imperial diarist, and Han Yŏnjo as general censor.

Sinmi (22nd day). Pirate ships belonging to eastern [Jurchen] tribesmen attacked the Tongjin guard post 桐津戍 in Samch'ŏk county, plundering the populace. The garrison commander set a trap for them in the grasses and weeds, waiting for the pirates to return. When they did, he launched

---

6. Wooden tokens indicating the amount of government salary (*nokbong* 祿俸) that officials received. *Nokbong* was a stipend paid semi-annually in rice.

a surprise attack to the clamor of beating drums and managed to capture or kill more than forty of them.

Imsin (23rd day). The king appointed Mun Samyŏng as vice director of the Censorate.

Third Month

Kyemi (4th day). The king appointed Hwangbo Yuŭi as vice director of the Chancellery with a concurrent assignment as Imperial Secretariat–Chancellery joint affairs manager, and Yu Chingp'il as commissioner of the Western Capital and senior governmental advisor.

Muja (9th day). The king went to Mount Samgak.

Kyehae (14th day). The king returned to the palace.

Musin (29th day). Eighty-two eastern [Jurchen] tribesmen, led by Chief Kwijŏng 貴正, came to the court with an offering of excellent horses.

Fourth Month, Summer

Imja (4th day). Since it was the start of summer (*ipha* 立夏),[7] ice was brought into the palace. The king issued a decree: "This year, the heat will not come early. Wait until the fifth month before bringing in ice." The relevant authorities submitted a petition.

> When the sun is in the Northern Lands[8] in the sky, ice is stored. When it is in the Western Lands,[9] it is taken out. A lamb is sacrificed, and the door

---

7. One of twenty-four divisions of the year in the East Asian solar calendar. As the first of the six subseasons of summer, *ipha* was the seventh of the twenty-four solar terms.

8. The Northern Lands, or Pugyuk 北陸, refers to one of the four directional quadrants in the sky, according to premodern East Asian astronomy. These four quadrants are further subdivided into seven mansions, or *suk* 宿, for a total of twenty-eight. These mansions correspond to longitudes along the ecliptic to track the position of the moon (or in this case the sun) in the sky. In this case, the Northern Lands specifically refers to the Emptiness Mansion (*hŏsuk* 虛宿), which has Beta Aquarii as its determinative star.

9. The Western Lands, or Sŏyuk 西陸, is another reference to the four directional quadrants in the sky. See previous note. Here it is specifically referring to the Hairy Head Mansion (*myosuk* 昴宿), which has Electra, also known as 17 Tauri, as its determinative star.

> to the ice storage is opened. If ice is carefully stored and properly used, then we will be spared the disaster of misery and hardship. Therefore, in general, ice is to be used up between the vernal equinox (*ch'unbun* 春分)[10] and the start of autumn (*ipch'u* 立秋).[11] If we start bringing it in in the fifth month, then this will be in violation of the old ways, and yin and yang will not be balanced. We request that the ice be brought in during the start of summer.

The king approved.

Kyech'uk (5th day). There was hail.

Kyŏngsin (12th day). Eighty-six Eastern Jurchens, led by Chief Obuha 烏夫賀, were granted an audience with the court.

Sinyu (13th day). There was frost.

Ŭlch'uk (17th day). Fifty-nine Northeastern Jurchens, led by Grand Preceptor Adogan 阿道間, were granted an audience with the court. The relevant authorities said, "Grand Astrologer is a Khitan office title. Since Adogan has already been naturalized, we request that his title be changed to Chŏngbo." The king approved.

The retired Chancellery executive Ch'ae Ch'ungsun died.

Kyeyu (25th day). A summer sacrifice for rain was held.

Chŏngch'uk (29th day). The king issued a decree.

> Although the former left vice director of state affairs Yi Kong was impeached twice when he served as state councilor in the court of the late king, he had been tasked with writing and other literary duties for a long time. For that reason, it would be fair to restore him to his office and title before he is sent into retirement.

Fifth Month

Kimyo (2nd day). Collecting firewood from or around famous mountains was prohibited across the country.

---

10. The fourth of the twenty-four solar terms.
11. The thirteenth of the twenty-four solar terms.

Sinmyo (14th day). The king issued a decree.

> Regarding families with four sons, I will allow one of them to leave home to become a Buddhist monk. Let him sincerely apply himself to the sutras and precepts of Buddhism at ordination platforms in monasteries such as Yŏngt'ong 靈通寺, Sungbŏp 嵩法寺, Powŏn 普願寺, and Tonghwa 桐華寺.

The relevant authorities submitted a petition.

> Little rain has come since spring. You should, in accordance with the old customs, screen wrongfully arrested prisoners, provide relief to the destitute, and bury exposed corpses. But first, in the northern outskirts of the capital, you should pray to the gods of the great mountains, great seas, and great rivers, and also of the small mountains and rivers, who hold the power to raise up clouds and bring rain. Second, you should offer prayers at the Imperial Ancestral Shrine once every seven days. If still no rain comes. repeat the same prayers to the mountains and seas as before. If the drought is severe, offer sacrifices for rain, relocate the markets, break the royal sun parasols, prohibit the butchering of livestock, and stop the feeding of government horses with food-grain.

The king approved. He avoided the main throne hall and reduced the number of side dishes served at meals.

Kihae (22nd day). There was hail.

Kyemyo (26th day). The king conducted a Buddhist ritual (*toryang* 道場)[12] in Mundŏk Hall and prayed for rain for five days.

Sixth Month

Ŭlmyo (8th day). The king conducted a Buddhist ritual in Mundŏk Hall and prayed for rain.

---

12. In Sanskrit, the term *bodhimaṇḍa* (K. *toryang*) means "seat of enlightenment" or "platform of enlightenment." In Koryŏ, it was used to refer both to the large courtyard in front of the main shrine hall and to the ceremonies held there and at other locations.

Ŭlch'uk (18th day). When the king personally conducted the Daoist Ch'o ritual, it started to rain.

Pyŏngin (19th day). The royal aides submitted a memorial.

> In ancient times, even though wise and holy rulers could not escape natural calamities, their high virtue and benevolent administration turned evils into blessings. With deep concern over the long drought that had stretched on since spring, you avoided the main throne hall, reduced the number of side dishes served at your meals, worked diligently, prayed earnestly day and night, and put the blame on yourself with deep reflection. Consequently, a timely rain has fallen to bathe the wide fields with the promise of rich crops. We ask you to return to the main throne hall so that you can preside over state affairs as usual, and also to return to having the normal number of side dishes served at your meals.

The king approved and issued a decree.

> Due to my own failings, a long drought was visited on this land. I still worry about the future even though we have been blessed with sweet rain. But since you have made this request, I cannot deny it.

Mujin (21st day). Earthquakes occurred in the capital, the Eastern Capital, Sangju, Kwangju, and Anbyŏn district. Many houses and huts were destroyed. In the Eastern Capital, the earthquakes continued for three days before they stopped.

Imsin (25th day). The relevant authorities submitted a petition.

> We request that ice be given to seventeen people, including the retired Chancellery director Yu Pang, once every ten days until the start of autumn.

The king approved.

Seventh Month, Autumn

Muin (2nd day). The Palace Secretariat (*chungch'uwŏn* 中樞院) submitted a petition.

> You decreed that an additional three hundred *kŭn* of ginseng must be brought in, but the one thousand *kŭn* that has already been collected can satisfy the demands of the Royal Household. The flesh and blood of the people are their tribute to the government, and it must not be extracted without thought. We beg that you not order any more.

The king was not pleased.

Then the Chancellery submitted a petition.

> The ancient kings controlled their desires, trimmed away luxuries, respected moral dictates, and admitted counsel into their hearts, receiving it in humility, in order to bring peace and prosperity to the myriads of people. As natural catastrophes visit this land so frequently, there is no other time for you to admonish your heart and reprimand your body. How can you imagine harming the flesh and blood of the people to satisfy your extravagance? We beseech you to heed the Palace Secretariat's memorial.

The king approved.

Sinsa (5th day). Sixty-seven Song merchants, led by Chen Liang 陳諒, made an offering of their native products.

Imo (6th day). The king issued a decree.

> Recently, we have seen strange things in Heaven and earth, all signifying my lack of virtue. Day after day, I observe caution, not daring to enjoy myself or a moment's peace. To prevent unforeseen calamities, I now command all the officials of my court and government to diligently attend to their official duties at all times. The only exceptions granted are when court business is suspended or when resting.

Kyŏngin (14th day). The director of military affairs and Palace Secretariat administrator Kim Ch'ungch'an died. He was given the posthumous title of Respecting Peace (*kongjŏng* 恭靖.)

Imjin (16th day). The king issued a decree.

> When the Khitans invaded our frontier in the year *ŭlmyo* (1015), the Astrological Service executive Kang Sŭngyŏng fought in the vanguard and fell in battle. His meritorious service in wartime is highly laudable, and I award him the posthumous title of Vice Director of the Weaponry

Directorate and bestow on his son Kang Hwa 姜和 an entry-level government post.

Japan repatriated eleven of our people, including Kyŏmjun 謙俊, who had drifted there.

Kyŏngja (24th day). The gracious consort Lady Han died.

This month, the State Affairs right office chief Kim Wŏnch'ung 金元冲 was dispatched to Song as a memorial envoy (*kojusa* 告奏使) and delivering goods envoy (*chinbongsa* 進奉使). He was on his way to Song when he lost his ship in Ongjin county and was forced to return.

Eighth Month

Imsul (17th day). The king appointed Hwangbo Yŏng as director of military affairs, Yi Chakch'ung as commissioner of the Palace Secretariat, and Kwak Sin as director of the Censorate.

Kyehae (18th day). The king fed ten thousand monks at the Polo Field.

Pyŏngin (21st day). The king issued a decree.

> Yesterday I saw the report on sentences for hanging and beheading from the Ministry of Punishments. During my mourning, we have witnessed repeated occurrences of strange and unusual events. I wish to act upon my love of life and express what lives in my heart for my people. Those who are to be hanged or beheaded shall have their sentences commuted and be exiled to an uninhabited island. Those who have committed crimes deserving of hanging or beheading but with extenuating circumstances shall be exiled to an inhabited island.

At this time, 116 people avoided death.

Mujin (23rd day). The king appointed Chin Hyŏnsŏk as Chancellery attendant (*chik munhasŏng* 直門下省), Kim Yŏnggi as left grand master of remonstrance (*chwa kanŭi* 左諫議), Im Yugan as right grand master of remonstrance (*u kanŭi* 右諫議), Pak Yangmyŏng as general censor, and Sŏ Yugŏl 徐維傑 as left executive of state affairs and right recipient of edicts.

Earthquakes sounding like thunder occurred in the Eastern Capital, Kŭmju, and Milsŏng.

Ninth Month

Chŏngch'uk (2nd day). A party of 135 Eastern Jurchens, led by General Agol, came to the court with an offering of excellent horses.

Tenth Month, Winter

Chŏngmyo (23rd day). Seventy-four Eastern Jurchens, led by General Supporting the State Yoya 要耶, were granted an audience with the court.

Eleventh Month

Kich'uk (15th day). The king held the Assembly of the Eight Prohibitions. Song merchants, Eastern Jurchens, and T'amna made offerings of their native products.
Chŏngyu (23rd day). Seventy-eight Eastern Jurchens, led by General Oŭlya 吾乙耶, were granted an audience with the court.

Twelfth Month

Musin (4th day). Seventy-four Eastern Jurchens, led by Grand General Supporting the State Yoŭldo 姚乙道, were granted an audience with the court.
Sinyu (17th day). The late King Tŏkchong was enshrined in the Imperial Ancestral Shrine

THIRD YEAR OF CHŎNGJONG (1037)

First Month, Spring

Kapsul (1st day). The king canceled the New Year Congratulations.

Second Month

Pyŏngjin (13th day). The retired Chancellery executive Pak Ch'ungsuk died. The king awarded him the posthumous title of Upright Behavior (*chŏngsin* 貞慎).

Kimi (16th day). The military commissioner of the Northwestern Frontier Circuit (*sŏbungno pyŏngmasa* 西北路兵馬使) captured fifty-five Eastern Jurchens, including Saira 沙伊邏, who had been secretly communicating with the Khitans. They were sent under escort to the Western Capital.

Kyeyu (30th day). Five comets appeared, each measuring five to six *ch'ŏk* in length.

Third Month

Kihae (26th day). No Yŏnp'ae 盧延霸 and others passed the state examination.

Fourth Month, Summer

Chŏngmyo (25th day). The king personally conducted the sacrifices at the Imperial Ancestral Shrine before issuing an amnesty decree.

A party of western [Jurchen] tribesmen led by Chief Saon 沙蘊 came to the court with an offering of their native products.

Intercalary Month

Imjin (20th day). Fifty-three Eastern Jurchens, led by the Chŏngbo Adohan, were granted an audience with the court.

Fifth Month

Kyech'uk (12th day). The king promoted fifty-seven Eastern Jurchens, including General Submitting to Virtue Nigudu 尼句豆, by one grade.

Ŭlch'uk (24th day). The king went to Hyŏnhwa monastery.

Sixth Month

Kimyo (8th day). The king personally hosted a banquet for the elders of the state at the Polo Field.

Seventh Month, Autumn

Imsul (22nd day). On the anniversary of the queen mother's death, officials submitted memorials of comfort to the king.

Ŭlch'uk (25th day). The king went to Kŏndŏk Hall and appointed a number of high officials 宣麻. These were Yu Chingp'il, appointed as vice director of the Imperial Secretariat with a concurrent assignment as Imperial Secretariat–Chancellery joint affairs manager; the Western Capital commissioner Hwang Churyang, appointed as vice director of the Imperial Secretariat with a concurrent assignment as Imperial Secretariat–Chancellery joint affairs manager; Ch'oe Chean, appointed as left vice director of state affairs, commissioner of the Palace Secretariat, and senior governmental advisor; and Ch'oe Chung, appointed as editor of national history and senior governmental advisor.

Eighth Month

Ŭrhae (6th day). The king invested his younger brother Wang Sŏ, the lord of Nangnang, with the titles of High Grand Preceptor and Director of the Imperial Secretariat.

Imo (13th day). The king invested his younger brother Wang Ki, the duke of Kaesŏngguk (*Kaesŏng kukgong* 開城國公), with the title of High Grand Guardian.

Ŭryu (16th day). Twenty Song merchants, led by Zhu Ruyu 朱如玉, came to the court.

Chŏnghae (18th day). The Song merchant Lin Yun 林贇 came with an offering of native products.

Ninth Month

Kiyu (10th day). Earthquakes occurred in the prefectures of Kwiju, Sakchu, Pakchu 博州,[13] T'aeju 泰州,[14] and at Wiwŏn Garrison.

Pyŏngin (27th day). The king went to Poje monastery 普濟寺.

This month, the Khitan-held Naewŏn Fortress, upon receiving an imperial decree, sent an official dispatch to Yŏngdŏk Garrison of Koryŏ.

> We understand that Koryŏ diligently sent its tribute in the past, but in recent years it has come to neglect this duty. If it wishes to fulfill its obligations, it should first demonstrate its sincerity by presenting a memorial, after which the emperor will be pleased to issue separate instructions.

Fourteen officials, including the Chancellery director Sŏ Nul, discussed this message and submitted a proposal: "It would be appropriate to send an envoy to the Khitans with a response."

Tenth Month, Winter

Kyŏngo (2nd day). Fifty-nine Eastern Jurchens, led by General Aryudae 阿留大, were granted an audience with the court.

Pyŏngja (8th day). The military commissioner of the Northwestern Frontier Circuit submitted a report: "The Khitans are invading. They are using warships to cross the Amnok River."

Eleventh Month

Kyech'uk (15th day). The king pardoned those sentenced to a punishment of flogging or less for public malfeasance.

---

13. Present-day Pakch'ŏn-gun, North P'yŏngan.
14. Present-day Taech'ŏn-gun, North P'yŏngan.

Twelfth Month

Chŏnghae (20th day). The king sent the Palace Administration vice director (*chŏnjung sogam* 殿中少監) Ch'oe Yŏnha to the Khitans with a memorial.

> Our country prostrates before you. Since the days when the late dowager empress and Emperor Sheng gave us the imperial investiture decree allotting fiefs with fixed duties to each domain, the Eastern Kingdom has looked up to the North Star [the Khitan emperor] with loyalty and has performed its duties generation after generation without cease. Recently, your former vassal, my brother, died after ruling as a sovereign of unsullied virtue and a dependent of the imperial court. Upon hearing of your accession, I presented a memorial that mentioned two state matters, but your approval has yet to arrive. From that time until today, the tribute offerings have been suspended although years have passed. However, when we received your gracious message, which fully accorded with our own wish, we felt a keen desire to uphold our allegiance to your court by adhering to our traditional role as a small state staunchly supporting the dowager empress's imperial will. To that end, we will attune ourselves to remaining in harmony with imperial rule, and we will act accordingly forever.

Ŭlmi (28th day). The king gave Mallyŏng Palace 萬齡宮 to the lady of Hyŏndŏk Palace (*Hyŏndŏk kungju* 玄德宮主), Lady Kim 金.

Fourth Year of Chŏngjong (1038)

First Month, Spring

Musul (1st day). The Khitans sent Ma Poŏp 馬保業.
Sinyu (24th day). General Submitting to Virtue Kojimun of the Eastern Jurchens was granted an audience with the court. The king promoted him to General Embracing Transformation and bestowed offices on his followers.

Second Month

Kyemi (16th day). The king went to Pongŭn monastery to hold the Lantern Festival and worship at the portrait of T'aejo. That evening, the king himself fired the incense at the Portrait Hall, and this became the custom thereafter.

Third Month

Sinhae (14th day). Ch'oe Yŏnha returned from the Khitans with an imperial edict from the emperor.

> Upon reading your memorial, we were apprised of your desire to renew your tribute offerings. That the small serve the great is the norm for all states, and discarding the old to promote the new is the proper course for all vassals. In the past, you received our calendars and edicts for generation after generation, and paid annual tribute. When the former Koryŏ king acceded to the throne, many years passed without contact, leaving our Celestial Court unaware of your intentions. It was not until recently, when we perused your memorial, that we recognized the sincerity in your wish to resume your duties as a vassal state. This means that you wish to follow the customs of the Great Bow without reservation and to observe the proper rite of offering arrows made from the thorn tree. When we reflect on this demonstration of your devotion, we find you worthy of our love and respect. We therefore approve of your tributary status with pleasure, and you are expected to perform your duties without fail, and thereby enjoy enduring peace and happiness.

Kyŏngsin (23rd day). Thirty-two Eastern Jurchens, led by General Submitting to Virtue Kujira 仇知羅, and thirty of their kinsman, including Hoep'al 恢八, who were convinced to accompany them, were granted an audience with the court.

Fourth Month, Summer

Chŏngmyo (1st day). The king invested Court Lady Han 韓 with the title of Gracious Consort (*yŏbi* 麗妃).
Mujin (2nd day). The affairs manager Yu So died.
This month, the king sent the left office chief of the State Affairs Department Kim Wŏnch'ung to the Khitans to present greetings, express gratitude, and request the era name.

Sixth Month

Ŭryu (20th day). The Chancellery director Yu Pang died.

Seventh Month, Autumn

Sinch'uk (6th day). Venus was visible during the day.
Musin (13th day). The Ministry of Punishments (*sangsŏ hyŏngbu* 尚書刑部) submitted a report: "In the entire country there are 103 people sentenced to be hanged or beheaded." The king decreed: "Those who are to be beheaded are to be flogged and exiled to uninhabited islands, and those who are to be hanged are to be flogged and exiled to inhabited islands."
Kabin (19th day). Kim Wŏnch'ung returned from the Khitans with an edict from the emperor.

> We received your memorial with summer greetings. Due to your able administration of your hereditary fief, which has been accomplished with surpassing designs and the expression of your allegiance to the [Khitan] North Palace, you are cherished by the people of the East Han [Koryŏ]. We are pleased to accept your official letter in this hottest season and express our gratitude for your tribute.

The emperor issued another imperial edict.

> We express our gratitude for your gifts of a gold drinking bottle, silver medicine bottle, official cap, silk cloth, ordinary cloth, *noewŏn* tea

腦原茶,[15] large paper, small ink sticks, and flower mats made with rushes. As you rule over a country that respects our imperial court, you have sent an envoy to renew your far-flung allegiance and to observe the traditional rite of offering tribute to become a permanent bastion. In your memorial, you described how, for generations, you wholeheartedly conformed to the diplomatic custom of maintaining regular communications, but in recent years failed many times to send an envoy, because the road was blocked, and how you wish to forever remain our loyal subject. When we approved of your allegiance, you sent a letter expressing your gratitude, together with boxes of tribute, which we received with astonishment and embarrassment.

He issued a further imperial edict.

From your memorial, we understand that you wish to use the era name of Chunghŭi 重熙[16] in your official documents. We assented at once when your envoy brought the memorial, and we are pleased with your loyalty.

Eighth Month

Ŭlch'uk (1st day). The court implemented the use of the Khitan era name Chunghŭi beginning on this day.

Due to the damage to the rice crops from the long and heavy rain, the order to mobilize the fall session of required labor in all the provinces was suspended.

Pyŏngin (2nd day). Forty-nine eastern [Jurchen] tribesmen, led by General Embracing Transformation Adu 阿豆, were granted an audience with the court.

Chŏngmyo (3rd day). The king sent the audience usher (*hammun chihu* 閣門祗候) Kim Hwaŏn 金華彥 as a sustaining rites envoy (*chiryesa* 持禮使) to the Khitan Eastern Capital.

Chŏngch'uk (13th day). Twenty-six Northwestern Jurchens, led by General Submitting to Virtue Yaban 耶半, were granted an audience with the court.

---

15. A unique tea made in Koryŏ that was used as a tribute offering or gift to foreign countries.
16. The era name for the Khitan emperor Hunjong from 1032 to 1055.

Muja (24th day). A party of 147 Song merchants, led by Chen Liang 陳亮 of Mingzhou 明州 and Chen Weiji 陳維績 of Taizhou 台州, came with an offering of their native products.

Tenth Month, Winter

Sinmyo (28th day). The Khitans sent Ma Poŏp with an imperial edict from the emperor.

> You have managed your state affairs with benevolence. The other day, you presented a memorial to our court containing an explanation of the interruption in our diplomatic relations and a declaration that you wish to resume communications. We accept what is stated in your memorial and will share our thoughts with you. We will not forget the deep loyalty that you have shown, and hereby send our envoy Ma Poŏp, who is the left general-in-chief of our Personal Guard (*chwa ch'ŏnuwi taejanggun* 左千牛衛大將軍) and commissioner of the Palace Audience Gate of the East (*tongsang hammunsa* 東上閤門使), to bring you encouragement.

Eleventh Month

Kabin (22nd day). The king appointed Hwang Churyang as executive of the Chancellery and Yi Chakch'ung as senior governmental advisor and a pillar of the state.

Ŭlmyo (23rd day). The commander-in-chief of the Righteous and Brave Army (*ŭiyonggun to jihwi* 義勇軍都指揮) Kang Tŏngnyŏng 康德寧 came to the court as a response envoy from the Khitan Eastern Capital (*tonggyŏng hoeryesa* 東京回禮使).

Kimi (27th day). The king dispatched Ch'oe Ch'unggong to the Khitans with a letter of congratulations on the Day of Eternal Life (*yŏngsujŏl* 永壽節)[17] and also for the new year.

---

17. The Day of Eternal Life was the Khitan emperor's birthday.

Twelfth Month

Kapsul (12th day). Fifty eastern Jurchens, led by General Submitting to Virtue Kojimun, were granted an audience with the court.

Kyemi (21st day). The Department of the Imperial Secretariat–Chancellery submitted a petition.

> The cost of daily feeding of the white cranes, ducks, geese, and goats of the Eastern Pond is considerable. An old text says, "If dogs and horses cannot subsist on their own, they should not be raised. Rare birds and strange beasts are not to be reared by the state." It also says, "Since birds, beasts, and winged or creeping insects each follow their own nature, we should refrain from using them for our own entertainment. This harms their nature." We request that they be released onto a sea island.

The king approved.

Fifth Year of Chŏngjong (1039)

First Month, Spring

Sinch'uk (10th day). Sacrifices were offered to the god of rain 雨師.

Pyŏngo (15th day). The king appointed the director of public works Wŏn Yŏng as the military commissioner of the Northwestern Frontier Circuit in the spring and summer (*ch'unhabŏn sŏbungno pyŏngmasa* 春夏番西北路兵馬使), the Palace Revenues Court vice director (*taebu sogyŏng* 大府少卿) Yang Taech'un 楊帶春 as the vice military commissioner of the Northwestern Frontier Circuit in the spring and summer (*ch'unhabŏn sŏbungno pyŏngma pusa* 春夏番西北路兵馬副使), the right scholarly counselor-in-ordinary Chin Hyŏnsŏk as the military commissioner of the Eastern Frontier Circuit, and the palace censors Im Chonghan and Wang Ibo as vice military commissioners of the Eastern Frontier Circuit (*tongno pyŏngma pusa* 東路兵馬副使).

Second Month

Imsul (1st day). The king sent the Palace Administration director Yi Sŏnggong to the Khitans with an offering of native products.

Chŏngmyo (6th day). The king sent the Revenue Ministry executive (*hobu nangjung* 戶部郎中) Yu Sŏn 庾先 to the Khitans with an expression of gratitude for the comfort mission and to request the dismantling of Khitan fortress walls east of the Amnok River.

Ŭrhae (14th day). The king went to Pongŭn monastery to hold the Lantern Festival.

Pyŏngja (15th day). The king went to Chunggwang Hall to watch a music performance.

Imo (21st day). Rites to the star Canopus were performed in the southern outskirts of the capital.

Sinmyo (30th day). Hwang Hangji 黃抗之 and others passed the state examination.

Third Month

Sinch'uk (10th day). The military commissioner of the Northeastern Frontier Circuit (*tongbungno pyŏngmasa* 東北路兵馬使) submitted a report: "Sixty Jurchen sons bearing gifts request entry to the court." The king approved.

Fourth Month, Summer

Sinyu (1st day). Yu Sŏn returned from the Khitans with the emperor's edict.

> From your memorial, we gather that the fortress walls east of the Amnok River seem to be hindering the daily lives of your people. You should know that those walls have defended our frontier since the time of our royal ancestors and do no harm to your land. We also have our own heritage to consider, and it will be difficult to make any such changes quickly. Your former king Wang Hŭm [King Tŏkchong] worried us many times with the same request and eventually stopped offering tribute. Since you

have just acceded to the throne and presented the tribute along with your memorial, your best option is to sustain the old bond between us and strengthen it with more frankness and diligence. You will secure your future by doing this, and it will certainly be in accord with my wishes. Your people can cultivate the land there, so do not feel anxious or troubled.

The Khitans sent the Judicial Review Court minister (*taerigyŏng* 大理卿) Han Pohyŏng 韓保衡 to preside at the ceremony of investiture for the king. He brought the emperor's edict.

Your land stretches out in the region to the east, and the stars you see surround the North Star [the Khitan throne]. As your worshipful mind has proved steadfast, it is only fit and proper that we confer on you a title of significant merit. We therefore dispatch an envoy from this great distance to hold the ceremony that will invest you as the sovereign ruler of your fief. This is a sign of imperial grace, which you may enfold in a duly grateful heart. Minister of the Judicial Review Court Han Pohyŏng will deliver your copy of the letter of investiture and our imperial edict. When he arrives, receive him with great courtesy.

The letter of investiture stated:

In accordance with the will of Heaven and in harmony with ancient ordinances, laws are enacted. At home, the majesty of our laws is seen in our embrace of faraway countries. Abroad, it is seen in the right we possess to regulate kingdoms. Trying to distinguish between the laws of the Celestial Empire and those of vassal states is a dangerous enterprise whether on land or sea. Our expectation is not that you will be so reckless but that you will uphold this great cause in concert with other heroic vassals. Emperor Xuanyuan practiced shooting with a bow and arrow, Yu 禹 used spears and shields to subdue rebels, but nothing could equal the division of the domain into vassal states in Zhou and the swearing by mountains and rivers in Han. Your achievements are greater than those of Duke Huan and Duke Wen, and your virtue outshines that of Chinhan and Pyŏnhan [ancient forebears of Koryŏ]. Soon after inheriting the territory of your ancestors, you sought to make amends for the inconsiderate policies of the preceding king [Tŏkchong] by offering tribute in advance of other kingdoms and proffering the same territory to expand our domain. With a loyal heart, you worked to restore peace and harmony, and we are therefore pleased to grant this special favor to you.

As befits the provisional king of Koryŏ (*kwŏnji Koryŏ kugwang* 權知高麗國王), your form is as beautiful as jade, and your generosity as deep and far-reaching as the abode of the immortals 鼇丘[18] in the middle of the sea, and your talents are as bright as the stars being born in the night sky. You have followed your duty and achieved supremacy. You have acted out of principle. Awake or asleep, you have shown that you can control your pride, and you have brought wealth to your country of a thousand *li*, allowing all the people to enjoy prosperity. You have thus restored the universal esteem that your noble family had sustained for generations and earned for your kingdom the means to flourish forever.

We therefore dispatch our envoy to your distant land to bestow this imperial decree. We hereby grant you all the lands of Hyŏnt'o 玄菟, which will redound to your glory, and give you the noble office of the Three Preceptors (*samsa* 三師).[19] In this way, we acknowledge your merits, elevate your rank, and award you exceptional titles as well as generous fiefs to inspire your loyalty.

Ah! It is fitting when the stars align themselves around the North Star, and it is telling that the rivers flow serenely when they follow their proper course to the sea. If you heed these words, you need no further instruction. We confer on you the titles of Commander Unequaled in Honor, Acting Grand Guardian, Director of the Chancellery, Supreme Pillar of the State, and King of Koryŏ as well as a fief of seven thousand households and an actual fief of one thousand households. In addition, we award you the six-character merit subject title of Fulfilling Loyalty (*such'ung* 輸忠), Preserving Righteousness (*poŭi* 保義), and Supporting Country (*pongguk* 奉國).

Fifth Month

Kyŏngja (10th day). Twenty-six Japanese men and women came to submit.

---

18. The legendary mountain of the immortals rested on the head of a giant sea turtle.
19. The office comprises the three titles of Grand Preceptor 太師, Grand Mentor 太傅, and Grand Guardian 太保.

Seventh Month, Autumn

The Khitans sent the Imperial Manufactories director (*sobugam* 少府監) Chin Mae 陳邁 with a letter of congratulations on the king's birthday.

The king sent the right scholarly counselor-in-ordinary Im Yugan to the Khitans to express his gratitude for the investiture.

Eighth Month

Kyŏngsin (1st day). Fifty Song merchants, led by Weiji 惟禃, came with an offering of their native products.

Eleventh Month, Winter

Sinch'uk (14th day). The king went to Sinbong Pavilion, where he hosted a banquet. Then he went to Pŏbwang monastery to hold the Assembly of the Eight Prohibitions.

Twelfth Month

Chŏngsa (1st day). The king sent the vice director of revenue Song Yung 宋融 to the Khitans to celebrate the emperor's Day of Eternal Life and to offer congratulations on the new year.

The king issued a decree.

> When the Great Cold descends, the wind and snow are especially severe. I am concerned that some of the poor will surely die of hunger or frost. I command the relevant authorities to distribute cotton cloth as a royal gift to naturalized foreigners and tribesmen over eighty, both men and women, to protect them from frostbite.

Intercalary Month

Chŏnghae (11th day). Nine Khitans, led by the Eastern Capital's response envoy Tae Kyŏnje 大堅濟, came to the court.

Sixth Year of Chŏngjong (1040)

First Month, Spring

Pyŏngjin (1st day). There was a solar eclipse.

The king appointed Ch'oe Yŏnha as deputy resident governor of the Western Capital.

Sinyu (6th day). Fifty Eastern Jurchens, led by Grand General Supporting the State Yoŏ 傜漁, came to the court with an offering of their native products.

Imsin (17th day). The king sent the right scholarly counselor-in-ordinary Chin Hyŏnsŏk to the Khitans with an offering of local products.

Pyŏngja (21st day). The esteemed grand lady of Ansan prefecture (*Ansangun taegun* 安山郡大君) Lady Kim accused her son Yi Konghyŏp 李公叶 of not being filial. The unfilial son was executed in the city market.

Kyŏngjin (25th day). Forty Eastern Jurchens, led by General Soothing Faraway Lands (*suwŏn changgun* 綏遠將軍) P'agŏl 巴桀, came to the court with an offering of excellent horses.

Kapsin (29th day). Forty-six Northeastern Jurchens, led by General Submitting to Virtue Kodu 高竇, came to the court with an offering of horses and their native products.

Second Month

Kyŏngin (5th day). The walkway and several hundred *kan* of Sŭngp'yŏng gate 昇平門 burned down. The fire extended to the Censorate.

Chŏngyu (12th day). The king appointed the assistant executive of civil personnel Kim Chŏngjun as provisional recipient of edicts (*kwŏnji sŭngsŏn* 權知承宣).

Musin (23rd day). Forty-eight Eastern Jurchens, led by General Embracing Transformation Yomae 傜賓, came to the court with an offering of excellent horses.

Imja (27th day). The king ordered the relevant authorities to standardize all weights and measures.

Kabin (29th day). The king invested the gracious consort Lady Han with the title of Queen. This was reported to the Imperial Ancestral Shrine on the following day. All the officials offered their congratulations.

Third Month

Sinyu (7th day). Thirty-three Eastern Jurchens, led by General Supporting the State Agol, came to the court with an offering of fifteen horses.

Imsul (8th day). Twenty-five Northwestern Jurchens, led by General Comforting the Frontier Ingbo 仍保, came to the court with an offering of their native products.

Kapsul (20th day). Twenty-six Northwestern Jurchens, led by Chief Kosamun 古史門, came to the court with an offering of their native products.

Imo (28th day). The king issued a decree.

> The Imperial Secretariat executive Yu Chingp'il was a descendant of a distinguished literary family that assisted the throne during the reigns of succeeding monarchs. His merit is worthy of special regard, so I wish to promote his son Yu Chak 劉綽 to the office of clerical scribe of the Public Works Ministry (*kongbu sŏryŏngsa* 工部書令史).

Fourth Month, Summer

Pyŏngsul (2nd day). More than twenty people from the Khitan Eastern Capital, led by Muŭiro 巫儀老 and O Chigŏl 吳知桀, came to submit. The king rewarded them with houses, fields, and assorted goods, and they settled in Yŏngnam 嶺南.[20]

Sinch'uk (17th day). The Chinju defense commissioner (*Chinju pangŏsa* 秦州防禦使) Ma Sejang 馬世長 came to the court as a Khitan special envoy bearing an imperial edict (*haengsŏnsa* 橫宣使).

Chŏngmi (23rd day). The king prayed for rain at Imhae Hall 臨海院.

---

20. The area around present-day Kyŏngsang.

Imja (28th day). The king awarded the Eastern Jurchen chief Ot'a 烏陁 the rank of General Commanding the Frontier (*toryŏng changgun* 都領將軍).
Kabin (30th day). Twenty-seven Northwestern Jurchens, led by General Supporting the State Aihwa 阿伊化, came to the court with an offering of their native products.

Fifth Month

Ŭlmyo (1st day). The king prayed for rain on Mount Pugak 北岳.
Sinyu (7th day). The king conducted the Daoist Ch'o ritual in Hoegyŏng Hall and prayed for rain.
Imsul (8th day). A great rain fell continuously for a whole month.
　The king appointed Yi Yŏnggan 李令幹 as compiler of national history (*sagwan susŏn* 史館修撰), and Yi Sangsŏn 李象先 as investigating censor.

Sixth Month

Ŭlsa (22nd day). The king sent Yu Paegin, the right office chief of the State Affairs Department, to the Khitans with an expression of gratitude.
　Fifty Eastern Jurchens, led by General Comforting the Frontier Moira 慕伊羅, came to the court with an offering of their native products.
Kyech'uk (30th day). A party of Heaga tribesmen led by Chŏgŭlgu 積乙仇 came from the northern frontier to submit.

Seventh Month, Autumn

Ŭlch'uk (12th day). Lightning struck Ŭich'un Pavilion 宜春樓.
　The Queen of Sunghwa Palace died.
　The Khitans sent the Haju surveillance commissioner (*Haju kwanch'alsa* 夏州觀察使) Cho Anin 趙安仁 with a letter of congratulations on the king's birthday.
Muchin (15th day). The retired left vice director of state affairs Yang Chin died.

Eighth Month

Ŭryu (3rd day). Yi Chujwa, superintendent of the Censorate and director of punishments, died.

The king sent the vice director of public works Yu Ch'ang to the Khitans with a letter of congratulations on the dowager empress's birthday.

Kyesa (11th day). Fifty-three Eastern Jurchens, led by Kododal 古陶達, came to the court with an offering of their native products.

Ninth Month

Ŭlmyo (3rd day). The king appointed Yi Hoe as right vice director of the State Affairs Department and Wŏn Yŏng as director of the Public Works Ministry.

A party of Northwestern Jurchens, led by General Yaban 耶盤, came to the court with an offering of thirteen excellent horses.

Chŏngsa (5th day). The king appointed Yi Chayŏn as administrator of the Palace Secretariat and Wang Ch'ongji 王寵之 (d. 1067) as administrator of memorials (*chungch'uwŏn chijusa* 中樞院知奏事).

Kyŏngsin (8th day). The Khitan commander-in-chief (*to chihwisa* 都指揮使) Ko Yuhan 高維翰 came to the court as a response envoy from the Eastern Capital.

Imsin (20th day). General Niuhwagolbo 尼迂火骨輔 of the Northern Jurchens came to submit. The king rewarded him with a house and field, and he settled within the capital.

Tenth Month, Winter

Kapsin (2nd day). Thirteen Northwestern Jurchens, led by Inghwaro 仍化老, came to submit. The king ordered that they be added to the tax registry.

Ŭryu (3rd day). A party of Northwestern Jurchens, led by the Chŏngjo Pugŏ 孚巨, came to the court with an offering of their native products.

Kyŏngin (8th day). The king made the Palace Secretariat administrator Kim Wŏnch'ung's daughter his queen.

Kyemyo (21st day). A large party of more than two hundred people was led to the court by General Sairo of the Eastern Jurchens, followed by another party of similar size led by General Tonghwaro 董化盧 of the Northwestern Jurchens. They made offerings of their native products.

This month, Yu Ch'ang returned from the Khitans with an edict from the emperor.

> Recently, many people have wished that our title be elevated even though we have refused to accept the idea on many occasions. The sincerity in their loud cries of acclamation did not pass unnoticed, however, and what is in their hearts arouses our pity and compels a feeling of approval. Thus we found that we could not persist in rejecting it, and we want to share our joy with our vassal countries by sending them a set of our imperial edicts. Furthermore, as we have decided to hold our coronation ceremony early in the twelfth moon, we now issue this decree.

Eleventh Month

Pyŏngin (15th day). A party of Arab merchants led by Ponagae 保那盍 came to the court with an offering of mercury, fossilized teeth, myrrh, champa incense, and sappan wood. The king ordered the relevant authorities to give them a warm reception and to send them off with rich gifts of gold and brocade.

Sinmi (20th day). The king sent the vice director of public works Yi Injŏng 李仁靜 to the Khitans to celebrate the emperor's Day of Eternal Life and to deliver a letter of congratulations on the new year.

Twelfth Month

Chŏngyu (17th day). Fifty Eastern Jurchens, led by the Wŏnyun Adugan 阿豆簡, were granted an audience with the court. They made an offering of thirty-five horses.

More than twenty households from the Khitan Eastern Capital came to submit.

Seventh Year of Chŏngjong (1041)

First Month, Spring

Kyŏngsul (1st day). The king canceled the New Year Congratulations.
Pyŏngjin (7th day). Fifteen Western Jurchens, led by the Taesŭng Kojiji 高支智, were granted an audience and made an offering of horses.

Second Month

Kyŏngjin (1st day). The Public Works Ministry (*sangsŏ kongbu* 尙書工部) submitted a proposal.

> Let us plant pine trees at the foot of the eastern and western slopes of Mount Songak to make the royal palaces more splendid.

The king approved.
Kich'uk (10th day). Yu Ch'ang 俞暢 and others passed the state examination.
Imin (23rd day). Eighteen Western Jurchens, led by General Supporting the State Niudae 尼于大, made an offering of excellent horses.

Third Month

Kyŏngsul (1st day). A party of Eastern Jurchens, led by the Chungyun Yasaro 也賜老, were granted an audience with the court.

Fourth Month, Summer

Kimyo (1st day). A party of Eastern Jurchens, led by the Taesang Chief Yigae, were granted an audience with the court.

Kyesa (15th day). The king held the Buddhist Tripitaka ritual in Hoegyŏng Hall. This event was observed twice a year, for six days in the spring and seven days in the autumn.

Fifth Month

Ŭlmyo (7th day). The king worshiped at Hyŏn Tomb.
Pyŏngjin (8th day). The king worshiped at Sŏn Tomb.[21] The king issued a decree.

> Some of the descendants of the officials who served Great King T'aejo when he unified the three kingdoms have now fallen in status and have become commoners without government office or slaves. I command the relevant authorities to test the literary and martial talents of these people. All those who pass the tests shall be elevated to official positions.

Then the king bestowed one horse each to the senior military protectors Hong Pin and Yun Sugi 尹修己, the grand generals Wi Chŏng 韋靖 and Kim T'angma 金琢磨, and on Sŏk Ch'ung 石忠, Yang P'ojil 梁抱質, Ha Hŭnghyu 河興休, Chi Maeng 智孟, O Kŭmbo 吳金甫, Han Sobo 韓所寶, Pu Ch'ang 敷暢, and the investigating censor Kim Kyŏng 金瓊.
Kyŏngo (22nd day). The king held the *Golden Light Sutra* ritual (*Kŭmgangmyŏng toryang* 金剛明經道場)[22] in Mundŏk Hall and prayed for rain.
Ŭrhae (27th day). Rain fell.

Sixth Month

Ŭryu (8th day). Twenty-six Eastern Jurchens, led by the Chŏngbo Obu 烏夫, were granted an audience with the court.

---

21. This was King Hyŏnjong's tomb.
22. Also known as the *Suvarṇa-prabhāsôttama-Sūtra* ritual, this Buddhist ceremony was intended to induce rainfall, prevent natural disasters, and ensure a long life.

Seventh Month, Autumn

Kimi (12th day). A party of Western Jurchens, led by General Submitting to Virtue Sojira 所智羅, were granted an audience with the court.

Sinyu (14th day). The Khitans sent the vice minister of the Imperial Regalia Court (*wiwi sogyŏng* 衛尉少卿) Kyŏng Ch'igun 耿致君 with a letter of congratulations on the king's birthday.

Eighth Month

Ŭlmi (18th day). Fifty Eastern Jurchens, led by General Soothing Faraway Lands P'aŭldal 波乙達, were granted an audience with the court.

This month, a comet was seen in the eastern quarter of the sky. It was around thirty *ch'ŏk* in length and disappeared after twenty days.

Ninth Month

Chŏngmi (1st day). The Military Affairs Ministry (*sangsŏ pyŏngbu* 尚書兵部) submitted a petition.

> The Military Recruitment Office (*sŏn'gun pyŏlgam* 選軍別監) recruits the sons of civil and military officials of the seventh rank and higher and sends them to the army to become common soldiers. Those studying literature or taking the civil service examinations are the only exceptions. Although this policy comes from a concern that we must be vigilant even in times of peace, the sons and grandsons of merit officials were never drafted for military service during the reign of King T'aejo. Between the years *kapcha* (1024) and *pyŏngja* (1026), there even were decrees prohibiting them from serving. Thus, not only is requiring them to serve at this time forgetting the merit earned by previous generations, but it also violates the old decrees. We request that we no longer use them to fill the rank and file.

The king approved.

Tenth Month, Winter

The king went to Hogyŏng [Western Capital].

A comet around thirty *ch'ŏk* in length appeared in the eastern sky for more than ten days.

Sinsa (5th day). When the king arrived on the Taedong River, the resident governor and senior governmental advisor Hwangbo Yŏng, who had come to the landing to welcome the royal procession, was granted an audience. After it, the king disembarked from the Dragon Ship and gave a banquet for his royal aides, commanding General Sŭnggae 承愷 and others to demonstrate their prowess at archery. But when the right reminder Kim Sangbin 金尙賓 remonstrated, the king withdrew his command and reentered the Sŏnŭn guesthouse 宣恩館.

Kich'uk (13th day). The king went to Yŏngbong gate 靈鳳門 to receive the congratulations of his officials. After giving them a banquet, he went to Hŭngguk monastery 興國寺 to hold the Assembly of the Eight Prohibitions and to burn incense. His residence was changed to Changnak Palace.

Kihae (23rd day). The king appointed Ch'oe Ch'ung as executive of the Imperial Secretariat and Hwangbo Yŏng as left vice director of state affairs and high minister of works.

Eleventh Month

Pyŏngo (1st day). The king returned from Hogyŏng.

The king awarded the title of Chungdaegwang 重大匡[23] to Sŏ Nul, Hong Pin, Yusŏm 有暹, An Po 安甫, and Ko Yŏl 高烈 (d. 1056).

Kimi (14th day). Song merchants led by Wang Nuo 王諾 came to the court with an offering of their native products.

Sixty-two Eastern Jurchens, led by General Soothing Faraway Lands Saira and General Comforting the Frontier Yaŏgae 耶於盖, were granted an audience and made an offering of horses.

---

23. A rank 1b title.

Twelfth Month

Sinsa (6th day). The king reviewed the archery units at Kuryŏng Pavilion 龜齡閣 on the Eastern Pond.

Imo (7th day). Fifty-five Eastern Jurchens, led by General Supporting the State Agaju 阿加主, were granted an audience and made an offering of their native products.

This year, the king sent the Hallim academician recipient of edicts Pak Yuin and the Ministries Department right office chief Yi Yuryang to the Khitans with a letter of congratulations on the accession of the emperor. The superintendent of the Imperial Regalia Court (*p'an wiwishisa* 判衛尉寺事) Yu Ch'am made an offering of native goods.

Eighth Year of Chŏngjong (1042)

First Month, Spring

Pyŏngo (1st day). The king canceled the New Year Congratulations.

Kiyu (4th day). A party of Eastern Jurchens with a leader named Kondu 昆豆 were granted an audience and made an offering of excellent horses.

Kabin (9th day). An Po 安保, supreme general of the Capital Garrison Division (*kŭmowi sangjanggun* 金吾衛上將軍) and the director of punishments, submitted a memorial requesting permission to retire due to old age. The king did not grant his request.

Kyŏngsin (15th day). The military commissioner of the Northwestern Frontier Circuit reported that the foreign households of Ipsŏk village 立石村 from east of the Amnok River to the area under the jurisdiction of Ch'ŏngsaek Garrison 淸塞鎭[24] had all been registered.

Kisa (24th day). Forty-nine Eastern Jurchens, led by General Submitting to Virtue Adogan 阿兜幹, were granted an audience and made an offering of their native products.

---

24. Present-day Hoech'ŏn city, Chagang province.

Second Month

Muin (4th day). Thirty-six Eastern Jurchens, led by General Soothing Faraway Lands Kojimun, were granted an audience and made an offering of their native products. The king appointed them to offices in accordance with their rank.

Muja (14th day). The king went to Pongŭn monastery to hold the Lantern Festival.

Pyŏngsin (22nd day). Twelve Western Jurchens, led by Chief Kojiji 高之知, were granted an audience and made an offering of their native products. The Foreign Relations Office (*yebinsŏng* 禮賓省) submitted a petition.

> Kojiji and his men were highly successful in expanding the two fortresses of P'yŏngno 平虜 and Yŏngwŏn 寧遠 last year. We request that goods be generously bestowed to them.

The king approved.

Kihae (25th day). The deputy resident governor of the Eastern Capital (*tonggyŏng pu yusu* 東京副留守) Ch'oe Ho 崔顥, together with the Eastern Capital executive (*pan'gwan* 判官) Na Chiyŏl 羅旨說, the Eastern Capital record keeper (*sarok* 司錄) Yun Kyŏm 尹廉, and the Eastern Capital chief secretary (*changsŏgi* 掌書記) Chŏng Konggan 鄭公幹, by order of the king, had both books of the *History of the Han Dynasty* [Former and Later Han] and the *History of the Tang Dynasty* newly engraved for presentation to the king. Receiving the books, the king awarded court titles to them.

Third Month

Ŭlsa (2nd day). The Imperial Secretariat–Chancellery submitted a petition.

> When you go to the palace to attend to state business, order each official to present his views and answer your questions.

The king approved.

Pyŏngjin (13th day). A party of Northwestern Jurchens, led by General Comforting the Frontier Yaŏgae, were granted an audience and made an offering of their native products.

Kapcha (21st day). Forty-seven [Western Jurchens], led by General Niubul, were granted an audience and made an offering of their native products.

Fourth Month

Pyŏngsul (13th day). There was frost.

Imin (29th day). The Eastern Jurchen Taesang Oŭdal 吳於達 requested cattle for plowing. The king gave him ten oxen from the Military Field Office of the Eastern Frontier Circuit (*tongno tunjŏnsa* 東路屯田司).

Fifth Month

Kisa (27th day). The king went to Hyŏnhwa monastery.

Sixth Month

Ŭrhae (4th day). The king visited Kaeguk monastery to conduct a Buddhist mourning rite for King T'aejo.

Chŏngch'uk (6th day). The king issued a decree.

> Since we have had no rain this busy farming season, I call on all the relevant authorities to recommend measures for dealing with a long drought.

Kyŏngjin (9th day). At the Royal Shrine, the king prayed for rain to the gods of the mountains and rivers.

Kapsin (13th day). The Imperial Secretariat director Sŏ Nul died.

Pyŏngsul (15th day). The Military and War Council (*tobyŏngmasa* 都兵馬使) submitted a petition.

Kan Hong 簡弘, a sublieutenant at the Yŏngp'a guard post (*Yŏngp'asu taejŏng* 寧波戍隊正) in Yŏlsan county 烈山縣 of the Eastern Frontier Circuit (*tongno* 東路), fought with the enemy even though he was outnumbered, his arrows were exhausted, and his strength was gone. He was killed in battle. We request that additional offices and posthumous rewards be granted to him.

The king approved.

Twenty-five Eastern Jurchens, led by General Submitting to Virtue Yaibul 耶伊弗, were granted an audience with the court.

Ŭlmi (24th day). The Imperial Secretariat executive Yu Chingp'il died.

Seventh Month

Ŭlsa (4th day). The consort of Yŏnch'ang Palace 延昌宮 died.

Ŭlmyo (14th day). The Khitans sent their Personnel Ministry administrator (*ibu nangjung* 吏部郎中) P'ungnip 馮立 with a letter of congratulations on the king's birthday.

Eighth Month

Muin (7th day). The king appointed Yi Chayŏn as vice commissioner of the Palace Secretariat.

Kyŏngjin (9th day). Sixty-eight Eastern Jurchens, led by General Soothing Faraway Lands Saira, were granted an audience and made an offering of their native products.

Kapsin (13th day). The king went to Sŏnjŏng Hall to pass judgment on cases proposed by the Ministry of Punishments.

Ninth Month

Chŏngsa (17th day). Fifty Eastern Jurchens, led by General Submitting to Virtue Agae, were granted an audience and made an offering of their native products.

Ŭlch'uk (25th day). A party of Northwestern Jurchens, led by General Soothing Faraway Lands Koduro, were granted an audience and made an offering of their native products.

Eleventh Month

Sinmyo (22nd day). The Khitans sent their minister of rites (*yebu sangsŏ* 禮部尙書) and censor-in-chief Wang Yŏngŏn 王永言 with an imperial edict.

> Since the ten prefectures south of Guannan 關南[25] once belonged to our old domain, we raised an army with the intention of restoring that territory. The Song, however, sent several intermediaries with earnest words offering annual gifts of gold and brocade as a replacement for the lost taxes, to be paid in addition to their previous tribute of three hundred thousand *nyang* of silver and three hundred thousand *p'il* of silk.[26] We renewed the peace treaty and will forever enjoy good and peaceful relations as a result. For our part, we gave them rich allowances and tax exemptions before sending them back, and we accomplished this great task with nothing but our small strength. Now, all our officials, civil and military, central and local, have submitted memorials urging us to assume an august title in keeping with our extraordinary achievements. Unable to dismiss their words, we have accepted their request and have chosen the third day of the eleventh month to hold a grand ceremony for the empress and myself. Since you have called yourself one of our vassals and have acknowledged us by oath as your suzerain, you will surely rejoice to hear this news. I therefore send Minister of Rites Wang Yŏngŏn to deliver this imperial edict and to give you formal instructions.

---

25. The Guannan (lit. "south of the passes") region was the southernmost part of the Sixteen Prefectures, a contested strategic area in northern China where important sections of the Great Wall were constructed. Shizong 世宗 of the Later Zhou dynasty (951–960) captured the Guannan region from the Khitan Liao in 959, and it was passed on to the Song dynasty (960–1279) following the collapse of the Later Zhou.

26. The Treaty of Shanyuan (1004) was a watershed moment in relations between the Northern Song (960–1127) and the Khitan Liao dynasty (916–1125). After many years of conflict, the Song dynasty finally recognized the legitimacy of the Liao dynasty as an equal empire. The treaty also stipulated that 200,000 *p'il* of raw silk and 100,000 taels of silver be sent annually as tribute, amounts that were subsequently increased.

Chŏngyu (28th day). General Comforting the Frontier Tongbul 冬弗 of the Eastern Jurchens was granted an audience and made an offering of horses.

Twelfth Month

Kyemo (4th day). Hwangbo Yuŭi, a retired Chancellery executive, died.
Kabin (15th day). The king appointed Yi Yŏnggan as vice director of the Royal Archives and Hallim academician lecturer-in-waiting.

NINTH YEAR OF CHŎNGJONG (1043)

First Month, Spring

Kyŏngo (1st day). The king canceled the New Year Congratulations.
Kyŏngjin (11th day). The king appointed Hwang Churyang as high grand guardian, director of the Chancellery, superintendent of the Civil Personnel Ministry, and supreme pillar of the state.
Kapsin (15th day). Thirty-six Western Jurchens, led by General Submitting to Virtue Kolgae 骨盖, were granted an audience and made an offering of their native products.

Second Month

Imin (4th day). The king appointed Ch'oe Chean as superintendent of the Revenue Ministry (*p'an sangsŏ hobusa* 判尙書戶部事) and vice director of the Chancellery with a concurrent assignment as Imperial Secretariat–Chancellery joint affairs manager; Ch'oe Ch'ung as high minister of education, editor of national history, and supreme pillar of the state; Hwangbo Yŏng as vice director of the Imperial Secretariat with a concurrent assignment as Imperial Secretariat–Chancellery joint affairs manager and supreme pillar of the state; Yi Chakch'ung as superintendent of rites and vice director of the Imperial Secretariat with a concurrent assignment as Imperial Secretariat–Chancellery joint affairs manager;

Kim Chŏngjun as left recipient of edicts; and Ko Suksŏng as right recipient of edicts.

Imja (14th day). The king went to Pongŭn monastery to hold the Lantern Festival.

Third Month

Pyŏngja (9th day). Forty Western Jurchens, led by Chief Koduro, were granted an audience and made an offering of their native products.

Kich'uk (22nd day). The king held the Hundred Seat ritual (*paekchwa toryang* 百座道場)²⁷ in Hoegyŏng Hall and fed ten thousand monks.

Imja (25th day). Forty Eastern Jurchens, led by General Kaero, were granted an audience and made an offering of horses.

Fourth Month

Musul (1st day). The military commissioner of the Northeastern Frontier Circuit submitted a report.

> General Soothing Faraway Lands Saira of the Eastern Jurchens has convinced 494 sea and land bandits, including their chief Nabul 羅弗, to accompany him to the Hwaju guesthouse to request an audience with the court.

The relevant authorities objected.

> This group wears men's faces but possesses the hearts of beasts. Let the military commander of the Northeastern Frontier Circuit reduce their number and permit entry to small groups by turn.

The king approved.

Imin (5th day). The king issued a decree.

---

27. Also known as the Paekkojwa toryang 百高座道場, this was a Buddhist ceremony held to ensure good fortune and prevent disasters.

> There has been no rain this season, causing concern over our crops. Could this be due to the resentment people feel for unfair criminal sentences? I command the relevant authorities to screen and release all criminals sentenced to a punishment of exile or less.

Kyemyo (6th day). The Eastern Jurchen general Nidabul 尼多弗 was granted an audience with the court.

Fifth Month

Chŏngmyo (1st day). There was a solar eclipse. The king issued a decree.

> Because of my shortcomings, our country has suffered from drought and repeated natural disasters. I therefore command the Food Service (*sangsikkuk* 尚食局) to prohibit fishing with fish traps and to reduce the taxes paid by falconers.

Kapsul (8th day). The king declared an amnesty.
Muin (12th day). The king avoided the main throne hall.
Kimyo (13th day). Rain fell.
Ŭlmi (29th day). Rain fell. The officials went to Kŏndŏk Hall 乾德殿 to submit memorials of congratulations.

Sixth Month

Pyŏngo (11th day). The king appointed Kim Yŏnggi as director of the Ministry of Punishments.
Chŏngsa (22nd day). Twenty-five Eastern Jurchens, led by Chief Yubuldal 紐弗達, were granted an audience with the court.

The military commissioner of the Northeastern Frontier Circuit submitted a petition.

> Hwangbo Kyŏng 皇甫瓊, a coastal branch province executive (*yŏnhae bundo p'an'gwan* 沿海分道判官), ventured far out to sea on his single warship and valiantly fought with sea pirates, killing and capturing them in great numbers. I request that he be rewarded.

The king approved the request.

Seventh Month

Chŏngmyo (2nd day). The Khitans sent the attendant censor (*siŏsa* 侍御史) Yo Gŏsŏn 姚居善 with a letter of congratulations on the king's birthday.
Chŏngch'uk (12th day). Sixty-six Eastern Jurchens, led by Chief Adugan 阿豆幹, were granted an audience with the court.

Eighth Month

Kimi (25th day). The king decided capital punishment cases across the country. Then he avoided the main throne hall, reduced the number of side dishes served at royal meals, and ceased his attendance at music performances.

Ninth Month

Imsin (8th day). The king personally conducted the Daoist Ch'o ritual at the Polo Field.
Chŏngch'uk (13th day). The relevant authorities submitted a petition.

> Chŏng Chang 鄭莊, the construction office commissioner for Chunggwang monastery (*Chunggwangsa chosŏng togamsa* 重光寺造成都監使), and the clerk Sŭng Chŏk 承迪 stole commodities that were under their care. We request that they be flogged and exiled according to law.

The king decreed that they be punished as light offenders, but the Censorate protested: "We beg you to follow the law without exception." The king approved.
Kyŏngjin (16th day). Eighty Jurchens, led by General Comforting the Frontier Tongbullo 冬弗老 and General Soothing Faraway Lands Saira of the Eastern Jurchens, were granted an audience with the court. They submitted a petition.

In former times, we the uncivilized were accustomed to creating disturbances and committing outrages in the frontier regions. But after receiving magnanimous treatment from the authorities in our area, we have thoroughly repented our past evil deeds. Together with our chiefs on land and sea, we now face the royal palace and prostrate ourselves to swear allegiance as loyal border people. In the future, we resolve to report on the movements of our enemies without fail.

The king was greatly pleased by this. He gave them promotions and special gifts of gold and silk.

Tenth Month

Imin (10th day). Eighty Eastern Jurchens, led by General Comforting the Frontier Yasagae 耶沙盖, were granted an audience and made an offering of their native products.

Eleventh Month

Muin (14th day). The acting left vice director of state affairs Chang Ch'angnyŏng 張昌齡 came as a response envoy from the Khitan Eastern Capital.
Sinsa (17th day). The Khitans sent a mission of 133 men, headed by the lead investiture envoy (*ch'aekpongsa* 冊封使) So Sinmi 蕭慎微 and the deputy investiture envoy (*ch'aekpong pusa* 冊封副使) Han Somun 韓紹文. They were followed by the chief administrative officer (*tobusŏ* 都部署) and Ich'ŏn province deputy surveillance commissioner (*Ich'ŏn kwannae kwanch'al yuhu* 利川管內觀察留後) Yu Irhaeng 劉日行, the investiture transmittal envoy (*apch'aeksa* 押冊使) and Palace Administration director Ma Chiyu 馬至柔, the investiture reading envoy (*tokch'aeksa* 讀冊使) and Palace Buildings vice director (*changjak sogam* 將作少監) Sŏ Hwahŭp 徐化洽, the edict delivery envoy (*chŏnsŏnsa* 傳宣使) and acting left cavalier attendant-in-ordinary Han Ison 韓貽孫, and others.

Chŏnghae (23rd day). The king built a platform to receive the Khitan emperor's commands. This was the imperial edict:

> With modest virtues, we have taken our place in the great enterprise. By relying on the achievements of past emperors, we have held dominion in every direction. Recently, in response to the pleas of our subjects, we received a magnificent title, and there will be tributes and festivals everywhere in our domain. For generations, you have venerated the imperial calendars and commands. You have inherited your territory and concluded the royal ceremonies. You have served us well. In keeping with the approaching celebrations, we will reward you for your achievements and elevate your title. We now send the generalissimo of the Left Palace Gate Guard (*chwa kammunwi sangjanggun* 左監門衛上將軍) So Sinmi as our lead investiture envoy and the vice minister of the Rites Ministry (*sangsŏ yebu sirang* 尚書禮部侍郎) Han Somun as deputy investiture envoy to present the letter of investiture. In addition, we are sending gifts of carriages, clothing, caps, swords, sealed ribbons, and official correspondence, as specified in the accompanying list. You should accept them with due respect.

The letter of investiture stated:

> When we bowed to the will of Heaven and accepted our part in the great task of our ancestors, people in every corner of the world submitted to us without a fight. We have invested all their officials and promoted them according to rule. Even faraway lands faithfully sent embassies across the sea to present letters of congratulation, strengthening their alliance with us. Therefore, during this time of great celebration, it is natural that we should grant special favors, and we award you the titles of Fulfilling Loyalty, Preserving Righteousness, Merit Subject Devoted to Country, Minister Unequaled in Honor,[28] Acting Grand Guardian, Director of the Chancellery, Supreme Pillar of the State, and King of Koryŏ, with a fief of seven thousand households and an actual fief of one thousand households. By maintaining your standing in the east, increasing your territory, and serving us well, you have faithfully carried

---

28. *Kaebu ŭidong samsa* 開府儀同三司, literally, Minister Who Chooses His Own Staff and Is Equal to Commander Unequaled in Honor.

out your duties in service to the royal household, and your name and merit are praised throughout the land.

Wherever we have traveled in the area of the capital, we have been welcomed by the common people and greeted by the provincial officials with respect. Even without weapons, there is order. By this, know that the sight of good governance in the provinces pleases us, even more than the jade and other gifts received from them. Neighboring countries recognize our preeminence as well, and hold it in awe, sending us gold and silk. With our country so prosperous, we have received a magnificent title, and to express our delight, we have given great things to the people and promotions to all of the officials, including fiefs and titles. We have also given this letter of investiture to our lead investiture envoy So Sinmi and our deputy investiture envoy Han Somun, who will bring it to you. With it, we invest you with the titles of Acting Grand Mentor (*su t'aebu* 守太傅) and Director of the Secretariat (*chungsŏryŏng* 中書令), and give you an additional fief of three thousand households and an actual fief of three hundred households. We also confer on you the additional titles of Gathering Virtue (*tongdŏk* 同德) and Serving Governance (*ch'iri* 致理) and reconfirm the rest.

Ah! By protecting the sage country under your rule, you have shown us that your virtue is prodigious, and that you are among the finest of our vassals. We have elevated you to this lofty position so that you may continue to live prosperously, bring honor to your ancestors, and serve us for all time. If you do this, your great achievements will continue to shine. Consider this!

Pyŏngin (2nd day). Eastern [Jurchen] tribesmen plundered Sŏgok county 瑞谷縣[29] with eight ships and took more than forty captives. The king punished the officers and men who had neglected their duties and failed to prepare adequate defenses.

---

29. Present-day Sŏgok-myŏn, Anbyŏng-gun, Kangwŏn.

Twelfth Month

Kyŏngsin (27th day). The Yugyŏk changgun 遊擊將軍[30] Kari 加利, ruler (*sŏngju* 星主) of the land of T'angna 乇羅,[31] submitted a petition.

> Prince Tura 豆羅 recently died. Since the succession cannot be broken for even a day, we ask that Hoing 號仍 be made our prince.

This was sent with an offering of native products.

Tenth Year of Chŏngjong (1044)

Fourth Month, Summer

Kyŏngsul (19th day). A party of 1,045 Eastern Jurchens bearing gifts requested an alliance. The king gave articles of clothing and silver vessels to each of them.

Kim Wŏnhyŏn 金元鉉 and others passed the state examination.

Fifth Month

Chŏngmyo (6th day). Twenty-five Eastern Jurchens, led by General Kura, were granted an audience and made an offering of their native products.

Sixth Month

Ŭlsa (15th day). The king received the bodhisattva ordination in Kŏndŏk Hall.

---

30. A rank 5b2 title for military officials.
31. Another name for T'amna, or present-day Cheju island.

Seventh Month

Kyeyu (14th day). The Khitans sent the acting grand guardian Yu Chongjŏng 劉從政 with a letter of congratulations on the king's birthday.

The king sent the right vice director of state affairs Yi Hoe and Accommodations Service director (*sangsa pongŏ* 尙舍奉御) Ch'oe Hŭijŏng 崔希正 to the Khitans with an expression of gratitude for his investiture.

Eighth Month

Kyemo (14th day). Forty-six Eastern Jurchens, led by General Adohan, were granted an audience and made an offering of their native products.

Ninth Month

Sinyu (3rd day). Sixty-six Eastern Jurchens, led by General Saira, were granted an audience and made an offering of their native products.
Kyehae (5th day). Fifty-nine Eastern Jurchens, led by General P'ogi 包伎, and twenty-seven Western Jurchens, led by Grand General Koduro, were granted an audience and made offerings of their native products.
Chŏngmyo (9th day). Twenty-six Eastern Jurchens, led by General Kunido 仇尼道, were granted an audience and made an offering of their native products.

Eleventh Month

Ŭrhae (18th day). The military commander Kim Yŏnggi submitted a petition.

The fortresses under construction at Ch'angju 長州,[32] Chŏngju 定州,[33] and Wŏnhŭng Garrison 元興鎭[34] will be completed sooner than expected, due

---

32. Present-day Chŏngp'yŏng-gun, South Hamgyŏng.
33. Present-day Chŏngp'yŏng-gun, South Hamgyŏng.
34. A location in present-day Kangwŏn.

to great effort. I recommend rewarding the local officials who oversaw the construction with suitable promotions. First, officials of rank seven or higher should be promoted by one grade and their parents invested with titles, while those of rank eight or lower should be promoted by at least one grade in rank and office and receive a promotion in prestige title according to the proper sequence. Second, other officials promoted in rank and office by one grade should receive a corresponding promotion in prestige title.

Also, since the territory of the three fortresses originally contained enemy strongholds, I have reason to be concerned about future disturbances and invasions. However, if a military detachment is deployed at each of these strategic points, I believe we will be able to defend them against enemy attacks by land or sea.

I recommend rewards for the soldiers as follows: First, officers at the rank of major or higher should be promoted by one grade and their parents invested with titles, while officers at the rank of sublieutenant (*taejŏng* 隊正) or higher should be promoted by one grade and receive a promotion in Koryŏ prestige title. Soldiers should also receive a promotion in Koryŏ prestige title. Second, ship's officers (*sŏndu* 船頭) as well as officers at the rank of sublieutenant or higher should receive one-grade promotions in official rank and Koryŏ prestige titles, while soldiers, sailors, and oarsmen should be given Koryŏ prestige titles. They should all be given gifts in accordance with their rank.

I also recommend that ten people in the first group receiving awards be given additional rewards, including the acting director of the Military Affairs Ministry (*sŏp pyŏngbu sangsŏ* 攝兵部尙書) Ko Yŏ. After the first ten, the next group of five should include the director of the Imperial Manufactories Directorate Yu Kyo, and the following group of five should include the executive of the Imperial Music Office (*taeaksŭng* 大樂丞) Chŏng P'ae, both of whom rendered meritorious service in battle during the construction of the fortresses. The purpose of these rewards is to inspire continued valor in the future.

The king approved.

Kyemi (26th day). A party of 144 male and female Eastern Jurchens, led by General Oŭldal 烏乙達, were granted an audience and made an offering of excellent horses. They also submitted a petition.

Living on the border of your esteemed country, we have long admired your benevolent rule. After serving you for many years, we are gratified to have been granted an audience as your loyal subjects. We once lived in constant fear of invasion from our enemies, which prevented us from establishing permanent homes and living in peace. But now three fortresses have been built, blocking the enemy's passage through our lands, and we have come to this audience with the court to express our gratitude.

The king rewarded them generously and sent them home.

Eleventh Year of Chŏngjong (1045)

First Month, Spring

Muo (1st day). The king canceled the New Year Congratulations.
Chŏngch'uk (20th day). The king offered sacrifices to the god of wind 風師 in the northern and eastern outskirts of the capital.

Fifty Eastern Jurchens, led by General Submitting to Virtue Aduju 阿豆主, were granted an audience and made an offering of their native products.

Second Month

Muja (1st day). The king gave the name Chaje monastery 慈濟寺 to Kwagyo station 課橋院[35] by the Imjin River. Before this, there was no ferry or bridge at the river port, so many who tried to get across the river would fall in and drown. The king ordered the relevant officials to make a floating bridge, and from then on, people and horses could cross the river as if on flat land.
Kabo (7th day). Sixty-five Eastern Jurchens, led by General Soothing Faraway Lands P'aŭldal 巴乙達, were granted an audience and made an offering of excellent horses.

---

35. The character *won* 院 can be interpreted as either a station or a monastery. It is translated here as Kwagyo station because this was a rest stop on journeys along or across the river.

Third Month

Kisa (13th day). Seventy-five Eastern Jurchens, led by General Embracing Faraway Lands (*hŏiwŏn changgun* 懷遠將軍) Yŏmhan 鹽漢, were granted an audience with the court.

Kyŏngo (14th day). The king went to Myot'ong monastery.

Pyŏngja (20th day). There was frost even though it was the time of the grain rain 穀雨,[36] so the king reviewed criminal cases.

Fourth Month

Chŏnghae (1st day). The Astrological Service submitted a report: "The expected solar eclipse did not appear due to dark clouds." The officials submitted memorials of congratulations.

Musul (12th day). Thirty-five Eastern Jurchens, led by Saŏdu 沙於頭, were granted an audience and made an offering of excellent horses.

Kihae (13th day). Seventy Eastern Jurchens, led by General Yoŏna 要於那, were granted an audience and made an offering of good horses.

Kyŏngja (14th day). Seventy Eastern Jurchens, led by General Comforting the Frontier Kod'ohwa, were granted an audience and made an offering of their native products.

Pyŏngo (20th day). The investigating censor Yi Ch'un 李春, who was serving as an executive in the Northwestern Frontier Circuit Military Commission (*sŏbungno pyŏngma p'an'gwan* 西北路兵馬判官), submitted a petition.

> More than one hundred bandit tribesmen attacked the Changp'yŏng guard post 長平戍 at Yŏngwŏn Garrison 寧遠鎭 and captured more than thirty garrison soldiers. I request that you punish those officers who failed to defend the fort.

The king approved.

---

36. The sixth of the twenty-four solar terms.

Musin (22nd day). The king offered sacrifices to the god of thunder 雷師 in the southern and western outskirts of the capital.

Kiyu (23rd day). The Imperial Archives (*pisŏsŏng* 秘書省) presented seventy new copies of the *Liji Zhengyi* 禮記正義[37] and forty copies of the *Maoshi Zhengyi* 毛詩正義.[38] The king ordered that one copy of each should be stored in the Royal Library (*ŏsŏgak* 御書閣) and the rest given to literary court officials.

Fifth Month

Kyŏngsin (5th day). The king decreed: "Since the lesser heat (*sosŏ* 小暑)[39] is almost here, prisoners with heavy sentences will be dealt with leniently and those convicted of minor crimes will be released."

Pyŏngin (11th day). A party of Song merchants from Quanzhou, led by Lin Xi 林禧, came to the court with an offering of their native products.

The king bestowed one horse from the Inner Stables (*naeguma* 內廐馬) to each soldier at the eastern frontier who had emerged victorious in battle against the tribal bandits.

Intercalary Month

Sinch'uk (16th day). Since it had continued raining for a long time, the king ordered the retrial of criminals and the release of those convicted of minor crimes.

---

37. A compilation of commentaries on the *Liji* by Zheng Xuan (127–200) and Kong Yingda (574–648).
38. A commentary on the *Maoshizhuan* by Kong Yingda.
39. The eleventh of the twenty-four solar terms.

Sixth Month

Kimyo (25th day). Yayul Sŏn 耶律宣, the acting grand mentor (*kŏmgyo t'aebu* 檢校太傅) and superintendent of the Three Ranks (*p'an sambanwŏnsa* 判三班院事), came from the Khitans as a special envoy bearing an imperial edict. *Kyŏngjin* (26th day). The king offered sacrifices to the Yŏng star 零星.[40]

Seventh Month, Autumn

Chŏngyu (14th day). The Khitans sent the acting right vice director of state affairs Ko Yugi 高惟幾 with a letter of congratulations on the king's birthday.

Ninth Month

Kyŏngin (8th day). Forty-five Eastern Jurchens, led by General Kojimun, were granted an audience with the court.

Eleventh Month, Winter

Kyŏngin (9th day). Due to the bitter cold, the king released those convicted of minor crimes and stopped all non-urgent required labor.

Thirty-six Eastern Jurchens, led by Koch'a 高遮, were granted an audience and made an offering of their native products.

Twelfth Month

Imja (1st day). The king ordered the retrial of criminals.

---

40. The character *yŏng* 零 in the original text is likely a misprint for 靈, the more commonly used character in this context. The Yŏng star represented the god of agriculture and was believed to oversee the success or failure of crops.

Twelfth Year of Chŏngjong (1046)

Second Month, Spring

Pyŏngin (15th day). The king held the Lantern Festival and dispensed food and drink.

Imsin (21st day). The king offered sacrifices to the Majo star 馬祖.[41]

Third Month

Sinsa (1st day). There was a solar eclipse. The king avoided the main throne hall, dressed in plain robes, and prayed for the sun to come out.

Sinmyo (11th day). Yi Injŏng 李仁挺 and others passed the state examination.

Sinch'uk (21st day). The king ordered the Chancellery director Ch'oe Chean to go to the Polo Field to burn incense, and that a sutra-chanting procession should be sent through the streets. The procession was divided into three groups that followed separate routes through Kaegyŏng. On each route, a colored box containing the *Prajñāpāramitā-sūtra* (*Panyagyŏng* 般若經) led the way, followed by monks in Buddhist robes chanting the sutra out loud, and by the supervisor of convoys (*kamapkwan* 監押官) in official robes, who walked through the streets praying for blessings for the people. This entire procession was called *kyŏnghaeng* 經行, and it became the custom from that year on.

Fourth Month, Summer

Sinhae (1st day). The king offered sacrifices to Chungnong 仲農.[42]

Chŏngmyo (17th day). The king fell ill and changed his residence to Sanho Hall 山呼殿.

Chŏngch'uk (27th day). The king moved to Pŏbun monastery 法雲寺 on the palace grounds.

---

41. The star that protected horses.
42. Another name for Hou Ji, the god of agriculture during the Zhou dynasty of China.

Fifth Month

Pyŏngsul (7th day). All the officials offered prayers at Buddhist monasteries.

Ŭlmi (16th day). The Civil Personnel Ministry submitted a petition.

> More than 180 days have passed since the Imperial Regalia Court director and Astrological Service administrator (*chi t'aesaguksa* 知太史局事) Sŏ Ung 徐雄 was granted sick leave. By regulation, any appointed official whose leave of absence exceeds one hundred days is dismissed from office. We request that Sŏ Ung be removed from office.

The king decreed: "Sŏ Ung performs his duties well as the head of the Astrological Service, so I award him a special grant of two hundred days."

Chŏngyu (18th day). The king was seriously ill. Believing he was near death, he summoned his younger brother Wang Hwi 王徽 (1019–1083), the lord of Nangnang, to his bedroom and issued an imperial edict ordering Wang Hwi to act on all state affairs.

> By the grace of the last ruler, I inherited the great and arduous task of my royal ancestors. For the past twelve years, with the aid of Heaven, there has been peace within this country. But since the spring and into the summer, due to ineffective medicines and a lack of proper care, my illness has grown worse. My wish now is to relinquish the throne to a virtuous person. Wang Hwi, the lord of Nangnang and director of the Imperial Secretariat, is my beloved younger brother, whose filial devotion, benevolence, civility, and restraint are well known to neighboring countries. It is right that I transmit to him the great treasure of the throne so that its radiance may continue to be seen.

> The king passed away that day.

King Chŏngjong was thirty-three and reigned for twelve years. His body lay in repose at Sŏndŏk Hall. The king was generous, benevolent, filial, friendly, broad-minded, resolute, and did not bother about trifles. His posthumous title was Holding Benevolence, and his temple name was Chŏngjong. His funeral was simple, and he was buried in Chu Tomb 周陵

in the northern outskirts of the capital, in accordance with his final will. The king was given the additional posthumous titles of Expansive Filiality in the tenth year of Munjong (1056), Wonderful Merit (*yŏngnyŏl* 英烈) in the eighteenth year of Injong (1140), and Brilliant Respect (*mun'gyŏng* 文敬) in the fortieth year of Kojong (1253).

Yi Chehyŏn's evaluation of the king:

> Since the Khitans were untrustworthy, greedy, and vicious, King T'aejo was always on his guard against them. But it was not good policy to break off long-standing relations with the Khitans over one disaster.[43] In the midst of difficulties, King Hyŏnjong settled the country but had little time to address foreign affairs. King Tŏkchong took the throne at a young age and had to be even more careful about going to war. However, Wang Kado's plan to sever peaceful relations was not as good as Hwangbo Yuŭi's plan to continue good relations with the Khitans and bring peace to the people. In the third year of his reign, King Chŏngjong sent Ch'oe Yŏnha to the Khitans on a diplomatic mission. In his fourth year, the Khitan envoy Ma Poŏp arrived, restoring the alliance thereafter. This was not accomplished due to sincerity, but through subtle diplomacy. The sage believed, "A good succession and good maintenance protect the state."

---

43. A reference to the events of 942 when T'aejo, seeing Khitan perfidy cause the collapse of the kingdom of Parhae, held a mission of Khitan envoys to Koryŏ captive on an island and let the camels they had brought him as a gift starve to death.

VOLUME 7

Compiled by Chŏng Inji, Chŏnghŏn grand master, minister of works, director of the Hall of Worthies, deputy director of the Royal Lectures Office and State Records Office, headmaster of the Royal Confucian Academy.

MUNJONG (1046–1056)

Munjong 文宗, reigned 1046–1083

Munjong, the Great King of Bright Holiness (*changsŏng* 章聖) and Benevolent Filiality (*inhyo* 仁孝), was named Sŏ 緒 at birth. His given name was changed to Hwi 徽, and his adult name was Ch'ogyu 燭幽. He was the third son of Hyŏnjong, and his mother was Lady Kim 金, the dowager empress Wŏnhye 元惠太后. He was born on *kyemi* (1st day) in the twelfth month of *kimi*, the tenth year of Hyŏnjong (1019). He was invested as the Lord of Nangnang in the thirteenth year of Hyŏnjong (1022) and as the Director of the Imperial Secretariat in the third year of Chŏngjong (1037).

On *chŏngyu* (18th day) in the fifth month of the twelfth year of Chŏngjong (1046), Chŏngjong passed away, and Munjong acceded to the throne. A procession of officials bearing the royal seal went to Chunghwang Hall, where they offered congratulations.

Accession Year of Munjong (1046)

Fifth Month

Kihae (20th day). The king issued a decree.

The late king's royal seat and footrest used nails decorated with gold and silver, and the bedclothes were made of woolen fabrics embroidered with gold and silver threads. Have the appropriate authorities replace them with copper, iron, twill damask, and silk.

Kyŏngja (21st day). The king led the officials to the funeral hall, where the late king's body lay in state, and wailed sadly in mourning.

Sixth Month

Kabin (5th day). The king sent the Public Works executive (*sangsŏ kongbu nangjung* 尚書工部郎中) Ch'oe Wŏnjun 崔爰俊 to the Khitans to inform them of the royal funeral.

Kimi (10th day). In the palace, the king conducted the Daoist Ch'o ritual using his personal star (*ponmyŏngsŏng* 本命星).[1] As the king was born in the year *kimi* (1019), he personally conducted the Daoist Ch'o ritual every year on this day.

Chŏngmyo (18th day). The king went to Sinbong Pavilion, where he proclaimed a general amnesty and promoted the officials by one grade.

Seventh Month, Autumn

Kimyo (1st day). The king went to Wangnyun monastery to attend a Buddhist mourning rite for the queen mother.

Sinsa (3rd day). The king issued a decree.

> The naval officer Ŭn Chil 殷質 of P'arŭm island 八音島[2] and naval officers Kwanghyŏp 匡協, Kwandal 寬達, and Yŏnggil 英吉 of Yang island 壤島[3] distinguished themselves in battle by capturing enemies. I award all of them the title of Chungyun.

---

1. The star that corresponded to the date and year of the person's birthday. Based on the birthday, one of the nine stars around the North Star became one's personal star.
2. Present-day Porŭm island, Sŏdo district, Kanghwa prefecture, Inch'ŏn city.
3. Present-day Chindo-gun, South Chŏlla.

Musul (24th day). The king issued a decree.

> When the eastern tribesmen besieged Chŏngbyŏn Garrison 靜邊鎭,[4] Major Chŏng Kwangsun 鄭匡順 fought valiantly and defeated the enemy before falling in battle himself. His meritorious deed is remarkable. I award him the posthumous title of Lieutenant Colonel of the Capital Garrison Division (*kŭmowi nangjang* 金吾衛郎將).

Eighth Month

Imja (5th day). The king held the *Avataṃsaka-sūtra* ritual (*Hwaŏmgyŏng toryang* 華嚴經道場)[5] in Kŏndŏk Hall.

Kyŏngsin (13th day). The king attended to state affairs in Kŏndŏk Hall. Then he went to Sŏnjŏng Hall and summoned the Chancellery director Ch'oe Chean and the affairs manager Ch'oe Ch'ung to discuss the moral considerations pertaining to current policies.

Ninth Month

Kimyŏ (2nd day). The king went to Poje monastery and provided food for the monks.

Kyemi (6th day). The king gave gifts of food, drink, and clothing to the left vice director of state affairs Ch'oe Posŏng, the right vice director of state affairs Cho Ong, the supreme general Yi Ŭngbo, and Kim Honggwang 金洪光, all of whom retired from office due to old age.

Ŭryu (8th day). The king held the three-day Hundred Seat ritual for the recitation of the *Humane Kings Sutra* (*paekchwa Inwanggyŏng toryang* 百座仁王經道場)[6] in the Inner Office.

Chŏngyu (20th day). A man of Imjin county named Pae Haeng 裴行 altered a royal decree to confer offices on seven people, including Cho Kyŏng

---

4. Present-day Kŭmya prefecture, South Hamgyŏng.

5. This Buddhist ceremony used the *Avataṃsaka-Sūtra* 華嚴經, to pray for the deceased and dispel natural disasters.

6. This was a ritual performed by one hundred Buddhist monks reading the *Humane Kings Sutra* in front of one hundred Buddhist statues to ensure the security of the country.

趙京. According to law, he should have been hanged. However, he was dismissed from office and returned home due to the proclamation of a general amnesty.

Kihae (22nd day). The king personally hosted a banquet at the Polo Field for elderly men who were eighty or older. Also included were filial sons and grandsons, virtuous husbands and wives, widows and widowers, orphans and the elderly without children, and the gravely ill or disabled. The king gave gifts to all in accordance with their rank.

Pyŏngo (29th day). The king went to Myot'ong monastery and burned incense.

Tenth Month

Kyech'uk (7th day). The relevant authorities submitted a petition.

> Palaces, gates, monasteries, government offices, and districts with names that have the same sound as the king's name should be changed without exception.

Pyŏngjin (10th day). The king held the Buddhist Calamity Dispelling ritual (*sojae toryang* 消災道場) in Hoegyŏng Hall.

Eleventh Month

Muja (12th day). The Chancellery director Ch'oe Chean died.

Kyŏngin (14th day). The king went to Pŏbwang monastery and held the Assembly of the Eight Prohibitions.

Twelfth Month

Pyŏngo (1st day). The officials went to Kŏndŏk Hall to offer their congratulations on the Day of Actualizing Peace (*sŏngp'yŏngjŏl* 成平節). The king hosted a banquet in Sŏnjŏng Hall for the state councilors, royal attendants 侍臣, and those in the Censorate at the rank of supervising secretary, executive assistant (*kŭpsa chungsŭng* 給舍中丞), and above. The Day of Actualizing Peace is the king's birthday. Beginning on the king's birthday, a state-sponsored ritual to protect the king's good fortune (*kisang yŏngbok toryang* 祈祥迎福道場) was held at the Outer Śakra monastery for seven days every year. The same ritual was observed at Hŭngguk monastery by civil and military officials and by the Eastern and Western Capitals, the four regional military commands, and the eight *moks* at their local monasteries. This became the custom thereafter.

Imsul (7th day). The Khitans sent the imperial diarist (*kigŏ sain* 起居舍人) Chu Chongbaek 周宗白 to offer condolences.

First Year of Munjong (1047)

First Month, Spring

Pyŏngsul (11th day). The king issued a decree.

> In the year *kapsin* (1044), when enemies attacked the Northeastern Frontier Circuit, a group of forty soldiers led by Yi Sŏmhan 李暹漢 stood in the vanguard leading our forces to victory. I award them gifts and titles in accordance with their rank.

Chŏnghae (12th day). The king issued a decree.

> The late Palace Secretariat commissioner Im Yugan rendered meritorious service by loyally assisting the throne. This was an exceptional case, and I confer on his son Im Yanggae 林良槩 an office of the eighth rank.

Chŏngyu (22nd day). The king issued a decree.

> Many *chus*, districts, prefectures, and counties hold an Assembly for Revolving Sutra Recitation (*yun'gyŏnghoe* 輪經會) every year. I fear that local administrative clerks may use this occasion to torment people by extorting money from them. Starting today, holding extensive banquets and music performances is forbidden.

Imin (27th day). The king appointed the director of the Water Control Court No U as administrator of the Northeastern Frontier District Military Commission (*chi tongbungmyŏn pyŏngmasa* 知東北面兵馬事), and the vice director of punishments and vice commissioner of state finance (*samsa pusa* 三司副使) Yi Injŏng 李仁靖 as the vice military commissioner of the Northwestern Frontier District (*sŏbungmyŏn pyŏngma pusa* 西北面兵馬副使).

Second Month

Pyŏngo (1st day). Yang Taech'un, the military commissioner of the Northwestern Frontier Circuit, submitted a petition.

> About eight hundred men serving under the Yŏnju defense commissioner (*Yŏnju pangŏsa* 連州防禦使), from local administrative leaders down to soldiers and commoners, reported to me that the Yŏnju vice defense commissioner (*Yŏnju pangŏ pusa* 連州防禦副使) So Hyŏn 蘇顯 has accomplished many great things in his promotion of agriculture since his arrival in office, and also in his provision of relief for the people there. It is for this reason that I thought it appropriate to memorialize the throne.

The king issued a decree: "I order the Civil Personnel Ministry to promote him properly according to the rules."

Kimi (14th day). The king went to Pongŭn monastery to hold the Lantern Festival. On the following day, he hosted a banquet for the royal family and his royal attendants.

Imsul (17th day). The Khitans sent the military commissioner of the Loyal Compliance Army (*ch'ungsun'gun chŏltosa* 忠順軍節度使) So Sinmi, the acting vice director of Palace Administration (*su chŏnjung sogam* 守殿中少監) Kang Hwasŏng 康化成, and other envoys to conduct the ancestral rites for King Chŏngjong at the funeral hall. The king participated.

Chŏngmyo (22th day). The Military and War Council submitted a petition.

> Chief Adogan of the eastern [Jurchen] tribesmen was granted royal gifts and benefits when he submitted to the authorities of Koryŏ. However, he rebelled against us after that and surrendered to the Khitans. His

crime is great. Kojimun, a leader [of the Eastern Jurchens], is now at the frontier with a few others. I request that the army be sent under cover to capture and bring them over to our jurisdiction, where we can interrogate them and impose punishment according to law.

The king approved.
Kapsul (29th day). The king went to the Outer Śakra monastery.

Third Month

Ŭrhae (1st day). There was a solar eclipse, and the Censorate submitted a petition.

> The spring astronomical observer (*ch'un'gwanjŏng* 春官正) Yu P'aeng 柳彭 and the Astrological Service executive Yu Tŭkso 柳得韶, being ignorant of astronomical observation, failed to report the eclipse beforehand. We request that they be discharged from their offices.

The king ordered their pardon. The Censorate submitted another remonstrance.

> The eclipse of the sun and moon are normal phases of yin and yang. If no mistakes are made in calculating the calendar, the changes can be predicted. Nonetheless, the officials in charge of astronomical observation are incompetent and have failed to fulfill their duties. How can this be tolerated? We request that they be punished as proposed in the previous memorial.

The king approved.
Kyemi (9th day). The king personally observed the *Prajñāpāramitā-sūtra* ritual (*Panya toryang* 般若道場)[7] in Kŏndŏk Hall for five days.
Pyŏngsul (12th day). A party of Eastern Jurchens, led by General Supporting the State Saira, was granted an audience and made an offering of native

---

7. A Buddhist ritual to promote the teachings of the *Prajñāpāramitā-Sūtra* 般若經. It was used to stop epidemics and other diseases from spreading, and to pray for rain. This ritual was also known as the Panyagyŏng toryang 般若經道場.

products. The king promoted him to the rank of Grand General Submitting to Virtue.

Sinmyo (17th day). The Chancellery executive Hwangbo Yŏng submitted a memorial.

> I have no heir [to carry on my name]. I request permission to adopt Kim Noksung 金祿崇, my daughter's son, as my heir.

The king approved and conferred on Kim Noksung an office of the ninth rank.

Musul (24th day). Six Eastern Jurchens, led by General Yaŏhae 耶於害, were granted an audience. As leaders of their respective tribes, they all submitted to Koryŏ. The king gave them land and houses and settled them in the country.

Fourth Month, Summer

Pyŏngo (2nd day). The king went to Kŏndŏk Hall to attend to state affairs. From there he proceeded to Sŏnjŏng Hall to discuss the moral considerations pertaining to current policies with his senior state councilors and members of the Censorate.

Chŏngmi (3rd day). The king appointed Ch'oe Ch'ung as director of the Chancellery, Kim Yŏnggi as executive of the Chancellery, Kim Wŏnch'ung as executive of the Imperial Secretariat, Pak Yuin as left vice director of the State Affairs Department and senior governmental advisor, and Yi Chayŏn as director of the Civil Personnel Ministry and senior governmental advisor.

Muo (14th day). The king awarded Yi Ŭngbo, who retired as a high grand marshal, the title of Kaebu ŭidong samsa.

Kyehae (19th day). There had been no rain through the spring. The king avoided the main throne hall and suspended regular court assemblies. He also prohibited the butchering of livestock and restricted royal meals to the use of dried beef and salted seafood. The king ordered the retrial of criminals across the country.

Kapcha (20th day). The king conducted the ancestral rites at the Imperial Ancestral Shrine.

Ŭlch'uk (21st day). The king appointed the military official Ko Yŏl as left vice director of the State Affairs Department and high minister of works, and Ha Hŭnghyu 何興休 as high director of the Public Works Ministry (*su kongbu sangsŏ* 守工部尙書).

Chŏngmyo (23rd day). The king personally observed the Hundred Seat ritual for the recitation of the *Humane Kings Sutra* in Hoegyŏng Hall. He fed ten thousand monks at the Polo Field.

Sinmi (27th day). Kim Chŏngsin 金鼎新 and others passed the state examination.

Kyeyu (29th day). A party of Eastern Jurchens, led by Agaju, came to the court with an offering of their native products. The king awarded Agaju the title of Grand General Pacifying Faraway Lands (*p'yŏngwŏn taejanggun* 平遠大將軍).

Fifth Month

Chŏngch'uk (3rd day). The Eastern Jurchen general Oŏnae 烏於乃 was granted an audience with the court.

Kimyo (5th day). There was a heavy rain.

Ŭlmi (21st day). The Chancellery submitted a petition: "Since the timely rain has come in abundance, please resume having the normal number of side dishes served at your meals." The king approved.

Musul (24th day). The Eastern Jurchen Taesang Obulch'a 烏弗遮 was granted an audience with the court.

Kihae (25th day). The king proceeded to Hyŏnhwa monestary to attend a Buddhist mourning rite for King Hyŏnjong.

Sixth Month

Ŭlsa (2nd day). The king went to Pongŭn monastery.

Musin (5th day). The king issued a decree.

The law establishes the standard for punishments. If it is clear, no punishment will be unjust or excessive. If it is not, punishments lose their weight. I am deeply concerned that many unfair provisions may remain in our current criminal and administrative codes. I therefore order the Chancellery director Ch'oe Ch'ung to gather jurists to carefully reexamine the codes in order to implement appropriate reforms. Also, be sure to examine the regulations governing the calligraphy and accounting examinations.

Ŭlmyo (12th day). The king led the court nobles to Pongŭn monastery, where he promoted the royal preceptor Kyŏrŭng 決凝 (964–1053) to state preceptor.

Chŏngsa (14th day). The king called Ch'oe Ch'ung and others to Mundŏk Hall and questioned them about military and state affairs.

Kyŏngsin (17th day). A party of Eastern Jurchens, led by General Comforting the Frontier Nodo 老道 and General Submitting to Virtue Yasaro 耶思老, were granted an audience and made an offering of their native products. The king awarded Yasaro the title of General Embracing Transformation.

Ŭlch'uk (22nd day). Ko Mujŏ 高無諸 and other Khitans came to submit.

Kyŏngo (27th day). Saibul 沙伊弗 and other Eastern Jurchens were granted an audience with the court.

Seventh Month, Autumn

Kapsul (1st day). The king went to Wangnyun monastery.

Kyŏngjin (7th day). The king issued a decree.

The left vice director of state affairs and high minister of education Chang Kŭngmaeng 蔣劇猛 rendered distinguished service on the frontier, forgetting his family's interests and caring solely for the country's welfare. To praise the extraordinary merit he displayed, it is appropriate for special favors to be granted. In addition to giving protected appointments (*ŭmjik* 蔭職)[8] to his descendants, I bestow on his sons and grandsons exceptional promotions to government offices.

---

8. Protected appointments gave the sons, grandsons, and other relatives of high-ranking officials the right to be appointed to entry-level government offices without taking the state examination.

Mun Han 文漢, a man of Changyŏn county 長淵縣,[9] killed his parents and four more people, his sister and children among them, and then claimed that he had been possessed by a spirit. He was beheaded and his dead body was placed in the street for public viewing.

The Punishments Ministry submitted a petition.

> The county governor (*hyŏllyŏng* 縣令) Ch'oe Tŏgwŏn 崔德元 and his assistant (*hyŏnwi* 縣尉) Ch'oe Sungmang 崔崇望 have failed to provide exemplary administration for the people [of Changyŏn]. They have not only delayed official reports but have caused many deplorable events and should be dismissed.

The king approved.

Sinsa (8th day). The king appointed the director of rites Yi Suhwa as military commander of the Northwestern Frontier District in autumn and winter (*sŏbungmyŏn ch'udongbŏn pyŏngmasa* 西北面秋冬番兵馬使), and the vice director of military affairs and State Finance vice commissioner Pak Chongdo 朴宗道 as vice military commissioner of the Northeastern Frontier District (*tongbungmyŏn pyŏngma pusa* 東北面兵馬副使).

Imo (9th day). The king called the senior state councilors to Mundŏk Hall and questioned them about the moral considerations pertaining to current policies.

Muja (15th day). The king appointed Ch'oe Yusŏn as miscellaneous affairs investigator, and Kim Ŭijin 金義珍 (d. 1070) as palace censor.

Imjin (19th day). The king appointed the Palace Secretariat commissioner Wang Ch'ongji as middle commander of the Northwestern Frontier District (*sŏbungmyŏn chunggunsa* 西北面中軍使) and military commissioner of the Mobile Headquarters (*haengyŏng pyŏngmasa* 行營兵馬使).

Eighth Month

Musin (6th day). The Censorate submitted a petition.

---

9. Present-day Changyŏn-gun, South Hwanghae.

Yi Hŭiro 李希老 and Hong Tŏgwi 洪德威 were recently appointed as investigating censors. As a quick-tempered man, Yi Hŭiro rendered no meritorious services even though he had held a number of previous posts in central and local government. Hong Tŏgwi, together with the Imperial Regalia Court assistant executive (*wiwi chubu* 衛尉注簿) Sŏ Kyŏngŭi 徐磬宜, hosted a reception with libations and a music performance on the fifteenth day of the first month of this year, devoting himself to pleasure before the mourning period for King Chŏngjong was over. In this he failed to fulfill his duties as a subject. Both are not fit to serve in the Censorate. They should be dismissed.

The king did not approve. The Censorate insisted on submitting a second memorial on the same subject. This time the king approved.

Sinhae (9th day). The king personally observed the *Golden Light Sutra* ritual (*Kŭmganggyŏng toryang* 金剛經道場) in Mundŏk Hall for five days.

Kapcha (22nd day). A party of Eastern Jurchens, led by Generals Soothing Faraway Lands Muiro 無伊老 and Adu, were granted an audience and made an offering of their native products.

Kisa (27th day). Thirty tribal chiefs leading their clans, including those from Mongnago village 蒙羅古村 and Anggwaji village 仰果只村, came to the court to submit.

Ninth Month

Ŭrhae (4th day). The king went to Poje monastery.

Chŏngch'uk (6th day). A party of Song merchants led by Lin Ji 林機 came to the court with an offering of their native products.

Imo (11th day). The Khitans sent the Pokchu district surveillance commissioner (*Pokchu kwannae kwanch'alsa* 福州管內觀察使) Song Lin 宋璘 as their investiture envoy. The letter of investiture stated:

> Mahan 馬韓 [Koryŏ] has been designated the land of a feudal lord. It has inherited a royal investiture for generation after generation, receiving titles of the highest rank. The emperor has conferred on the Mahan kings a golden seal with colored tassels in recognition of Koryŏ's status as the highest of tributary states, as well as red and black bows for

conquering territories in all directions. Now it is time to bestow that royal inheritance from your forefathers on the most qualified person of all, and we take pleasure in following precedent with a grand ritual.

The provisional king of Koryŏ (*kwŏnji Koryŏ kugwangsa* 權知高麗國王事) Wang Hwi, born with the destiny of governing his country, possesses extraordinary talent. Besides showing auspicious signs like that of the celestial giraffe topping the tortoise and dragon, you have faithfully illuminated the right path in the same way that the Riguan summit 日觀峰[10] dominates Mount Song and Mount Hua.[11] You are talented in both the literary and the martial arts, you firmly grasp the deep roots of filial devotion and loyalty, and your bearing has been sincere from your youth. Inheriting the great achievements of the late king, you have appointed wise and able men while upholding virtue with proper and harmonious decorum. Moreover, admiring the hegemony of Duke Huan of Qi 齊桓 and Duke Wen of Jin, you have mastered the military strategies of Wei Qing 衛青 (d. 105) and Huo Qubing 霍去病 (d. 117), creating opportune advantages with rich and grand schemes. As the lord of a tributary state, you have submitted to our imperial court and sent us your envoys. But as king, you have bestowed regal benefits on your country and gained the trust of the people.

Now we cannot delay granting our favor, and with this message we issue the decree that will confirm and uphold your kingdom. We appoint you our Left Councilor and raise your rank to that of the Three Preceptors. To acknowledge your merits, we give you noble titles and award you generous fiefs to illuminate them.

King Wen of Zhou 周文王 (r. 1056–1052 BCE) appointed Jiang Taigong 姜太公 to an important position but gave the remote land of Qi as a fief, and Han Taizi 漢高祖 (247–195 BCE) sacrificed a white horse to promise that emperors would only come from the Liu 劉 family. Looking back to ancient times, the exceptional respect we have bestowed on you has been rare. From this you may infer that you have been enjoined to enjoy happiness and wealth forever.

If you heed our instructions, you will receive assistance from Heaven. We confer on you the titles of Commander Unequaled in Honor, Acting

---

10. The highest summit of Mount Tai 泰山 in Shandong province.
11. Mount Song 嵩山 is in Henan province, and Mount Hua 華山 is in Shaangxi province.

Grand Guardian (*su t'aebo* 守太保), Director of the Chancellery, and Supreme Pillar of the State. We invest you as King of Koryŏ and give you a fief of seven thousand households and an actual fief of one thousand households. In addition, we award you the titles of Rectifying the Age (*kwangsi* 匡時), Serving Governance, and Merit Subject for Perfecting Integrity (*kalchŏl* 竭節).

Tenth Month

Kapchin (3rd day). The retired Chancellery executive Hwangbo Yŏng died.
Ŭlsa (4th day). Forty Eastern Jurchens, led by General Kododal 高都達, were granted an audience and made an offering of their native products.
Chŏngmi (6th day). A party representing 312 Eastern Jurchen households from Mongnago village, led by Komujŏ 古無諸 and others, came to submit.
Kyŏngsin (19th day). The Chinju *mok* administrator (*Chinju moksa* 晋州牧使) and Water Control Court director Ch'oe Pokkyu 崔復圭 submitted a report: "I located the family members of 13,000 displaced households and called them back to return to their livelihoods." The king praised him.

Eleventh Month

Chŏngch'uk (7th day). Forty-six Eastern Jurchens, led by Generals Maji 馬志 and Kosa 高謝, were granted an audience and made an offering of excellent horses.
Kich'uk (19th day). The king called the senior state councilors to Mundŏk Hall to discuss the moral considerations pertaining to current policies.
Pyŏngsin (26th day). The Civil Personnel Ministry submitted a petition.

> The king ordered that all central and local government offices, with the sole exception of the Frontier Patrol Office (*sunbyŏn kwansa* 巡邊官司), should reduce their personnel by one man. We find that regional offices responsible for administering *chus* and *moks* in the P'aesŏ 浿西道 and Sannam 山南 provinces have more issues than a reduced staff can handle, so that governance in those areas suffers from frequent delays. We request that the working staff responsible for the mountains

(*ak* 岳), *moks, chus,* and districts in those areas be restored to their former number and that this practice be made permanent.

The king approved.

Twelfth Month

Sinch'uk (1st day). The retired Chancellery executive Yi Tan died.
Kiyu (9th day). The consort of Yŏndŏk Palace (*Yŏndŏk kungbi* 延德宮妃), Lady Yi 李, gave birth to a son. The king named him Hyu 烋 (1047–1083).[12]
Kyŏngsul (10th day). The Civil Personnel Ministry submitted a petition.

> According to the old system, all officials who have not [voluntarily] requested retirement before the age of sixty-nine are dismissed at the end of the same year. The vice director of imperial medicine (*t'aeŭi sogam* 太醫少監) in the Tea Ritual Office (*tabang* 茶房), Kim Chingak 金徵渥, has now reached the age of retirement. He should be dismissed.

The king issued a decree: "Kim Chingak is a renowned doctor and a royal attendant. Let him remain in office a few more years."
Pyŏngjin (16th day). The king appointed the Revenue Ministry director Pak Sŏnggŏl 朴成傑 as military commissioner of the Mobile Headquarters of the Northwestern Frontier District (*sŏbungmyŏn haengyŏng pyŏngmasa* 西北面行營兵馬使).
Chŏngsa (17th day). The Eastern Jurchen Yago 也古 and Western Jurchen Kosa 高舍, accompanied by others, were granted an audience with the court.

---

12. Wang Hyu was renamed Hun in 1053 and ruled as King Sunjong for barely three months in 1083.

Second Year of Munjong (1048)

First Month, Spring

Kyŏngo (1st day). The king canceled the New Year Congratulations.

Ŭrhae (6th day). Forty Eastern Jurchens, led by Generals Embracing Transformation Kura and Maribul 麻里弗, were granted an audience and made an offering of fine horses. The king gave them gifts in accordance with their rank.

Intercalary Month

Kyŏngja (1st day). The king performed the rite for Distributing the Calendar at the Imperial Ancestral Shrine.

Pyŏngo (7th day). Thirty-five Eastern Jurchens, led by General Submitting to Virtue Saira and General Soothing Faraway Lands Sasiha 沙時賀, were granted an audience and made an offering of native horses.

Kyŏngsul (11th day). Thirty-eight Eastern Jurchens, led by General Embracing Transformation Togura 都仇羅, were granted an audience and made an offering of their native products.

Sinhae (12th day). Twenty-four Western Jurchens, led by General Comforting the Frontier Kojiji 高之智, were granted an audience and made an offering of their native products.

The Khitans sent the chief general of the Personal Guard Wang T'aek 王澤 and other officials to deliver a state letter.

Second Month

Sinsa (13th day). The king ordered the retrial of criminals.

Kapsin (16th day). The Lantern Festival was held on this day because the Cold Food day fell on *kyemi*, the fifteenth day of the month.[13]

---

13. The Lantern Festival was usually held on the fifteenth day of the second month, but it could be postponed by one day if there was a conflict with other special events.

Third Month

Kyŏngja (2nd day). The Censorate submitted a petition.

> Last month, you issued a decree that said, "I am concerned about the lack of timely rain when the sowing of seeds has started. If any unexecuted amnesty decrees or orders to relieve the destitute remain among my edicts in the year *pyŏngsul* (1046), the relevant authorities should carry out the edict with all possible haste." We implemented your order, but laborers who had been conscripted for the construction of Taeun monastery 大雲寺 and Taean monastery 大安寺 were forced to abandon their farm lands while the construction of the two monasteries was still in progress. If someone is not farming, then someone must be starving. How can we disturb people's farming during the three seasons?[14] Moreover, everyone was deeply affected by your merciful edict to suspend construction projects for three years, and the entire country was joyous, but the edict was not fully implemented in the end. Integrity is a state treasure that should not be neglected. As we fear that people will criticize you for breaking your word, we request that the construction of the two monasteries be postponed until the offseason for cultivation.

The king approved.

Kyemyo (5th day). The king installed Queen Chŏngsin 定信王妃 as the Dowager Queen Yongsin 容信王后.

Sinhae (13th day). The king held the Buddhist Calamity Dispelling ritual in the Inner Office. He released those convicted of minor crimes and forgave back taxes.

Kabin (16th day). The lady of Yŏnch'ang Palace 延昌宮主, Lady No 盧, died.

Ŭlch'uk (27th day). The king prayed for rain.

---

14. The three agricultural seasons are spring, summer, and autumn.

Fourth Month, Summer

Kyŏngo (2nd day). The king went to the Outer Śakra monastery to listen to the sutra chanting on the Hŏllan 軒欄 stage.[15] In the past, a king would stop at the monastery after visiting the pine forests on Mount Songak, and a monk would greet the king's carriage while sutras were chanted in the hall. This was the origin of the custom.
Kapsul (6th day). The king went to Myot'ong monastery.
Kabo (26th day). There was frost in T'osan county.

Fifth Month

Kapcha (27th day). The king went to Hyŏnhwa monastery.

Sixth Month

Mujin (1st day). The king went to Pongŭn monastery.
Kyemi (16th day). The king performed a rite for the earth god 中霤.[16]
Chŏnghae (20th day). The king performed a rite for Lord Millet 後農.
    Twenty-six Eastern Jurchens, led by Osa 吳史, were granted an audience with the court.
Kich'uk (22nd day). The king ordered the retrial of criminals.

Eighth Month, Autumn

Kyŏngo (4th day). The king observed the *Golden Light Sutra* ritual in Hoegyŏng Hall.
Pyŏngja (10th day). The king enshrined King Chŏngjong's mortuary tablet in the Imperial Ancestral Shrine.

---

15. This was likely a railed platform in the monastery hall.
16. A ritual held at the Imperial Ancestral Shrine in the sixth month of the year.

Ninth Month

Kabin (19th day). Thirty-six Eastern Jurchens, led by General Submitting to Virtue Adu, were granted an audience with the court.

Pyŏngjin (21st day). The king held the three-day Hundred Seat ritual for the recitation of the *Humane Kings Sutra* in Hoegyŏng Hall. He fed ten thousand monks at the Polo Field and twenty thousand monks at famous monasteries on mountains across the country.

Tenth Month, Winter

Kapsul (9th day). Riding a carriage decorated with ivory, the king went to the purification chamber (*chaegung* 齋宮)[17] and spent a night.

Ŭrhae (10th day). The king performed the Joint Ritual (*hyŏpche* 祫祭) in the Imperial Ancestral Shrine. After that, he went to Sinbong Pavilion and declared an amnesty.

Eleventh Month

Ŭlmi (1st day). The king promoted officials in the State Council (*yangbu* 兩府) by one grade,[18] including the Chancellery director Ch'oe Ch'ung, officials of the fifth rank and higher, and officials in charge of rituals.

Musin (14th day). The king went to Pŏbwang monastery and held the Assembly of the Eight Prohibitions.

Kimi (25th day). The Khitans sent the vice minister of imperial entertainments Hyŏng P'aengnyŏn 邢彭年 with a letter of congratulations on the king's birthday.

Sinyu (27th day). The Ch'eju regional inspector (*chasa* 刺史) Ko Kyŏngsŏn 高慶善 came to Koryŏ as a response envoy from the Khitan Eastern Capital.

---

17. A building or room where the king purified himself before performing sacrifices. *Chaegung* were a functional part of the ancestral shrine and royal tombs.

18. Senior members of the Secretariat-Chancellery (*chungsŏ munhasŏng* 中書門下省) and Palace Secretariat (*chungch'uwŏn* 中樞院) formed the State Council.

Twelfth Month

Ŭlch'uk (1st day). The king went to Kŏndŏk Hall to receive his officials' congratulations on his birthday.

Kabo (30th day). There was a solar eclipse.

Third Year of Munjong (1049)

First Month, Spring

Ŭlsa (11th day). Thirty-two Eastern Jurchens, led by Agol, were granted an audience and made an offering of excellent horses.

The Khitans sent So Yudŏk 蕭惟德 and Wang Sudo 王守道 as investiture envoys bearing the emperor's edict.

> You have taken possession of the throne to continue the unfinished work of governing. You have faithfully communicated with our imperial court and sent tribute offerings of linen and silk. By the rules of our Office of Protocol (*koktae* 曲臺), it is appropriate that we should invest you now and send you gifts to show our warm wishes. Accordingly, we have sent our Personal Guard generalissimo (*ch'ŏnuwi sangjanggun* 千牛衛上將軍) So Yudŏk as our lead investiture envoy, and our chief censor Wang Sudo as our deputy investiture envoy, to provide the requisite courtesies and bring you a number of gifts, including a sword and crown, an official seal, articles of clothing, rolls of silk, and saddled horses, as specified in the accompanying list. You may accept them all.

The investiture decree stated:

> Our inheritance of the imperial throne was entirely due to the virtue of our ancestors. In the provisioning of countries, a great country is led by a king and a small country is led by a lord. Although rival leaders can be suppressed militarily and far-off officials appeased, justice must be continually maintained for the preservation of the great enterprise. When you inherited the throne, you sent messages to inform us of your work, and you have ruled well. Although you reside in the east, you have

fulfilled your pledge of loyalty and shown that you revere the emperor. So we have sent our envoys to perform the investiture ceremony.

We invest you, Wang Wi, with the titles of Rectifying the Age, Serving Governance, Merit Subject for Perfecting Integrity, Commander Unequaled in Honor, Acting Grand Guardian, Director of the Chancellery, Supreme Pillar of the State, and King of Koryŏ, with a fief of seven thousand households and an actual fief of one thousand households. Now, with your helmet warm in all seasons, musical instruments make an enchanting sound. Your broad generosity contains the immensity of the sea, and your august presence is more imposing than the highest peak in the Kunlun mountains 崑崙山. You have studied the ancient texts and learned the art of politics. You have become well versed in military tactics and deepened your knowledge of strategy. And from the beginning of your reign over the Samhan, you have acted like the five hegemons 五霸.[19] Therefore, we have sent this edict and invested you as ruler of the eastern land [Koryŏ]. Your blessings are being recounted in every direction, and your fame will last throughout history. Even though your country's customs may change completely, your pervasive moral influence will still guide your people. Yet you are humble and gentle in person, and far from arrogant. Your filial devotion is unmatched, and neighboring countries attest to your sincerity. You have continuously sent envoys to our court with bountiful tribute offerings, so in accordance with the rules promulgated by the Office of Protocol, we now give you instructions, promote you to the highest rank and positions, confirm your inheritance of the throne, and expand your fief. We further give you an era name that acknowledges your merit, and we bestow on you our special grace.

We have entrusted this investiture decree to the generalissimo of our Personal Guard and lead envoy So Yudŏk and our censor-in-chief and deputy envoy Wang Sudo, who will convey the letter and provide the requisite courtesies. We now invest you as Acting Grand Mentor, Director of the Secretariat, and in particular as King of Koryŏ with an additional fief of three thousand households and an actual fief of three hundred households. In addition, we give you the four-character merit subject

---

19. During the Spring and Autumn period, the five hegemons were the feudal lords of Ji 齊, Jin 晉, Chu 楚, Wu 吳, and Yue 越.

title of Offering Loyalty (*chach'ung* 資忠) and Dedicating Superiors (*pongsang* 奉上) with the same rank and commendations as before.

Ah! The Zhou gave their vassal lords a red arrow 彤弓 as a sign of their authority to subjugate other countries. The Han gave their vassal lords an iron axe while expanding the scope of their authority over uncivilized countries. In past and present times, the special favor of the emperor is just like this. Consider the responsibility that you have been given for your country and never forget the emperor's sincerity. Revere his words and you will enjoy happiness and prosperity.

Pyŏngo (12th day). The king received the investiture decree in the southern outskirts of the capital.

Second Month

Ŭrhae (12th day). The king appointed Ch'oe Ch'ung as high grand protector, Yi Chayŏn as high minister of education, Wang Ch'ongji as high minister of works and supreme pillar of the state, Chŏng Kŏl 鄭傑 (d. 1051) as deputy administrator of the Palace Secretariat (*tongji chungch'uwŏnsa* 同知中樞院事), Ch'ae Ch'unghyŏn as director of the Rites Ministry, and Ch'oe Yŏn'ga and Yang Kam 楊鑑 as left and right scholarly counselors-in-ordinary, respectively.

Kapsin (21st day). The king invested his younger brother Wang Ki, the duke of P'yŏngyang (*P'yŏngyanggong* 平壤公), with the titles of High Grand Preceptor and Director of the Imperial Secretariat.

Third Month

Kyesa (1st day). The royal commissioner of warehouse inspection for the Northeastern Frontier Circuit (*tongbungno kamch'angsa* 東北路監倉使) submitted a petition.

> The Kyoju Defense Office executive (*Kyoju pangŏ p'angwan* 交州防禦判官) Yi Yubaek 李惟伯 not only repaired fortress equipment but restored the lands around it. Comparatively speaking, he is the most competent

official in these counties. Also, the local officials and people in Yŏnsŏng 連城[20] and Changyang 長楊[21] prefectures have all told me, "Once Yi Yubaek came here, he has given farming his support and helped us all." Although his term has ended and it is time to replace him, he should be allowed to remain in his post.

The king thought this was admirable and forwarded the petition to the Civil Personnel Ministry.

Kyŏngja (8th day). The king hosted a banquet in the garden inside the Audience gate 閣門 for elder statesmen eighty or older, which included the right vice director of state affairs Ch'oe Posŏng, the Water Control Court director Cho Ong 趙顒, and the Crown Prince's Household Management director (*t'aeja ch'ŏmsa* 太子詹事) Yi T'aeksŏng 李澤成. The king himself went to the tables and poured wine for them. He gave one suit of official dress, two official caps, and thirty *kak* 角 of *noewŏn* tea 腦原茶 to Ch'oe Posŏng and Cho Ong, and one suit of official dress to Yi T'aeksŏng. He also gave them permission to be conveyed by horse from the Audience gate and leave the palace from the Chŏnga gate 正衙門, but the three elder statesmen obstinately refused.

   The next day, the king hosted a banquet at the Polo Field for the elderly, virtuous husbands and wives, filial sons and grandsons, widows and widowers, elderly without children, orphans, and the disabled. Gifts were bestowed in accordance with their rank.

Kyemo (11th day). The king appointed Wi Chŏng 韋靖 as right vice director of the State Affairs Department, Wi Sung 魏崇 as acting director of the Revenue Ministry, and O Yŏn 吳演 as director of the Public Works Ministry.

Ŭlsa (13th day). Thirty people from Pongju, led by Hŭidal 喜達, all of whom had been prisoners of the Khitans, returned to Koryŏ.

Kabin (22nd day). Twenty Eastern Jurchens, led by Marihae 麻離害, were granted an audience and made an offering of good horses.

---

20. Yŏnsŏng Prefecture 連城郡 is present-day Hoeyang-gun, Kangwŏn province.
21. Changyang Prefecture 長楊郡 is present-day Hoeyang-gun, Kangwŏn province.

Muo (26th day). The king appointed Yi Injŏng as left vice director of the State Affairs Department and pillar of the state, Kim Chŏngjun as commissioner of the Palace Secretariat and superintendent of the Censorate, Chŏng Kŏl as director of the Imperial Archives and administrator of the Palace Secretariat, and Kim Wŏnjŏng as director of the Foreign Relations Office and deputy administrator of the Palace Secretariat.

Fourth Month, Summer

Ŭlch'uk (3rd day). Twenty Western Jurchens, led by Pugŏ 符巨, were granted an audience and made an offering of good horses.
Chŏnghae (25th day). Seventy-nine Eastern Jurchens, led by General Supporting the State Saira, were granted an audience and made an offering of excellent horses.
Muja (26th day). The king took the daughter of the affairs manager Kim Wŏnch'ung as a consort.

Fifth Month

Kapcha day. The king went to Mundŏk Hall to retest the examination candidates. Pak Insu 朴仁壽 and others passed the state examination.

Sixth Month

Mujin (7th day). Pirates from the eastern tribes attacked Imdo county 臨道縣[22] and took seventeen people captive.
Imsin (11th day). The military commissioner of the Northeastern Frontier Circuit submitted a report.

> Eleven soldiers from Unam county 雲嵒縣,[23] led by Sublieutenant Yugo 惟古 from the Assault Resisting Garrison (*chŏlch'unggun* 折衝軍隊正), were

---

22. Present-day Kosŏng-gun, Kangwŏn.
23. Present-day Kosŏng-gun, Kangwŏn.

on night patrol when they encountered approximately forty tribesmen at the Ch'ŏnjŏng guard post (*Ch'ŏnjŏngsu* 泉井戍). The eleven soldiers fled and tried to hide, but Yugo stayed and led the fight against the enemy, who were defeated and forced to retreat. I request that his meritorious service be recognized with appointment to a government post.

Muja (27th day). The king issued a decree.

From the beginning of the sixth month until the start of autumn,[24] distribute ice once every three days to retired royal aides, and once every seven days to vice directors of state affairs, directors of ministries (*sangsŏ* 尚書), directors of courts (*kyŏng* 卿), directors of directorates (*kam* 監), grand generals, and above. Do this every year, and make it permanent.

Seventh Month, Autumn

Chŏngyu (6th day). Pirates from the eastern tribes attacked Kŭmyang county 金壤縣[25] and took twenty people captive.

Eighth Month

Kisa (9th day). Seventy-one people from Song, led by the Taizhou merchant Xu Zan 徐贊, came with an offering of their native products.
Sinsa (21st day). Sixty-two people from Song, led by the Quanzhou merchant Wang Yicong 王易從, came with an offering of treasures.

Ninth Month

Kyŏngja (10th day). The consort of Yŏndŏk Palace gave birth to a son. The king named him Chŭng 王蒸 (1049–1094).[26]

---

24. One of the twenty-four solar terms. In the lunar calendar, autumn was considered to begin in the seventh month.
25. Present-day T'ongch'ŏn-gun, Kangwŏn.
26. Wang Chŭng became King Sŏnjong in 1083.

Tenth Month, Winter

Chŏnghae (28th day). The king ordered the retrial of criminals.

Eleventh Month

Imin (13th day). Seventy-seven people from T'amna, led by the Chinwi kyowi 振威校尉[27] Pu Ŭring 夫乙仍, and twenty Northern Jurchens, led by Pu Kŏ 夫擧, were granted audiences and made offerings of their native products.

Muo (29th day). The Naval Administration Office of the Southeastern Sea (*tongnamhae sŏnbyŏng tobusŏsa* 東南海船兵都部署司) submitted a report.

> The government office on Japan's Tsushima island sent a party led by Akitō 明任 to return twenty shipwrecked Koryŏ people, including Kim Hyo 金孝. They arrived at Kŭmju.

The king gave gifts to Akitō and the others in accordance with their rank.

Twelfth Month

Kimi (1st day). The Khitans sent the Palace Administration vice director Mau 馬祐 with a letter of congratulations on the king's birthday.

Fourth Year of Munjong (1050)

First Month, Spring

Kich'uk (1st day). The king canceled the New Year Congratulations.

The chief military commissioner of the Northeastern Frontier District, Park Sŏnggŏl, submitted a report.

---

27. A rank 6b2 title for military officials.

Immediately after pirates seized and took away two warships from Chinmyŏngp'o 鎭溟浦 in the tenth month of last year, the chief registrar of the military commission, Mun Yangnyŏl, led armed vessels in pursuit. With Song Chehan 宋齊罕, a Wonhŭng Naval Administration executive (*Wonhŭng tobusŏ p'an'gwan* 元興都部署判官), he chased the pirates to their hideout and torched their houses and beheaded twenty before retreating. Meritorious deeds like these should be rewarded.

The king wrote: "Send this to the Military and War Council."

Kyemo (15th day). The king appointed the Chancellery director Ch'oe Ch'ung as high grand mentor.

Pyŏngo (18th day). The assistant executive of the Imperial Regalia Court Park Yongjae 朴庸載, newly appointed as the chief registrar of the Military Commission of the Northeastern Frontier District, met the king on his way to take up his post. The king said, "If you should meet eastern tribesmen seeking an audience with the court, do not give permission to any except for their chief Nabul 那拂." This was because three hundred tribesmen were already detained at the capital guesthouse for foreign officials.

Ŭlmyo (27th day). The king appointed Kim Wonch'ung as executive of the Chancellery and superintendent of the Ministry of Punishments (*p'an sangsŏ hyŏngbusa* 判尙書刑部事), Yi Chayŏn as executive of the Imperial Secretariat, and Chŏng Kŏl as commissioner of the Palace Secretariat and Hallim academician recipient of edicts.

Third Month

Pyŏngo (19th day). Several groups of Eastern Jurchens came to the court, including twelve led by General Comforting the Frontier Yŏmhan 塩漢, thirty led by General Soothing Faraway Lands Agaju, four led by the Chungyun Inguhŭn 仍亏憲, and thirty-eight led by General Yorana 要羅那. They made offerings of good horses. Six of them, including General Embracing Transformation Agaju, presented leopard skins. The king gave them gifts in accordance with their rank. A party of fifteen, led by Yŏmhan, was detained because they had known border violations in the past.

Fourth Month, Summer

Sinyu (5th day). The king worshiped at Hyŏn Tomb and Sŏn Tomb. He issued an amnesty decree.

Kyeyu (17th day). Kaeho and others from Parhae came to submit.

Kyemi (27th day). The king issued an order to the relevant authorities: "Define the borders around the Eastern Jurchen villages of Taegŏllani 大乞羅尼 and Sogŏllani 小乞羅尼 to prevent enemy incursions."

Sixth Month

Mujin (13th day). Pirates from the eastern tribes invaded the Yŏngp'a guard post 寧波戍 in Yŏlsan county and took eighteen men and women captive.

Kimyo (24th day). The king issued a decree.

> The commoners and soldiers living in each of the coastal fortifications in the Northeastern Frontier District have suffered from a recurring disruption of their lives. As selecting a trustworthy commander (*wŏnsu* 元帥) is the most important step that can be taken to protect subjects in outlying regions, the Military Affairs director Yang Kam shall be appointed the military commissioner in autumn and winter of this year.

Seventh Month, Autumn

Pyŏngsul (1st day). Eastern tribesmen invaded P'ach'ŏn county 派川縣.[28]

Kyŏngja (15th day). Because of the midsummer heat, maintenance work on the outer walls was discontinued.

Musin (23rd day). A party of Eastern Jurchens, led by Chief Kollagae 骨羅介, were granted an audience and made an offering of their native products. Kollagye had paid the ransom for four Koryŏ men and women who had been kidnapped by tribesmen and subsequently returned to Koryŏ. The king rewarded him with gold and silk.

---

28. Present-day T'ongch'ŏn-gun, Kangwŏn.

Eighth Month

Sinsa (27th day). Agaju, Yŏmhan, Saira, and other Eastern Jurchen generals returned the Chŏngbyŏn Garrison deputy commander (*Chŏngbyŏnjin pujang* 靜邊鎭副將) Hwangbo Ch'ung 皇甫冲 and the sublieutenant Song Yong 宋迎, who had been kidnapped by the tribesmen.

Ninth Month

Chŏnghae (3rd day). The Khitan commander-in-chief of the Loyal Intrepid Army (*ch'ungyonggun to jihwisa* 忠勇軍都指揮使) Ko Changan 高長安 came as a response envoy from the Eastern Capital.

Kihae (15th day). The military commissioner of the Northeastern Frontier District submitted a petition.

> When pirates invaded Yŏlsan county, the king sent the military commission's chief registrar Mun Yangnyŏl 文揚烈 with twenty-three warships to chase the enemy all the way to Ch'oja island 椒子島, where he courageously fought and defeated them. He beheaded nine and set fire to about thirty houses in the village. He destroyed eight warships and captured more than one hundred weapons. I request that you reward him for his meritorious deeds.

The king approved.

Ŭlsa (21st day). The king held the three-day Hundred Seat ritual for the recitation of the *Humane Kings Sutra* in Hoegyŏng Hall.

Eleventh Month, Winter

Kiyu (26th day). The vice commissioner of the Chinmyŏng Naval Administration Office Kim Kyŏngŭng 金敬應 led naval forces in driving back three pirate ships at Yŏl island 烈島. He beheaded dozens and many of the enemy drowned. The king ordered the relevant authorities to evaluate his merit and reward him.

Intercalary Month

Imsul (9th day). The Khitan military commissioner of the Expanding Justice Army (*kwangŭigun chŏltosa* 匡義軍節度使) So Chil 蕭質 came to Koryŏ as a special envoy bearing an imperial edict.
Sinmi (18th day). A Chinese man named Cao Yi 曹一, who had been residing among the Khitans, came to Koryŏ to submit.

Twelfth Month

Kapsin (1st day). The Khitans sent the Koju surveillance commissioner (*Koju kwanch'alsa* 高州觀察使) So Ok 蕭玉 with a letter of congratulations on the king's birthday.

Fifth Year of Munjong (1051)

First Month, Spring

Kyech'uk (1st day). The king canceled the New Years Congratulations.
Kyehae (11th day). The king went to Chin'gwan monastery and skipped sections in the chanting of the new *Avataṃsaka-sūtra* and *Prajñāpāramitā-sūtra*.

Second Month

Kyesa (12th day). A fire that had broken out at the capital marketplace office (*kyŏngsisŏ* 京市署) burned down 120 households. The relevant authorities were ordered to supply construction materials and roof tiles for the restoration.
Ŭlmi (14th day). The king went to Pongŭn monastery to hold the Lantern Festival. On the following day, he ordered that a flower festival be held and invited his royal attendants to participate.
Kyŏngja (19th day). A fire broke out in Paengnyŏng Garrison 白翎鎭, burning twenty-eight *kan* of the fortress walls as well as seventy-eight households.

Regarding this, the Military Affairs assistant executive Yu Suk 劉肅 and the vice commissioner for pacification (*anch'al pusa* 按察副使) submitted a memorial of impeachment.

> The carelessness of the garrison commander Ch'oe Sŏngdo 崔成道 and the deputy garrison commander (*pujang* 副將) Ch'oe Sungmang, among others, was responsible for the fire. They should be relieved from their posts and punished.

The king approved.

Third Month

Imsul (11th day). The king conducted ritual prayers for rain on the riverside.
Mujin (17th day). The left vice director of state affairs Yi Suhwa died.
Imsin (21st day). The king conducted ritual prayers for rain on the riverside.

Fourth Month, Summer

Sinsa (1st day). The king conducted rain rituals.

The king passed Ch'oe Sŏk 崔錫 and others in the state examination.
Imo (2nd day). The king went to Poje monastery for the Five Hundred Arhats rite (*obaek nahanjae* 五百羅漢齋).[29]
Ŭlmi (15th day). The king issued a decree: "Release Chief Agol and the seventy-seven Eastern Jurchens detained in Kwangin guesthouse 廣仁館."[30]
Kyŏngja (20th day). The Imperial Secretariat–Chancellery submitted a petition.

> Although the new construction or restoration of monasteries such as Chunghŭng 重興, Taean, and Taeun have begun, it must be questioned whether projects like these are urgently required. When artisans and laborers work day and night, the burden of carrying food to them,

---

29. A Buddhist ritual to ward off accidents and anxiety.
30. A guesthouse for northern tribesmen, including the Jurchens, who were visiting the capital.

undertaken by the wives and children who travel back and forth without a moment to rest, is heavy. Moreover, there is a shortage of food after last year's famine, which renders laborers unable to perform difficult work. If these projects must be carried out, at least postpone them until the off-season for farming.

The king approved.

Chŏngmi (27th day). The Imperial Secretariat–Chancellery submitted a petition.

> Earlier, you ordered a number of appointments, including Hwangbo Yŏn 皇甫延 as grand general of the Imperial Army (*ŭngyanggun taejanggun* 鷹揚軍大將軍) and acting director of the Palace Revenues Court (*sŏp taebugyŏng* 攝大府卿), Chin Ŏn 秦彦 as grand general of the Royal Guard Division (*chwauwi taejanggun* 左右衛大將軍), and No Nŭnghun 盧能訓 as grand general of the Envoy Escort Division (*shinhowi taejanggun* 神虎衛大將軍). In the past, however, these three were relieved of their posts due to various offenses. Although they were granted amnesty and restored to their posts, they have not accomplished anything meritorious since that time. Because of this, selecting them for promotion does not seem appropriate. We ask that you rescind the order.

The king wrote: "Let it be done, but Hwangbo Yŏn must remain on the appointment list."

Musin (28th day). The king himself conducted the Daoist Ch'o ritual at the Polo Field.

Fifth Month

Chŏngsa (8th day). The king issued an amnesty due to the drought.

Sinmi (22nd day). The king again conducted rain rituals.

Seventh Month, Autumn

Kyŏngsul (2nd day). The king went to Hŭngwang monastery 興王寺.

Kimi (11th day). Envoys were sent from Tsushima island 對馬島 to retrieve three criminals, including Yanghan 良漢, who had committed crimes in Japan and fled to Koryŏ.

Muin (30th day). Twenty-six Eastern Jurchens, led by the Wŏnbo Kosa, were granted an audience and made an offering of their native products.

Eighth Month

Kimyo (1st day). The Palace Secretariat commissioner and Rites Ministry director Chŏng Kŏl died.

Sinch'uk (23rd day). The king himself attended a reception at the Polo Field for 1,343 monks and laymen who were eighty or older, 653 monks and laymen with disabilities or a serious illness, and 14 filial sons, filial grandsons, and virtuous women. He gave out gifts in accordance with the recipient's rank.

Kapchin (26th day). The Kwiju lieutenant colonel (*nangjang* 郎將) Kang In 康隣 and Ch'angju subcolonels (*pyŏlchang* 別將) Kang Ŏn 康彥 and Ch'oe Nip 崔立 captured six tribesmen and killed them.

Ŭlsa (27th day). Thirty-one Eastern Jurchens, led by General Submitting to Virtue Tuyabul 豆也弗, were granted an audience and made an offering of their native products.

Ninth Month

Kiyu (1st day). The vice military commissioner of the Northeastern Frontier District Kim Hwasung 金化崇 submitted a report:. "The Jurchens attacked the border and soldiers were sent. Fifty-nine enemies were beheaded." The king dispatched secretarial attendant and receptionist Sŏ Tan 徐亶 with a royal edict.

> You have defended the frontier with outstanding strategy. You took note of when the tribesmen blocked the roads and penetrated our borders. Then you assisted the commander with a brilliant plan to achieve a victory. You succeeded in killing many of the enemy and also took

numerous prisoners, and this good work has earned my highest praise. I now send to you my secretarial attendant and receptionist Sŏ Tan with my commendation. I also bestow on you silver dishes together with clothing and silks. To the other generals and soldiers who participated in the battle, I bestow rolls of silk in accordance with their rank.

Kabin (6th day). The military commissioner of the Northwestern Frontier District Pak Chongdo submitted a report.

> Yesterday, while my soldiers and I were on patrol in the pass, we encountered a group of eastern tribesmen, whom we fought. In the end, we beheaded approximately ten of them and captured twenty war horses, as well as numerous weapons and pieces of armor.

The king rewarded them generously.

Tenth Month, Winter

Chŏnghae (9th day). The military commissioner of the Northeastern Frontier District submitted a report.

> Because the tribesmen have been attacking along the borders, the Military Commission's chief registrars Yun Po 尹甫 and Kyŏngch'ung 敬忠, together with the Changju defense commissioner 長州防禦使 Kim Tan 金旦, were sent to chase after them. They beheaded approximately twenty of the enemy.

Kyŏngin (12th day). The king went to Mount Samgak.
Imin (24th day). The king returned to the capital.
Chŏngmi (29th day). The Khitan acting minister of works Yayul Suhaeng 耶律守行 came as a response envoy from the Eastern Capital.

Eleventh Month

Kyŏngsin (13th day). The king held the Assembly of the Eight Prohibitions. Because a lunar eclipse was expected, the ceremony was held on the thirteenth day for the first time.

Twelfth Month

Muin (1st day). The Khitans sent the Ŭnju 恩州 regional inspector Yu Chongbi 劉從備 with a letter of congratulations on the king's birthday.

Sixth Year of Munjong (1052)

First Month, Spring

Musin (1st day). The king canceled the New Year Congratulations.
Kabin (7th day). The king appointed Ch'oe Yusŏn as Hallim academician.
Pyŏngjin (9th day). A party of Eastern Jurchens, led by General Embracing Transformation P'ogaju 包加主, were granted an audience and made an offering of good horses.
Pyŏngin (19th day). Forty-eight Eastern Jurchen men and women, led by the Chŏngbo Map'a 馬波, came to the outskirts of Chŏngju and requested enrollment in the household register. The king gave them land and houses and allowed them to live in Koryŏ.
Kapsul (27th day). A substantial party of Western Jurchens, led by General Comforting the Frontier Kobanji 高反知, and another party of Eastern Jurchens, led by General Submitting to Virtue Taro 多老, were granted audiences and made offerings of good horses.

Second Month

Chŏngch'uk (1st day). An earthquake occurred in the Western Regional Military Command (*ansŏ tohobu* 安西都護府).

Muin (2nd day). The king invested the lady of Yŏndŏk Palace, Lady Yi 李, with the title of Queen.

Kyŏngjin (4th day). Twenty-nine eastern tribesmen, led by the Wŏnbo Arin 阿麟, were granted an audience and made an offering of good horses.

Sinsa (5th day). A new Altar of the Gods of Earth and Grain was completed on the western side of the capital.

Muja (12th day). The king went to the new Altar of the Gods of Earth and Grain to personally perform a rite at its consecration. He gave gifts to the soldiers who carried his litter in accordance with their rank, and promoted by one grade the officials and clerks who participated in the ceremony. He also promoted by one grade the officials and clerks who had supervised the consecration of the Altar of the Gods of Earth and Grain.

Third Month

Chŏngmi (2nd day). The king went to Taean monastery and fed the monks.

Kyŏngsul (5th day). The king appointed Yi Chayŏn as high grand marshal.

Ŭlmyo (10th day). The king appointed Kim Wŏnjŏng as director of the Censorate.

Muo (15th day). The king ordered the grand astrologer Kim Sŏngt'aek 金成澤 to compile *Sipchŏngnyŏk* 十精曆, Yi Inhyŏn 李仁顯 to compile *Ch'iryoryŏk* 七曜曆, Han Wihaeng 韓爲行 to compile *Kyŏnhaengnyŏk* 見行曆, Yang Wŏnho 梁元虎 to compile *Tun'gamnyŏk* 遁甲曆, and Kim Chŏng 金正 to compile *T'aeillyŏk* 太一曆.[31] This was in preparation for any events, inauspicious as well as auspicious, that could occur during the year.

Imsul (17th day). The king went to Hyŏnhwa monastery and fed the monks.

Imsin (27th day). The State Finance Commission (*samsa* 三司) submitted a petition.

> The country of T'amna offers tangerines each year. The amount should be revised to one hundred *p'o* 包, and this should become a fixed amount hereafter.

---

31. These compilations were different types of calendars.

The king approved.

Fourth Month, Summer

Kimyo (4th day). The king appointed Wang Musung 王務崇 as left deputy recipient of edicts (*chungch'uwŏn chwa pu sŭngsŏn* 中樞院左副承宣) and Ch'oe Sŏngjŏl 崔成節 as right deputy recipient of edicts and palace censor.

Pyŏngsul (11th day). The king went to Taean monastery upon completion of the monastery's restoration to participate in its ritual opening (*naksŏng toryang* 落成道場).

Chŏnghae (12th day). The king appointed Yi Injŏng as left vice director of state affairs and eminent minister of education (*kŏmgyo sado* 檢校司徒), and then gave him permission to retire.

Imin (27th day). Moajin 毛阿眞, who had been captured by the eastern tribesmen, returned with sixteen men and women.

Fifth Month

Kyŏngsul (6th day). Ko Yŏn 高演, the bandit leader from Samsal village 三撒村[32] in the Northern Circuit 北路, joined with tribal soldiers to besiege Ch'idam station 淄潭驛. The Military Commission's chief registrar Kim Ch'unggan 金忠簡, together with the Chaju Defense Office executive (*Chaju pang'ŏ p'an'gwan* 慈州防禦判官) Chang Ipsin 張立身 and others, led their soldiers out to fight the invaders and defeated them soundly. Energized by victory, they pursued the bandits and captured or killed about fifty of them.

Kabin (10th day). Due to the drought, the king avoided the main throne hall, reduced the number of side dishes served at royal meals, and ordered retrials for criminals across the country.

Ŭlmyo (11th day). Twenty-five Eastern Jurchens, led by Chief 酋長 Kojimun, were granted an audience and made an offering of their native products.

Muo (14th day). The king issued a decree.

---

32. Present day Pukch'ŏng, South Hamgyŏng.

During the T'onghwa era, Khitan soldiers invaded for an entire year and my late father, Hyŏnjong, withdrew to the south. At that time, the right vice director of state affairs Pak Sŏm took the bridle of my father's horse and diligently attended to his needs. When Kaegyŏng was recaptured and hostilities ended, Pak Sŏm stabilized the government. His portrait shall be placed in the Hall of Merit Subjects so that later generations can learn from his example.

Kyehae (19th day). The king ordered all civil and military officials of the fifth rank and higher, including retired officials, to each submit a memorial on the moral considerations pertaining to current policies.

Sixth Month

Ŭrhae (2nd day). The king held the *Golden Light Sutra* ritual in Mundŏk Hall and prayed for rain. Afterward, there was a heavy rain.

Muin (5th day). The king appointed Chang Chŏng (Ch. Zhang Ting) 張廷, a literary licentiate candidate from Song, to the position of collator in the Imperial Archives (*pisŏ kyosŏrang* 秘書校書郎) and issued a royal edict.

> Yue Yi 樂毅 of Wei 魏 helped both the king of Yan and Lu Ji 陸機 of Wu 吳 return to the government of Jin 晉. The events occurred fortuitously, a circumstance they shared in common. Your lofty reputation reminds us of the Xie brothers,[33] and your distinguished family name recalls the three generations of Zhang.[34] Your body appears disciplined, and you stand before us as a shining example of honest Confucian loyalty. You are also widely traveled and have never been tied down, capable always of pursuing your objectives. Now fate has brought you to our country, and the joy of receiving a scholar like you relieves our chronic longing to meet people who are truly benevolent. I appoint you without examination to a civil post so that you can assist us in determining the proper rituals and procedures of government. While you are a man of talent from another country, I perceive that you will fit in quite well,

---

33. Xie An 謝安 and Xie Wan 謝萬 were famous gentlemen from Jin.
34. Zhang Zai 張載, Zhang Xie 張協, and Zhang Kang 張亢 from Western Jin were well known for their writings.

and having sworn your allegiance, you may now put aside any thought of going back. Instead, with a constant heart, you will help us to discern and achieve the destiny that shapes our country to the end. I therefore issue this edict and bestow on you an official's dress and belt together with silks, silver, and other gifts that it may please you to accept.

Kimyo (6th day). A band of Eastern Jurchens, Kojimun among them, came by sea to attack the Imwŏn guard post 臨遠戍 in Samch'ŏk county. The guard post general (*sujang* 守將) Ha Churyŏ 河周呂 said to his soldiers in the fortress before leading them out: "We are outnumbered, but if each of us fights to the end without thought of preserving our life, we will certainly prevail." With a shout, they raised their swords and shields and charged the enemy. Then, it so happened that the Anbyŏn Regional Military Command executive (*Anbyŏn toho p'angwan* 安邊都護判官) Kim Sungjŏng 金崇鼎, who was was conducting an inspection of guard posts in the area, arrived on the scene. The enemy heard Kim's drums and bugles from a distance and thought that reinforcements were about to arrive, so they panicked and fled. Ha Churyŏ and his men killed or captured about ten of the enemy during the fight.

Seventh Month, Autumn

Muo (15th day). The king appointed Ch'oe Yusŏn as director of the Punishments Ministry, Yi Yŏnggan as director of the Rites Ministry, Wang Cho 王祚 as director of the Revenue Ministry, Yu Kyu 庾逵 as director of the Public Works Ministry, and Kim Hyŏn as scholarly counselor-in-ordinary (*san'gi sangsŏ* 散騎常侍).

Eighth Month

Kyeyu (1st day). The king issued a decree.

> When my late father, Hyŏnjong, withdrew to the south, Han Sik 韓式, Mun Chil 文質, U Kiri 牛奇里, and Kim Yŏl 金悅 among others attended to his needs and achieved merit. I award them the posthumous title of

Supreme General of the Royal Guard Division (*chwauwi sangjanggun* 左右衛上將軍).

Ŭryu (13th day). The retired eminent grand preceptor and left vice director of state affairs Ch'oe Posŏng died. The king suspended court business for one day.

Thirty-five merchants from Song, led by Lin Xing 林興, came with an offering of their native products.

Sinmyo (19th day). Gao Shiwen 高士文, a man from Xianzhou 咸州 in Song who had been captured by tribesmen, came over from the Eastern Jurchens and submitted.

Ninth Month

Kyemyo (1st day). The king appointed Kim Wŏnjŏng as deputy administrator of the Palace Secretariat, and Yi Yŏnggan as Hallim academician.

Twenty-six merchants from Song, led by Zhao Shou 趙受, came with an offering of their native products.

Imja (10th day). Forty merchants from Song, led by Xiao Zongming 蕭宗明, came with an offering of their native products.

Kimi (17th day). Forty Eastern Jurchens, led by General Sasiha, were granted an audience and made an offering of excellent horses.

Kyŏngsin (18th day). The king held the three-day Hundred Seat ritual in Hoegyŏng Hall and fed thirty thousand monks at the Polo Field and well-known monasteries.

Tenth Month, Winter

Kyemi (11th day). The king invested his nephew Wang Kyŏng 王璥 with the titles of High Grand Protector and Director of the State Affairs Department.

Pyŏngsul (14th day). So Kanghan 蘇康漢, who died at the battle of P'yŏngno Garrison 平虜鎮,[35] had his merit recorded. He was given the posthumous

---

35. Present-day P'yŏngwŏn-gun, South P'yŏngan.

title of Supreme General of the Capital Security Division (*hŭngwiwi sangjanggun* 興威衛上將軍).

Kabo (22nd day). The king invested his nephew Wang Kae 王暟 (d. 1062) with the titles of High Grand Marshal and Director of the State Affairs Department.

Eleventh Month

Kapchin (3rd day). The king went to Sŏnjŏng Hall. The Censorate submitted a memorial to the king on the moral considerations arising from current policies.

Ŭlch'uk (24th day). The king appointed Chang Chŏng as right reminder.

Twelfth Month

Imsin (1st day). The Khitans sent the Yŏngju regional inspector (*Yŏngju chasa* 永州刺史) Yayul Sach'ŏng 耶律士淸 with a letter of congratulations on the king's birthday.

Kabo (23rd day). The retired Chancellery executive Kim Yŏnggi died. The king suspended court business for three days.

Seventh Year of Munjong (1053)

First Month, Spring

Pyŏngo (5th day). White vapors pierced the sun and permeated the sky.

Pyŏngjin (15th day). Venus was visible during the day.

Second Month

Ŭrhae (5th day). A comet emerged from the Centaurus constellation (*korusŏngjwa* 庫樓星座) and entered the Wing constellation (*iksŏngjwa* 翼星座). It was approximately ten *chŏk* in length.

Chŏngch'uk (7th day). Thirty-three Eastern Jurchens, led by Abuhan 阿夫漢, were granted an audience and made an offering of excellent horses. They also paid the ransom for the return of six people who had been kidnapped by tribesmen. Because of this, the king gave them official positions and rewards in accordance with their rank.

Suunna 殊雲那, a prince of T'amna, sent a party led by his son the Paeyung kyowi Komul 古物 with an offering of ox bezoar, oxhorns, oxhide, conch meat, nutmegs, seaweed, and tortoise shells. The king awarded Komul the title of Chungho changgun 中虎將軍[36] and gave him an official's dress, a silver belt, colored threads 彩段, and medicines.

Third Month

Musin (8th day). U Sang 禹相 and others passed the state examination.

Fourth Month, Summer

Chŏngyu (28th day). The king himself conducted the Daoist Ch'o ritual at the Polo Field.

Sixth Month

Kyemi (15th day). The king received the bodhisattva ordination in Kŏndŏk Hall.

Seventh Month, Autumn

Muo (21st day). The Rites Ministry submitted a petition.

According to the *History of the Tang Dynasty*, "On *kyŏngin* of the intercalary sixth month of the eighth year of Tian Bao 天寶 (749), Emperor

---

36. This rank 4a title for military officials was originally called Chungmu changgun 中武將軍, but *mu* 武 was replaced by *ho* 虎 to avoid an overlap with King Hyejong's given name, Wang Mu 王武.

Xuanzong 玄宗 personally worshiped at Taqing Palace 大清宮 and presented posthumous titles to five people, including Laozi 老子, whose posthumous title became Sagacious Ancestor and Thearch of Mysterious Origin (*shengzu xuan yuan huangdi* 聖祖玄元皇帝). Then the emperor went to Hanyuan Hall 含元殿, received letters of congratulations from his subjects, and declared an amnesty for all the world." We beseech you to follow this precedent by attending the court assembly at the Royal Council Hall (*p'yŏnjŏn* 便殿) on the first day of every intercalary month.

The king approved.

Kimi (22nd day). The king appointed Yi Chayŏn and Wang Ch'ongji as executives of the Chancellery, and Kim Chŏngjun and Park Sŏnggŏl as senior governmental advisors.

Sinyu (24th day). Thirty Eastern Jurchens, led by General Embracing Transformation Kododal 古刀達, were granted an audience and made an offering of horses. They also returned men and women who had been taken captive by tribesmen. The king gave them assorted goods and promotions in rank.

Intercalary Month

Kyemi (16th day). There was a great flood in Munju 文州[37] and Yongju 湧州[38] in the Northeastern Frontier Circuit. One hundred commoner households were washed away, and the king sent commissioners to console the people.

Eighth Month

Chŏngyu (1st day). The Censorate submitted a memorial.

Your earlier decree to the Public Works Ministry said, "The reason the levee on the southeastern side of the capital's outer walls was built high was to compensate for the geomantically weak spaces in the

---

37. Present-day Munch'ŏn city, Kangwŏn.
38. Present-day Tŏkwŏn-myŏn, Munch'ŏn city, Kangwŏn.

capital. With the outer walls now threatened by the rising water in the stream, recruit three or four thousand laborers to repair the levee." The Censorate has examined the area and found that the land protected by the levee is good farmland. We are concerned that a construction project there will impair farming, and we urge you to postpone construction until the end of the harvest.

The king approved.

Ninth Month

Kapsin (18th day). The Censorate submitted a petition.

Royal attendants who belong to government offices outside the palace come to the palace to attend to their duties from early morning until late at night, yet they are not provided with overnight lodging. In the Chinese system, officials charged with literary composition 詞臣 are attached to the Document Drafting Office (*sherenyuan* 舍人院). We request that you allow all officials preparing your decrees to stay at the Hallim Academy.

The king approved.
Pyŏngsul (20th day). The king went to the Western Capital.
Kyŏngin (24th day). The king traveled to the Western Regional Military Command and stayed in the countryside for three days.
Sinmyo (25th day). The king stayed at Sin'gwang monastery on Mount Puksung 北嵩山. He observed the [Five Hundred] Arhats ritual and held a banquet for the royal family, the state councilors, and his royal attendants.
Kyesa (27th day). The king climbed the southernmost mountain 南山 in the Regional Military Command. He summoned the royal family, the state councilors, and his royal attendants to a reception with libations, and the party ended when night fell.

Tenth Month, Winter

Pyŏngsin (1st day). There was a solar eclipse.

Kyŏngja (5th day). The king traveled to the Taedong River, boarded a floating pavilion 樓船, and hosted a banquet for the royal family and state councilors.

Imin (7th day). The king went to Hŭngbok monastery 興福寺. He again went to the Taedong River and boarded a floating pavilion, where he hosted a banquet for officials ranked supreme general and higher.

Kapchin (9th day). The king provided food for filial sons and grandsons, virtuous husbands and virtuous wives, widows and widowers, orphans, and the elderly without children. He also gave them assorted goods in accordance with their rank.

Kiyu (14th day). The king went to Hŭngguk monastery and held the Assembly of the Eight Prohibitions.

Kyech'uk (18th day). At Changnak Hall 長樂殿, the king hosted a banquet for civil officials of the fifth rank and higher and military officials ranked lieutenant colonel or higher. He presented gifts of silk in accordance with their rank.

Kabin (19th day). The king went to Chunghŭng monastery.

Ŭlmyo (20th day). The king departed from the Western Capital and boarded a floating pavilion on the Taedong River. As he gazed at the eastern bank of the river, he ordered eight people, including General Chŏng Chŭng 鄭曾, to shoot arrows across the river. When Lieutenant Colonel Yuhyŏn's 惟現 arrow hit the eastern bank, the king commended him. Afterward, the king hosted a banquet for the royal family, the state councilors, and his royal attendants.

Pyŏngjin (21st day). The Western Capital commissioner and director of revenue Wang Ibo led a party of officials to Saengyang station 生陽驛 to send the king off. The king gave an official's dress to each of them.

Chŏngsa (22nd day). The king stayed at Maitreya monastery (*Mirŭgwon* 彌勒院) in Chabiryŏng 慈悲嶺,[39] where he burned incense and donated articles of clothing. As the king's procession moved through Chŏllyŏng 岊嶺 on

---

39. Chabiryŏng, a militarily strategic place between Kaegyŏng and the Western Capital, was located between present-day Hwangju-gun and Sŏhŭng-gun, North Hwanghae. As it was the site of Chŏllyŏng station, Chabiryŏng was also known as Chŏllyŏng.

the following day, he saw a woman holding up two children to his view. Feeling pity, he gave them a gift of rice.

Sinyu (26th day). The king returned to the palace from the Western Capital.

Eleventh Month

Kich'uk (24th day). The king issued a decree.

> The *Book of Classics* 書經 says, "When the ruler is supremely good, the whole world functions in the right order." The crown prince is the cornerstone of the kingdom. The distinction between legitimate and illegitimate sons affirmed in the installation of the crown prince has the purpose of upholding royal descent and unifying public sentiment. For this reason, rulers of a kingdom usually consider this to be a matter of some urgency. Accordingly, the name of the consort of Yŏndŏk Palace's eldest son is now changed from Wang Hyu 王烋 to Wang Hun 王勳, and he will be installed as the Crown Prince.

Twelfth Month

Pyŏngsin (1st day). The Khitans sent the Iju regional inspector 利州刺史 So So 蕭素 with a letter of congratulations on the king's birthday.

Eighth Year of Munjong (1054)

First Month, Spring

Pyŏngin (1st day). The king canceled the New Year Congratulations.
Imsin (7th day). Eighteen Eastern Jurchens, led by the Chungyun Yŏngson 英孫, were granted an audience and made an offering of fine horses.

Second Month

Kyemyo (9th day). Wang Hun was installed as the Crown Prince. The letter of investiture stated:

For people to live together, there must be a king who controls every aspect of a country's rule. It follows, then, that the king must select a son to be his successor. This tradition has not changed for a hundred generations, so it is not a matter of personal preference. It is a law that is binding for all. Having the audacity to lead our people, I have long wished to bring them a happiness that endures. The foundation of our country must be kept strong for their lives to be secure, and now they can expect to have a bright future when they see what Heaven has bestowed. Over the years, wishing to avoid confusion in the order of succession, I have waited for someone endowed with wisdom to whom I could entrust the fate of this country. And so, Heaven blessed me with a precious son. Not only that, but the admiration that others have expressed for his wisdom and honesty has made it clear to all that he deserves to have the honor of succeeding me.

Ah! My eldest son, Hun 勳, is broad-minded, generous, and admirably mature. Even in childhood, he did not engage in child's play but instead sought the company of older and wiser people who could tell him about virtue 善道. People who saw this sang his praises, and all the officials watched their prince grow with the highest expectations. Then I saw his place in the hall of the kings 紫殿 and conferred on him the rank of Crown Prince 靑墻. On this auspicious day, with lavish words of praise 綸音, I send the grand marshal and acting vice director of the Chancellery (*su munha sijung* 守門下侍郞) Wang Ch'ongji as the lead investiture commissioner, and the minister of education and right vice director of state affairs Pak Sŏnggŏl as the deputy investiture commissioner, to arrange your installation as Crown Prince with all due ceremony.

Ah! It was so beautiful when Liu Che 劉徹 (156–87 BCE)[40] became crown prince at the age of seven, and so admirable when King Wen of Zhou 周 文王 sincerely asked about his father, through a palace servant, three times in a single day. You must work hard to model yourself after the merits attained by our ancestors as you strive to accomplish their vision for our country. Remember that the higher one rises in position, the more careful one needs to be. Listen to honest advice as you would to a teacher, for it will redound to your honor, and when contemplating the affairs of the state and military, never neglect your duty to rule. If you can remember this exhortation always, how splendid it will be!

---

40. Liu Che 劉徹 was Emperor Wu of Han, r. 141–87 BCE.

Pyŏngo (12th day). The king went to Sinbong Pavilion. He declared a general amnesty and promoted officials by one grade.

Kyech'uk (19th day). The king went to the Imperial Ancestral Shrine and the royal tombs to conduct several rites. He hosted a banquet for the officials in Kŏndŏk Hall and presented gifts in accordance with their rank.

Third Month

Kapsul (10th day). The king showed his consideration to fifty-nine Eastern Jurchens, including Agol, who had been detained. He gave them gifts of cloth and other goods in accordance with their rank.

Fourth Month, Summer

Kyŏngsul (17th day). The king rewarded Yi Chayŏn with the additional title of High Grand Tutor. Also, the king issued a decree reinstating officials and clerks who had been purged before the amnesty to their former offices.

Imja (19th day). Thirty-nine Northern Jurchens, led by General Comforting the Frontier Koch'a 高遮, were granted an audience and made an offering of excellent horses.

Kimi (26th day). Yu Sŏnyŏ 柳善餘 and others passed the state examination. This month, the king sent the supervising secretary Kim Yangji 金良贄 to the Khitans with a message informing them of the crown prince's installation.

Fifth Month

Kimyo (16th day). Characters for *chŏng* 正, "upright," and *ch'ong* 聰, "intelligent," were added to the merit titles designating the gods of the important mountains and rivers of Koryŏ.

The country of T'amna sent envoys with a letter of congratulations on the installation of the crown prince. The king gave additional government posts to thirteen envoys and presented gifts to their boatmen and members of their retinue in accordance with their rank.

Ŭryu (22nd day). Lightning struck Hoegyŏng Hall.

Sixth Month

Chŏngmi (15th day). The king received the bodhisattva ordination in the Inner Office.

Seventh Month, Autumn

Kyŏngo (9th day). Sixty-nine Song merchants, led by Zhao Shou 趙受, were granted an audience and made an offering of rhino horns and ivory.

Kich'uk (28th day). A prince was born. He was named Ong 顒 (1054–1105).[41] This month, the Khitans began to build a barricade with arrowslits (*kunggumullan* 弓口門欄)[42] in the field to the east of P'oju Fortress 抱州城.

Eighth Month

Imja (21st day). The king appointed the Palace Secretariat commissioner Kim Wŏnjŏng as the military commissioner of the Northwestern Frontier District.

Kyŏngsin (29th day). The military commissioner of the Eastern Frontier Circuit submitted a petition.

> Since the terrain in Changju is steep and rough and the fortress there does not have a well, I recommend that the flat area outside the south gate be protected with a wooden fence. The residents can be settled near the fence and allowed into the fortress when there is an emergency.

The king approved.

---

41. Wang Ong 王顒 became King Sukchong in 1095.

42. Built from stones or wood, this defensive fortification was also known as *kunggumun* 弓口門, *kunggunanja* 弓口欄子, or *kungnan* 弓欄.

Ninth Month

Kisa (9th day). The king recognized the meritorious service of the soldiers who defeated the enemy at the battle of Ch'idam station in the year *imjin* (1052). He gave them rich gifts and official positions in accordance with their rank.

Kyŏngo (10th day). Forty-eight Song merchants, led by Huang Zhu 黃助, were granted an audience.

Tenth Month

Ŭlmi (5th day). Twenty-eight Eastern Jurchens, led by General Soothing Faraway Lands Idabul, were granted an audience and made an offering of excellent horses. They returned three tribesmen who had previously been captured in Koryŏ, Sin'gŭm 信金, Wibong 位奉, and Sŏmnye 暹禮, and said of the others, "The tribesmen Silbin, Yŏmhan, Pidan 比丹, and Maribul have received official posts and titles from the Khitans. We brought them to you because they wanted an audience with the Koryŏ king when they heard that he treats foreign people with respect and is inclined to benevolence."

The king gave government positions and promotions to Silbin, Yŏmhan, Pidan, and Maribul and presented gifts to the others in accordance with their rank.

Kapchin (14th day). The Ikchu regional inspector 益州刺史 Yayul Pang 耶律芳 came as a Khitan special envoy bearing an edict from the emperor.

Eleventh Month

Kapcha (5th day). The Khitans sent the Ikchu regional inspector Yayul Kan 耶律幹 as a special envoy and imperial lecturer (*sŏnyusa* 宣諭使).

Twelfth Month

Kyŏngin (1st day). The Khitans sent the Pokchu regional inspector Yayul Sin 耶律新 with a letter of congratulations on the king's birthday.

The relevant authorities submitted a petition.

The posthumous rank of the Taegwang Ch'ŏnmyŏng 千明 and some 3,200 other merit subjects of King T'aejo should be promoted in accordance with their rank.

The king approved.

Sinhae (22nd day). The king ordered the selection of higher and lower pages for the heir apparent's honor guard (*tonggung siwi* 東宮侍衛).

Ninth Year of Munjong (1055)

Second Month, Spring

Ŭlsa (17th day). Twenty-seven Eastern Jurchens, led by General Supporting the State Idabul, were granted an audience and made an offering of their native products.

Musin (20th day). For the Cold Food day, the king hosted a banquet for 87 Song merchants, led by Ye Dechong 葉德寵, in the Obin guesthouse 娛賓館. There also were banquets for 105 people, led by Huang Zheng 黃拯, in the Yŏngbin guesthouse, for 48 people, led by Huang Zhu, in the Ch'ongha guesthouse 淸河館, and 158 people from the country of T'amna, led by Ko Han 高漢, in the Chojong guesthouse 朝宗館.

Fourth Month, Summer

Sinch'uk (13th day). Hail fell, and then it snowed.

Fifth Month

Sinyu (4th day). The Khitans sent Yayul Hyŏk 耶律革 and Chinŭi 陳顗 as investiture envoys bearing the emperor's edict.

> Following the achievements of your ancestors, you have made culture and learning flourish in Koryŏ, and also presented tribute offerings to the imperial family with the greatest sincerity and respect. You have brought good fortune to your feudal land 藩圭 and peace to the east. Now, since we have just received a ceremonious title, it has occurred to us to share this pleasure with you. So, as a sign of our favor, we have prepared this letter of investiture 冊函 with numerous gifts to demonstrate to all how honored you are, and we dispatch the commissioner of the Expending Justice Army Yayul Hyŏk with other envoys to conduct the investment ceremony with the proper courtesies. The bestowal of carriages 車輅, official robes 冠服, scepter 圭 and sword 劍, and other gifts is fully accounted for in the accompanying list. You may accept them when they arrive.

The letter of investiture said:

> To enjoy harmonious relations with other countries, an emperor shows his regard for a feudal lord by giving him red and black bows, and also commends his merit and the achievements of his royal family with bestowals of meat for the royal shrine 膰胙. By the good fortune that has blessed our reign, order in this court was reestablished 縣蕝之儀 through the efforts of our officials, and we were compelled to accept a grand title by the will of our subjects. Since by our rules, you are truly deserving of a similar privilege, it is entirely appropriate that the emperor's gifts 蓼蕭之澤 be extended to the farthest reaches of the sea.
>
> We therefore proclaim this order of investiture 昆命 on the auspicious day 靈辰 that has been chosen. To Wang Hwi, blessed with a gentle and understanding personality, we award the titles of Rectifying the Age, Serving Governance, Completing Integrity, Offering Loyalty, Merit Subject Demonstrating Dedication to Superiors, Commander Unequaled in Honor, Acting Grand Guardian, Director of the Secretariat, Supreme Pillar of the State, and King of Koryŏ with a fief of ten thousand households

and an actual fief of thirteen hundred households. The king has faithfully performed his duties, and possessing the virtue of wood 木德,[43] he has governed benevolently. Neighboring peoples and countries look to him and see that he has been endowed by Heaven with the exceptional qualities of the old sages 珠衡. He is descended from the ancestor who equaled the feats of Duke Huan of Qi and Duke Wen of Jin by pacifying the feudal lands of Chinhan and Pyŏnhan. From his royal ancestors, he inherited his kingdom and has renewed it with virtuous administration, eliciting from his people a beautifully echoing song of delight. As a subject king 賓王 requesting our calendar 朔, he has been steadfast in sincerely serving the great country, and at the same time he has remained faithful to the duty of protecting his country. By carefully observing the progression of the seasons, and the weather, he has accumulated the strength to serve the emperor 北面 as a guardian of the imperial court, relieving anxiety about affairs in the east and causing his own prestige to rise among the subject countries. Now, since we have just observed a happy occasion and are ever mindful of his long-standing merit, we dispatch our envoys with this letter of investiture from the imperial court.

In keeping with prior precedent, we reach out to your distant land and reward a faithful merit subject by promoting you to the rank of Grand Preceptor (*t'aesa* 太師), and giving you appropriate fiefs. Accordingly, we send Yayul Hyŏk, commissioner of the Expending Justice Army, Yoju regional inspector 饒州刺史, and censor-in-chief, as our lead investiture envoy; and Chinŭi, minister of the Imperial Entertainments Court and military protector (*hogun* 護軍), as our deputy investiture envoy. With the order entrusted to them, we invest you, with all due ceremony, as Acting Grand Preceptor (*su t'aesa* 守太師) and confer on you a fief of five thousand households with an actual fief of five hundred households. Your other titles and fiefs remain as before.

Ah! We also present you with special gifts, such as a beaded crown 冕冠 with embroidered luan bird 鸞, eight kinds of official dress, and a carriage decorated with ivory 象輅 and nine flags, all prepared in strict conformity with legal requirements. Having your gifts made by

---

43. This is an invocation of Koryŏ's position in the east, one of the five directions, and hence of benevolence (*in* 仁), one of the five virtues. In yin-yang philosophy, the east is identified with wood and benevolence, the west with metal and righteousness, the south with fire and etiquette, the north with water and wisdom, and the center with earth and fidelity.

the Office of Protocol is a high honor 榮暉 rarely extended to rulers of other countries, so you may receive them with proper respect and dedicate yourself to realizing the plan you've devised for your country. As we are in a prosperous time, your achievements in sustaining your people and uniting them under your rule will serve as a model for other feudal lords to emulate. They will also create the peaceful realm you bequeath to your descendants. Keep this exhortation in mind, and you will receive great fortune.

The king received the letter of investiture on the southern outskirts of the capital.
Kyehae (6th day). The Khitans sent the Iju regional inspector So Nok 蕭祿 to install the crown prince. The letter of investiture stated:

In days of yore, feudal lords usually had a crown prince because maintaining order was important, and preserving the dynasty was difficult. The wish to honor one's ancestors forever meant that one had to choose a legitimate son as a successor. We found the sincerity of your recent memorial most admirable. Indeed, your courtesy as a fief lord 專封之禮 since the time you paid us your respects and requested our calendar has been excellent. By requesting an order of investiture from your emperor, you sought our indulgence while you installed a crown prince 樹本之恩. As the traditional ceremony will now be held, you should confirm the titles you hold in good faith: Rectifying the Age, Serving Governance, Completing Integrity, Offering Loyalty, Merit Subject Demonstrating Dedication to Superiors, Commander Unequaled in Honor, Acting Grand Guardian, Director of the Secretariat, Supreme Pillar of the State, and King of Koryŏ with a fief of ten thousand households and an actual fief of thirteen hundred households.

Wang Hwi's son, Wang Hun, was guided by the virtue that has accrued for generations, and he has inherited his ancestors' exceptional wisdom. From childhood, he was endowed with excellent talent. He showed his respect for his elders whenever he attended the royal lectures, and sought out teachers of his own and attended their lectures to discern the truth. The lineage of the Koryŏ kings is unbroken, and the kingdom's prosperity going back in time has deep roots. The royal descendants have inherited their ancestors' achievements and successfully maintained their ancient traditions. Samhan was originally the old land of Paekche.

Thus, installing the son after the father accords with the protocols of our court. In becoming the crown prince, you will discover the extent of our generosity and consideration, and within that span your great fortune will be revealed. Ah! Since you have the honor of receiving an imperial edict in your youth, it is certain that the duty of riding in a royal carriage and wearing royal robes will be yours. Serve your parents with filial devotion and respect, and be a worthy representative of your family's bounty and integrity. If you refrain from indulging in pride or indolence and always keep our advice in mind, you will never stain the benevolence shown you in this kind exhortation. As a special favor, we now invest you as Duke of Samhan 三韓國公.

The crown prince received the letter of investiture in the garden inside the Audience gate.

Ŭrhae (18th day). There was heavy hail.

Seventh Month, Autumn

Chŏngsa (1st day). The Military and War Council submitted a memorial.

> The last Khitan dowager empress issued an imperial decree granting us the land east of the Amnok River, which became our kingdom's border. Yet the Khitans violate the border by building bridges, fortresses, and barricades with arrowslits on our side. This shows they are intent on invading our frontier without any qualms. They have even dared to build post houses in our territory. This calls to mind the statement in the *Spring and Autumn Annals*: "Do not let creeping vines spread. Once they spread, they are difficult to control." We suggest sending a message at the state level to the resident governor of the Eastern Capital, to warn him about the extent of their actions. If they do not heed our warning, it would then be best to send an envoy with a report to the emperor.

Consequently, the king sent a letter to the resident governor of the Eastern Capital.

As the inheritors of Jizi's [Kija] land, our kingdom has traditionally had the Amnok River as our border. Furthermore, when the last dowager empress and emperor granted us a fief in their letter of investiture, the Amnok River officially became the border between the Khitan empire and Koryŏ. In spite of this, the Khitans in that region have crossed over the border to build bridges and strongholds. We have always paid our sincere respects to the emperor by sending envoys to a distant land. We have also submitted memorials requesting the return of our former territory, but failed to receive an answer until just recently. We cannot but hope that the land along the Amnok River will be returned to its rightful king. Yet it has also been reported that your soldiers in Naewŏn Fortress recently built a barricade with arrowslits near our P'oju Fortress and are preparing materials for building a watchtower 亭舍. These activities are highly concerning to our people in the frontier region, as their purpose is not yet known. To preserve friendly relations with a neighboring country, we ask you to report our concerns to the emperor and urge him to restore to us the land that the Khitan dowager empress and emperor acknowledged was ours. We also request that you order your soldiers to dismantle the aforementioned bridges, fortresses, barricades with arrowslits, and watchtowers.

Kyŏngsin (4th day). The king appointed Ch'oe Ch'ung as director of the Imperial Secretariat before giving him permission to retire. The king also appointed Yi Chayŏn as superintendent of the Civil Personnel Ministry and director of the Chancellery; Kim Chŏngjun as executive of the Imperial Secretariat; Pak Sŏnggŏl as executive of the Imperial Secretariat and supreme pillar of the state; and Kim Wŏnjŏng as left vice director of the State Affairs Department, senior governmental advisor, and junior guardian of the crown prince (*t'aeja sobo* 太子少保).

Fifteen Khitans, led by Kang Kyŏngjun 康慶遵, came to submit. They returned fifty-three Koryŏ people who had been taken captive by the tribesmen.

Kyehae (7th day). The king appointed Chi Maeng 智猛 (988–?) as high minister of works, Kusŭng 仇勝 as director of the Ministry of Punishments, Kim Sobo 金所寶 as director of the Revenue Ministry, and Hwangbo Yŏn as director of the Public Works Ministry. All four were military officers receiving concurrent appointments to civil positions.

Imsin (16th day). Twenty-six Eastern Jurchens, led by Yasiro 耶時老, were granted an audience and made an offering of their native products. The king gave them official positions and gifts in accordance with their rank.

Kyeyu (17th day). The king issued a decree.

> Lady Kim 金氏, the elder sister of my deceased mother, looked after my elder brother King Tŏkchong and me when we were children. My wish is that she should be granted titles and fiefs as recompense for her devoted work. The Palace Secretariat will execute this order in accordance with the relevant regulations.

Eighth Month

Kyŏngin (5th day). The king ordered the retrial of criminals.

Kihae (14th day). The Civil Personnel Ministry submitted a petition.

> The eminent vice director of construction and maintenance (*kŏmgyo changjak sogam* 檢校將作少監) Yu Kongŭi 庾恭義 is a great-grandchild of the Taegwang Yu Kŭmp'il, but because he committed a crime, he has never received a prestige title higher than the one he holds. Since this contravenes your decree that descendants of the merit subjects venerated in King T'aejo's shrine be appointed to government office even if they have been guilty of a criminal offense, it is appropriate that you award him now the title of Sukchu Defense Commissioner (*Sukchu pangŏsa* 肅州防禦使).

The Chancellery, however, submitted their own memorial.

> Yu Kongŭi should not be appointed a Sukchu defense commissioner because the offense he was guilty of was flattery. Everyone knows that local governance is more difficult than weaving silk, so it follows that the prestige of this position will be undermined if a less than qualified person is appointed to it. We ask you to reject the petition.

The king approved the Chancellery's memorial.

Ninth Month

Kyehae (8th day). The Khitans sent Chang Sabok 張嗣復, the vice minister of their Dependencies Court (*hongnyŏ sogyŏng* 鴻臚少卿), as a demise-announcing envoy to Koryŏ (*koaesa* 告哀使). When the king learned that Chang Sabok had crossed over the Amnok River, he ordered a reduction in the number of side dishes served at royal meals, suspended music performances in the court, and prohibited hunting and the butchering of livestock.

Ŭlch'uk (10th day). Wearing mourning robes, the king went to the Ch'angdŏk gate with all the officials to receive the imperial edict from Chang Sabok. The king conducted a rite of mourning for the Khitan emperor and ordered a suspension of court business and marketplace activity for three days.

Sinmi (16th day). The Foreign Relations Office submitted a petition.

> Huang Xin 黃忻, the Dugang from Song, sent us a letter with the appeal, "I came with my sons, Huang Puan 黃蒲安 and Huang Shian 黃世安, to submit to Koryŏ, but I cannot help being concerned about my eighty-two-year-old mother in my homeland." We request that the king send the eldest son, Huang Puan, back to his homeland to support his grandmother.

The king said, "When even a bird from Yue 越 nests in the branches facing south, how can human beings not miss their homeland?" The king approved the request.

Pyŏngja (21st day). The king sent the Palace Secretariat administrator Ch'oe Yusŏn and the vice director of public works Yi Tŭngno 李得路 as envoys bearing condolences to the Khitans and to represent him at the funeral of Emperor Hŭngjong.

Tenth Month, Winter

Ŭryu (1st day). The vice director of revenue Ch'oe Chongp'il 崔宗弼, who had been sent to the Khitans as an envoy bearing the king's grateful response on his birthday (saengsin hoesasa 生辰回謝使), returned and submitted a report.

> The Khitan Rites Ministry (yebu 禮部) informed me: "The emperor's name is Chongjin 宗眞. Since having the same Chong 宗 in your name is a violation of the naming rule, your name must be rewritten." I therefore altered my name on the memorial to Ch'oe P'il 崔弼.

The Chancellery submitted a memorial.

> Ch'oe Chongp'il should have replied, "We did not know the emperor's name at the time, so it is Koryŏ's mistake. Still, I cannot change the content of the memorial as requested." Even though the Khitans demanded that he change the memorial, he should have known that erasing a single dot or stroke on it would not have been in accord with propriety. By inappropriately changing its content, Ch'oe Chongp'il has disgraced your royal command. We ask that he be punished.

The king forgave his deed.

Pyŏngsin (12th day). The king issued a decree.

> Old texts confirm that former emperors and kings used to worship the Buddha's teachings 釋敎, and Buddhist monasteries have been built here to pray for good fortune since the reign of King T'aejo. After my accession to the throne, the repeated disasters that occurred were due to my failure to properly govern the kingdom. Therefore, since it is imperative that we entreat the Buddha to bring good fortune to our kingdom, let the relevant authorities choose an appropriate plot of land for constructing a monastery.

The Chancellery submitted a memorial.

> In the past, there was no wise king or holy emperor who ever achieved prosperity by building monasteries and pagodas. Kings may follow Buddhism while still weighing its effect on public edification and governance, and if they avoid driving the people to exhaustion, their dynasty will last forever. Long ago, Bodhidharma explained to Emperor Wu of Liang (r. 502–549) that building monasteries and pagodas does not earn

merit. What he meant is that true merit is not produced through calculated acts but accrues from effortless action. Furthermore, the reason King T'aejo built monasteries was to channel the energy of our mountains and rivers as well as to repay the Buddha for granting his wish to unify our land. If you build another monastery now, the additional labor that will be required from people will push them to exhaustion, bringing resentment and slander. We must also be sure that it will not harm the energy flow of our mountains and rivers, causing natural disasters and arousing the ire of gods as well as people. This is not the way to achieve prosperity.

The king did not approve.

Eleventh Month

Ŭlch'uk (11th day). The king went to the Eastern Pond. When the eminent vice director of imperial regalia (*kŏmgyo wiwi sogyŏng* 檢校衛尉少卿) Ch'oe Sŏngjŏl entered the king's pavilion without a reason, the king was startled and ordered his imprisonment. The authorities in charge of law enforcement submitted a memorial pointing out that "the punishment for the offense of intruding on the king's privacy is execution by beheading." In response, the king said, "Although mandated by law, execution is too severe a punishment for such an offense. Moreover, since he has useful writing talent, I shall forgive him." When the Chancellery remonstrated with a second memorial, the king rejected both.

The Khitan acting minister of works Yayul To 耶律道 came to Koryŏ as a response envoy from the Eastern Capital.

Twelfth Month

Kabin.[44] The Khitans sent the Kŭmju regional inspector 金州刺史 Yayul Changjŏng 耶律長正 with a letter of congratulations on the king's birthday.

---

44. *Kabinsak* 甲寅朔, meaning the first day of the eighth month, in the original text. The actual date is unknown.

Tenth Year of Munjong (1056)

First Month, Spring

Sinmi (18th day). A meteor fell in Hwangju, making a sound like thunder.

Kapsul (21st day). Fifty Eastern Jurchens, led by General Supporting the State Agaju, were granted an audience and made an offering of thirty-two excellent horses.

Second Month

Kabo (12th day). The relevant authorities submitted a petition.

> Yŏm Kach'ing 廉可偶, a former captive of tribal people, is the son of the Weaponry Directorate executive (*kun'gisŭng* 軍器丞) Yŏm Wi 廉位 and the grandson of the minister of education and unification merit subject Yŏm Hyŏngmyŏng 廉邢明. In the year *kyŏngsul* (1010), he was recruited to the Noble Guard Army (*hwanwi kongjagun* 環衛公子軍), and when the Khitan army invaded and Kaegyŏng fell into chaos, he tried to flee to Pongsŏng county 峯城縣[45] with his parents. That was when he was taken captive by tribesmen. He escaped in the first month of the first year of Ch'ŏngnyŏng 清寧 (1055) and returned to Koryŏ with a son. We would like the hereditary land (*yŏngŏpchŏn* 永業田)[46] and the house of his father and grandfather returned to Yŏm Kach'ing.

The king issued a decree.

> Yŏm Kach'ing, a descendant of a merit subject, was taken captive in his youth. That his hair turned gray before he returned to Koryŏ, leaving his wife and children behind, except for a son, is pitiful. His hereditary land and house shall be returned to him.

---

45. Present-day P'aju city, Kyŏnggi.
46. Stipendiary land that was permanently assigned to a civil or military official and his descendants and could also be granted to a meritorious soldier.

Kyemyo (21st day). The construction of Hŭngwang monastery began in Tŏksu county.

Kiyu (27th day). The country of T'amna sent a tribute offering of its native products.

Third Month

Kabin (2nd day). The king invested Wang Chŭng with the title of Marquis of Kugwŏn 國原侯 and entered the Royal Council Hall unobserved to watch the ceremony of investiture. Then he summoned the Chancellery director Yi Chayŏn, the senior governmental advisor Kim Wŏnjŏng, the left vice director of state affairs Chi Maeng, and several others to celebrate with him. With libations, the party lasted until dawn.

Intercalary Month

Kyemi (1st day). The king performed the rite for Distributing the Calendar at the Imperial Ancestral Shrine.

Ŭryu (3rd day). The retired right vice director of state affairs and high minister of works Ko Yŏl died. In his time, he was a great general who excelled at archery and had distinguished himself in war more than once. Everyone grieved when they heard the news. The king suspended court business for three days and ordered all officials to attend the funeral.

Fourth Month

Pyŏngin (15th day). The king appointed Chi Maeng as high minister of works.

Pyŏngja (25th day). The king went to Kŏndŏk Hall to retest the examination candidates. Yi Kanbang 李幹方 and others passed the state examination.

Seventh Month, Autumn

Chŏngyu (17th day). With the eastern tribesmen repeatedly invading the frontier region, the king ordered the vice military commissioner of the Eastern Frontier Circuit and general censor Kim Tan to suppress them. Addressing his soldiers, Kim Tan said, "It is our duty to fight the enemy without letting personal concerns come before our devotion to country. Today's battle is a matter of life or death." Deeply moved and inspired, the Three Armies summoned their courage and crushed the enemy, destroying twenty villages and capturing numerous weapons and livestock.

Eighth Month

Mujin (19th day). On the day for executing condemned criminals across the country, the king avoided the main throne hall, ate only simple foods, and suspended music performances.

The resident governor of the Western Capital submitted a report.

> The books that people in the Western Capital use to study for the state examinations have many misspelled or misprinted words in them. This is because most of them are copies of the literary licentiate course and the classics examination course (*myŏnggyŏnggwa* 明經科) that were made at different times by many people. Since this is a serious problem, we request that copies of books like the Nine Classics 九經,[47] the histories of the Han, Qin, and Tang dynasties, the *Analects of Confucius*, and the *Classic of Filial Piety* be sent from the library of the Imperial Archives (*pigak* 秘閣) so that we can put them in our schools. Books about other masters, literary collections, and histories, together with books about medicine, divination, geography, and mathematics, would also be useful.

The king ordered the relevant authorities to make copies of the books requested for transmission to the schools in the Western Capital.

---

47. The *Book of Songs, Book of Classics, Book of Changes, Book of Rites, Book of Filial Piety, Spring and Autumn Annals, Analects of Confucius, Works of Mencius,* and *Rites of Zhou.*

Kyŏngo (21st day). The king fed thirty thousand monks.

Ninth Month

Kapsin (5th day). The king issued a decree.

> Send commissioners to check the service record and integrity of *mok* administrators (*moksa* 牧使), regional chiefs (*chasa* 刺史), regional military executive assistants (*t'ongp'an* 通判), county governors (*hyŏllyŏng* 縣令), county governor assistants (*wi* 尉), and local administrative leaders. Check also on the well-being of the people and the difficulties they are facing.

The relevant authorities proposed the suspension of this order, because having to provide for the new commissioners would exhaust the officials and personnel of the stations the commissioners would use. The king responded:

> My impression is that governors in the various regions, in previous reigns, worked hard as upright officials and the people under them lived comfortably, because the kings frequently sent commissioners out to check on their difficulties. Recently, however, even though we all see that discipline among the officials is deteriorating, we still do not have adequate means to punish their wrongdoing. Instead of being devoted to serving the state, regional officials prefer to pursue their own interests by colluding with the wellborn and powerful. Rather than help people engage in farming or sericulture, they only want a slice of the income from properties to feather their own nest. Some regions produce fish, others salt, or lumber, or sap from the lacquer tree, and still others raise domestic animals or make handicrafts. Yet corrupt governors exploit them all. If people refuse to succumb, they are falsely accused and severely punished, even killed. People caught in this plight, with hearts full of resentment, have nowhere to turn. The rare official who tries to set things right eventually fails because powerful superiors and aristocrats 要路 look after the governors they employ. With parasites like this multiplying every day, how can anyone hope to live comfortably? While I try day and night to cure this malady, I wonder why the ones who should

be carrying out my orders are making unnecessary arguments to dissuade me.

Now, send the assistant executive of the Punishments Ministry (*hŏngbu wŏnoerang* 刑部員外郎) and general censor Yi Yujŏk 李攸績 as consolation and pacification commissioner for three provinces (*samdo mumunsa* 三道撫問使) to Chungju, Kyŏngju, and Sangju in the Sandong 山東 and Sannam 山南 regions. Send the executive of the Military Affairs Ministry and miscellaneous affairs investigator Kim Yakchin 金若珍 (d. 1082) and the Rites Ministry executive Ch'oe Sang 崔尙 as consolation and pacification commissioners for seven provinces (*ch'ilto mumunsa* 七道撫問使) to Chinju 晉州,[48] Naju, Chŏnju, Ch'ŏngju, Kwangju, Kongju, and Hongju 洪州[49] in the Sannam region. Send the de facto assistant executive of the Palace Administration (*si chŏnjung naegŭpsa* 試殿中內給事) and investigating censor An Minbo 安民甫 as consolation and pacification commissioner for three provinces to the Kwansŏ 關西, Kwannae 關內, and Kwanbuk 關北[50] regions; and send the investigating censor Min Ch'angsu 閔昌壽 as consolation and pacification commissioner of the eastern province (*tongdo mumunsa* 東道撫問使) to the Kwannae region. All of them should depart for their assigned posts without delay.

Kich'uk (10th day). The king conducted the North Star rite (*t'aeilsŏng* 太一星) in Such'un Palace 壽春宮 to prevent fires.

Kyesa (14th day). The king ordered the crown prince to host a reception with libations in the East Pond Pavilion 東池樓 for members of the royal family. He invited the examination candidates Ch'oe Ŭng 崔應 and Yi Sŏ 李曙 and Wang Ch'ung 王忠, a royal relative, to each compose a "Poem while Gazing at the East Pond" (*Tongjisimsŭngsi* 東池尋勝詩), and he presented rolls of silk to each of them.

The king issued a decree.

---

48. Present-day Chinju city, South Kyŏngsang.
49. Present-day Hongsŏng-gun, South Ch'ungch'ŏng.
50. Kwannae 關內 refers to the province of Kwannae. The Ten Provinces System (*siptoje* 十道制) was established in 994. Kwannaedo included Kyŏnggi and parts of Hwanghae and Ch'ungch'ŏng provinces. Kwansŏ 關西 was the region located to the west of Kwannae and included P'yŏngan province, North Korea. Kwanbuk 關北 was the region to the north of Kwannae and included the former Hamgyŏng province.

When I recently read the astrologer's memorial, I saw that many extraordinary calamities have occurred, undoubtedly because of my lack of virtue and inconsistent governance. Because of this, I cannot avoid a feeling of uneasiness both day and night as my pulse quickens from worry. Starting this month, I will answer to this reprimand from Heaven by avoiding the main throne hall and reducing the number of side dishes served at royal meals. I expect every official to carry out his duties to the fullest and to point out my misconduct without fear or concealment.

Pyŏngsin (17th day). The king issued a decree.

Buddha taught that achieving purity 淸淨 must come first, and that people had to keep away from contamination to eliminate their greed. Recently, however, people have begun to assume the role of Buddhist monk to avoid required labor, even while they accumulate wealth by farming or ranching. When they are outside, they violate the Buddhist precepts. When they are in their homes, they violate the purity taught by the Buddha. Their monk robes become covers for wine crocks, and the place to hear a Buddhist lecture becomes a field for garlic and green onions. These so-called monks also associate with merchants and trade products with them. They frequent taverns to indulge in drunkenness and other amusements, they patronize brothels and defile the Ullambana 蘭盆.[51] Wearing secular clothes and caps, they play music around commoners' houses while pretending to manage and repair a monastery with flags and drums. They roam through town fighting with commoners, which often leads to bloodshed. To restore discipline, we must maintain distinctions between good and evil. I hereby order the reform of every monastery across the country. Monks who faithfully follow Buddhist precepts will be allowed to stay in their monasteries. Those who violate the precepts shall be punished according to law.

---

51. A Buddhist ritual to save the spirits of people sent to hell, based on the *Ullambana-sūtra* 盂蘭盆經.

Tenth Month, Winter

Kiyu (1st day). A mission with thirty envoys led by a Fujiwara 滕原 carrying the designation of servant with superior rank and authority (*shōjō ikenrei* 正上位權隸) and the court officer Yoritada 賴忠 came from Japan and stayed in Kŭmju.

Sinhae (3rd day). The crown prince conducted the ancestral worship rites at the Imperial Ancestral Shrine.

Imsul (14th day). The king personally conducted the Joint Ritual at the Imperial Ancestral Shrine and awarded additional posthumous titles to nine generations 九廟 of his ancestors. After the rite, he went to the purification chamber and received the congratulations of the officials. He then went to Sinbong Pavilion and issued an amnesty decree.

> Along with the audacity to claim my ancestors' achievements, I have been given the duty to preside over the mountains and rivers. I seek to renew my strength day after day and want to rest, but often cannot. I continually pray for the eternal prosperity of my kingdom and perform the ancestral rites at my ancestors' shrines. Today I have reverently performed the rite honoring all my ancestors, and to uphold their high virtue, I wish to share the merit of this event with all my people. I hereby order a general amnesty for criminals across the country.

Eleventh Month

Sinsa (3rd day). Twenty-nine Song merchants, led by Huang Zheng, came with an offering of their native products.

On this day, it snowed for the first time this year. All the officials offered congratulations.

Imo (4th day). The king went to the Inner Śakra monastery (*Nae Chesŏgwŏn* 內帝釋院), where he appointed the monk Haerin 海麟 (984–1067) to the position of royal preceptor.

Imjin (14th day). The king went to Pŏbwang monastery and held the Assembly of the Eight Prohibitions.

Kabo (16th day). Fifty Eastern Jurchens, led by Yasaro 耶賜老, were granted an audience and made an offering of their native products.

Twelfth Month

Musin (1st day). The Khitans sent the Yŏngju regional inspector So Yusin 蕭惟新 as an envoy to attend the celebration of the king's birthday.

Pyŏngjin (9th day). Letters of congratulations on the Day of Long Prosperity (*changhŭngjŏl* 長興節)[52] were received from central and local officials by the crown prince in Such'un Palace.

Two Eastern Jurchens were executed for pillaging the people of Sakchu prefecture. One of them was General Soothing Faraway Lands Sabokha 沙攴何.

This year, Changwŏn Pavilion 長源亭 was constructed on the south side of Mount Pyŏng 餠嶽 near the Western River (*sŏgang* 西江).[53]

---

52. The birthday of the crown prince.
53. Present-day Yesŏng River.

VOLUME 8

Compiled by Chŏng Inji, Chŏnghŏn Grand Master, minister of works, director of the Hall of Worthies, deputy director of the Royal Lectures Office and State Records Office, headmaster of the Royal Confucian Academy.

MUNJONG (1057–1071)

Eleventh Year of Munjong (1057)

First Month, Spring

Muin (1st day). The king canceled the New Year Congratulations.

Kich'uk (12th day). The king appointed Ko Yu 高維 as right reminder. The Secretariat submitted a memorial.

> Ko Yu, being from T'amna, is not a suitable remonstrance official. If his talent must be put to use, we request that he be appointed to another government position.

The king approved the request.

Ŭlmi (18th day). A meteorite fell in Hwangju with a sound like thunder.

Second Month

Kyeyu (27th day). The king held the Calamity Dispelling ritual in Kŏndŏk Hall for five days.

Third Month

Ŭryu (9th day). The Khitans sent a mission led by the investiture envoys So Kyejong 蕭繼從 and Wang Sujol 王守拙. The emperor's edict stated:

> You acceded to the throne following the late king and have become a vassal of our court. Now that our officials have presented us with a title and performed the ceremony, it is appropriate that we celebrate this happy occasion in the land of Koryŏ by giving you the special privilege of investiture as well. Therefore, we will bestow these blessings to show our favor, and we appoint the military commissioner of the Heaven Blessing Army (*ch'ŏndŏkkun chŏltosa* 天德軍節度使) So Kyejong as our lead investiture envoy, and the chief general of the Left Personal Guard Wang Sujol as our deputy investiture envoy, and send them to you. In addition, we send you gifts including official robes, carriages, silverware, rolls of silk, saddled horses, and bows and arrows, as specified in the accompanying list. You may accept them when they arrive.

The letter of investiture stated:

> As recipients of Heaven's grace and will, successive sage-emperors of our country have bequeathed wealth and happiness down through the generations. In extending their trust and blessings to every region under Heaven, would they have made a distinction between this country and foreign countries? In rewarding the meritorious service of officials, would they have discriminated between those who are distant and and those who are near? The grand territory of Samhan was located outside our borders when the country of Koryŏ was founded and when it submitted to our court. Taking its place under the mighty rule that called feudal lords to rectify all under Heaven, it proceeded to cultivate the loyalty of a tributary vassal, and as a descendant of the former Koguryŏ, it received investiture as a fief. It therefore has accepted our moral influence, provided aid, and even uses the same script we use. Now, to reward this meritorious service and to share in the happy occasion, we have chosen an auspicious day to bestow this special favor.
>
> We invest you, Wang Hwi, with the titles of Rectifying the Age, Serving Governance, Completing Integrity, Offering Loyalty, Merit Subject for Dedication to Superiors, Commander Unequaled in Honor,

Acting Grand Preceptor, Director of the Secretariat, Supreme Pillar of the State, and King of Koryŏ, and bestow a fief of fifteen thousand households and an actual fief of eighteen hundred households.

Wang Hwi, by accumulating the vital force in the dragon constellation (龍宿), was born in Koryŏ (雞林) as an outstanding prodigy. He was bright enough to understand music and rituals at birth and was erudite from childhood, becoming exceptionally well versed in poetry and calligraphy. With a powerful and expansive imagination, he has always investigated precious books like treasures in a gold chest, and once wrote out an anthology of brilliant and beautiful ideas, calling it a gold pavilion. As the heir of the country of Chumong 朱蒙之國,[1] he brought civilization to the people in the Xuantu commandery 玄菟, commanded the military with bravery and generosity, and revived venerable customs with gentleness and grace. Like fecund rain, he has showered his kingdom with blessings, and like an auspicious star (*kyŏngsŏng* 景星), he shines as an augury of eternity.

When our father was emperor, you served him with propriety. When we ascended the throne, you demonstrated firm loyalty. You have sent letters on fine paper and tributes wrapped in blue ribbons, tokens of your unchanging sincerity and faith. Recently, many officials pressed us with unfeigned fervor to accept an additional title, so we had no choice but to hold a magnificent ceremony. As we now bestow our imperial blessings, the strategies of Duke Huan of Qi 桓公 and Duke Wen of Jin 文公 are something to consider. Just as a Jin dynasty minister[2] rose to a seat in the carriage, and a Han dynasty subject[3] became sole seat (*tokchwa* 獨坐), we will bestow on you titles and fiefs to confirm our wish to give you encouragement. Accordingly, we have ordered our lead investiture envoy, the military commissioner of the Heaven Blessing Army So Kyejong, and our deputy investiture envoy, the chief general of the Left Personal Guard Wang Sujol, to deliver to you the imperial command to add Director of the State Affairs Department to your titles

---

1. Chumong was the legendary founder of Koguryŏ in the first century BCE; hence Koguryŏ was known as the country of Chumong.

2. In the time of Emperor Wu of Jin, He Qiao 和嶠 was given a carriage to show that the emperor considered him an exalted person.

3. In the reign of Emperor Guangwu of Han, Xuan Bing 宣秉 held the top three government positions—the meaning of "sole seat."

with a fief of five thousand households and an actual fief of two hundred households.

After ascending the throne, we made a pledge to your country. We gave you red bows as a token of our favor, elevating your status to the highest rung over those of the five marquises and nine earls (五侯九伯). The honored position you now hold, like a supporting leg of a jade vessel (*okhyŏn* 玉鉉), gives you authority that is higher than that of the four royal aides (*sabo* 四輔) and three dukes (*samgong* 三公). Furthermore, your country is one that your father and elder brother ruled before you. If you serve us well, you can expect the virtue of that succession to extend to posterity. We wish to bring comfort to your country so that we can live in harmony with you. With grand policies and formidable accomplishments, attained with help from Heaven and the gods, you will long enjoy supernal happiness and wealth. Be ever mindful to protect honor and fortune forever.

The king led his officials to the southern outskirts of the capital, where he received the order of investiture. The Khitans also sent So So and Si Tŏkcha 柴德滋 to invest the crown prince. The emperor's edict stated:

Your birth was precious for you came into the world as the first son of a king. Then you were bright from childhood, and your fame spread. Your title was elevated to the rank of Duke, and you received a gracious order of investiture. Recently, we conducted a magnificent ceremony attended by all the feudal lords and court officials. To celebrate this happy occasion, it is appropriate that we share our happiness by bestowing blessings and issuing a letter of investiture. So we send the Iju 利州 district surveillance commissioner So So as our lead investiture envoy and Si Tŏkcha, minister of the Imperial Granaries Court (*sanonggyŏng* 司農卿), as our deputy investiture envoy to deliver the letter and present you with gifts including official robes, carriages, silverware, rolls of silk, saddled horses, and bows and arrows, as specified in the accompanying list. You may accept them when they arrive.

The letter of investiture stated:

In the imperial succession, we inherited the glorious enterprise of ruling all under Heaven. Following the recommendation of our ministers, we recently conducted a magnificent ceremony attended by all the feudal lords and court officials. At the highest station, the dowager empress was given an additional honorific title. Among those below, even we, though still unworthy, received a title. To share our happiness, it is appropriate now that we include you in the ceremony of investiture.

Wang Hun 王勳, the son of Wang Hwi, has auspicious talent, like a phoenix, and an outstanding record, like a swift horse. With a warm and intelligent bearing, he has been educated in a fine family and has studied the deepest wellsprings of virtue. When he succeeds to the royal enterprise, he will use the teachings of his ancestors to properly govern the country. He has already known the glory of investiture from an earlier time, when he was elevated to a high position. But as with amnesties and good fortune, now is again the time for all under Heaven to share in the joy of investiture, and it is appropriate that you, as the heir of this family, should receive the blessing of imperial grace.

We therefore bestow on you a special letter of investiture and send the Iju district surveillance commissioner So So as our lead investiture envoy and the minister of imperial granaries Si Tŏkcha as our deputy investiture envoy to present the token (*pujŏl*) that invests you in the proper manner as Military Commissioner of the Obeying Justice Army (*sunŭigun chŏltosa* 順義軍節度使), Supervisory Surveillance Commissioner of Sangju and Muju Provinces (*Sangmu tŭngju kwanch'al ch'ŏch'i tŭngsa* 朔武等州觀察處置等使), Grand Master of Imperial Entertainments (*sungnok taebu* 崇祿大夫), Acting Grand Marshal, Secretariat-Chancellery Joint Affairs Manager (*tong chungsŏ munha p'yŏngjangsa* 同中書門下平章事), Commissioned with Extraordinary Military Powers in Sakchu (*sajijŏl sakchu chegunsa* 使持節朔州諸軍事), Acting Regional Inspector of Sakchu (*haeng sakchu chasa* 行朔州刺史), Supreme Pillar of the State, and Duke of Samhan with a fief of three thousand households and an actual fief of five hundred households.

Ah! When placing titles into the five categories, your position is above that of marquis. Furthermore, you have the additional seal of a minister, and your duties will become still heavier when you govern a country. Let this special favor abide deep in your heart and honor it forever.

The crown prince led the officials serving in his own palace and all the court officials to the southern outskirts of the capital, where he received the investiture. The king went unobserved to observe the ceremony.

Pyŏngsin (20th day). The Civil Personnel Ministry submitted a petition.

> Based on the amnesty decree declared at the Joint Ritual in the year *pyŏngsin* (1056), we request that Ch'oe Mu 崔懋, the great grandson of the Chancellery director Ch'oe Suk, who is enshrined as a merit subject in the king's shrine 配享功臣, be promoted to the position of equivalent clerk in the Revenue Ministry (*hobu yŏngsa tongjŏng* 戶部令史同正) through a protected appointment.

The king approved.

Kyemyo (27th day). The king appointed Yi Yuchung 異惟忠 (d. 1072) as deputy administrator of the Palace Secretariat, Im Chongil 任從一 as right vice director of the State Affairs Department, Wang Musung 王懋崇 as director of the Censorate, and Kim Wŏnhwang 金元晃 (d. 1062) as director of the Public Works Ministry.

Fourth Month, Summer

Pyŏngjin (10th day). The king went to Puril monastery and fed the monks.

Imsul (16th day). The king issued a decree.

> Last year, I sent an envoy to the Khitans to request the removal of a station located near a barricade with arrowslits (*kunggumun* 弓口門), but it has not yet been demolished. In addition, they are expanding the reclaimed land to the northeast of Songnyŏng, installing thatched cottages in some spots and stationing people and goods. This appears to be a scheme to invade our territory, and we must immediately request its removal.

The Secretariat submitted a remonstrance.

> The Khitans have not as yet provoked a border dispute. Furthermore, the new emperor has taken the throne and elevated our title as a feudal domain, but we have not yet expressed our gratitude. It would seem inappropriate for us to raise the border issue at this time.

The king responded.

> If they install a fortress and a palisade before we do, what is the use of regretting it after the fact? They must think that we are not aware of the issue. Envoys shall be sent in mid-autumn to express gratitude for the investiture, and then to request the removal of the new construction.

Pyŏngin (20th day). The king issued an imperial edict.

> The parties of the lead investiture envoy and the deputy investiture envoy both arrived at the same time from the Khitan capital. Consequently, officials and personnel of the stations receiving them are exhausted across the country. Therefore, prisoners who were punished for serving them improperly shall be released. All those living in districts and counties through which the envoy parties passed shall have their taxes reduced by half. Officials who were in charge at the time of our investiture, the ritual-performing officials (*sŭngdan paewigwan* 升壇陪位官), and officials of the fifth rank and higher shall be promoted. Officials who have Koryŏ prestige titles shall receive equivalent positions. The storehouse clerk (*changgo* 掌固), accountant (*sansa* 筭士), copyist (*sŏsu* 書手), and head of the Royal Guards (*kŭnjang kundu* 近仗軍頭) shall be appointed to government positions, and gifts shall be given to the other soldiers in accordance with their rank.

Kyeyu (27th day). Yi Chun 李畯 and others passed the state examination.

Fifth Month

Chŏngch'uk (2nd day). The king held the Buddhist ritual to avert calamities in Such'un Palace for three days.

Muin (3rd day). The Rites Ministry submitted a memorial.

> We have not had a timely rain since early summer. Now there is a report from Kwangju 廣州 that the fields and paddies have dried up, so the harvest this year is about to be abandoned. We recommend that prayers for rain should be addressed to the gods of the mountains and rivers and offered once every seven days at Mount Songak, Tongsin

Shrine 東神堂, local shrines,[4] and the Pagyŏn 朴淵 waterfall. In addition, Kwangju and other prefectures and districts should be ordered to add their own prayers for rain.

The king approved.

Imo (7th day). All shrines prayed for rain.

Pyŏngsul (11th day). Twenty-five Eastern Jurchens, led by General Embracing Transformation Kododal, were granted an audience and made an offering of their native products.

Chŏnghae (12th day). The consort of Hŭngsŏng Palace, Lady Sŏ 徐, died.

Muja (13th day). The king prayed for rain again, and rain fell soon after.

Sixth Month

Chŏngmi (2nd day). The Khitans sent the acting minister of works Yayul Kahaeng 耶律可行 as the Eastern Capital's message envoy for gratitude response (*tonggyŏng chirye hoesasa* 東京持禮回謝使).

Mujin (23rd day). Twenty-five Eastern Jurchens, led by General Soothing Faraway Lands Yoŏnae 要於乃, were granted an audience and made an offering of their native products.

Seventh Month, Autumn

Muja (14th day). The king held the Buddhist ritual for averting calamities in Kŏndŏk Hall for five days.

Imjin (18th day). The king ordered that Zhang Wan 張琬, who had come from Song to submit, be tested on the *dunjia sanqi* 遁甲三奇法[5] and *liuren* 六壬占,[6] after which Zhang was appointed as an astronomical observer (*t'aesa kamhu* 太史監候).

---

4. Shrines to the village deity and other gods in the provinces.
5. Astrological method for determining auspicious days and locations for the construction of houses and tombs.
6. A method of divination based on the five elements (*wuxing* 五行).

Kabo (20th day). The king gave food and other gifts to the elderly aged eighty or older, and to filial sons and grandsons, virtuous husbands and virtuous wives, widows and widowers, orphans, those living alone, and those with disabilities or critical illness. The gifts were distributed on the Polo Field in accordance with the recipient's rank.

Sinch'uk (27th day). The king went to Sŏnjŏng Hall to judge the cases of criminals deserving severe punishment across the country.

Eighth Month

Chŏngmi (3rd day). Twenty-five people led by the Song merchant Ye Dechong came to the court with an offering of their native products.

Pyŏngin (22nd day). The king appointed the proofreader (*pisŏsŏng kyogam* 秘書省校勘) Kyŏng Chŏngsang 慶鼎相 as provisional attendant in the Hallim Academy (*kwŏnji chik hallimwŏn* 權知直翰林院). The Secretariat submitted a memorial of remonstrance.

> Kyŏng Chŏngsang is the descendant of a metal worker. As such, he is unsuitable for appointment to a reputable and prestigious office 清要職. We request cancellation of the appointment.

The king denied the request, and added this response:

> The *Book of Songs* says, "When pulling up turnips, there is no need to look at their roots." This means we should value all things that can be used. Kyŏng Chŏngsang is a man of talent worthy of recruitment. Why should his family lineage be discussed?

Chŏngmyo (23rd day). Thirty-three people led by the Song merchant Guo Man came with an offering of their native products.

Sinmi (27th day). The king went to the Western Capital after ordering the Chancellery director Yi Chayŏn, the affairs manager Wang Ch'ongji, and others to stay behind to protect Kaegyŏng.

Ninth Month

Kapsin (11th day). The king sent Wang Ibo and Ch'oe Wŏnjun to the Khitans with an expression of gratitude for the investiture.

Tenth Month, Winter

Chŏngsa (14th day). The king went to Changgyŏng monastery 長慶寺 and held the Assembly of the Eight Prohibitions.

Kyehae (20th day). The T'aeju regional inspector 泰州刺史 Yayul Koeng 耶律宏 came from the Khitans as a special envoy bearing an imperial edict.

Eleventh Month

Pyŏngja (4th day). The king returned from the Western Capital.

Chŏngch'uk (5th day). The king appointed Kim Chŏngjun as vice director of the Chancellery with a concurrent assignment as Imperial Secretariat–Chancellery joint affairs manager.

Twelfth Month

Kyemyo (1st day). The Khitans sent the right grand master of remonstrance Wang Chongnyang 王宗亮 with a letter of congratulations on the king's birthday.

Chŏngmi (5th day). The king sent the vice director of revenue (*sangsŏ hobu sirang* 尙書戶部侍郎) An Minbo to the Khitans with a letter of congratulations on the grand dowager empress's birthday.

Kiyu (7th day). The king sent the vice director of public works (*sangsŏ kongbu sirang* 尙書工部侍郎) Ch'oe Kyeyu 崔繼游 to the Khitans with a letter of congratulations on the Day of Heavenly Peace (*ch'ŏnanjŏl* 天安節).[7]

---

7. The birthday of Emperor Tojong 道宗 (r. 1055–1101) of the Liao dynasty.

Sinhae (9th day). When the left vice director of state affairs Chi Maeng submitted a memorial requesting permission to retire, the king denied his request. The Secretariat submitted a petition: "Resigning is the proper courtesy for those who reach the age of seventy. Please grant his request." The king issued a decree.

> Chi Maeng's ancestors performed meritorious deeds for our country. I therefore granted him, even before he requested retirement, an armchair and a walking staff[8] so that he could serve the court for a few more years. If I accede to your request and go back on my previous words, I fear that Chi Maeng will no longer take the king's word seriously.

The Secretariat submitted another petition.

> The rules of decorum stipulate that elderly subjects acquainted with worldly matters be given an armchair and a walking staff. However, Chi Maeng became a government official through a protected appointment, and he knows nothing of worldly matters, much less achieved any merit in war. As for state affairs in general, there are no policy areas on which we would seek his advice. You could allow him to remain in office for one year given the achievements of his ancestors. But giving him an armchair and a walking staff together with several more years in office would be seen as excessive solicitude. Please withdraw the previous order.

The king approved.

Sinyu (19th day). The king appointed Kim Wŏnjŏng as vice director of the Imperial Secretariat with a concurrent assignment as Imperial Secretariat–Chancellery joint affairs manager, Kim Hyŏn as left vice director of state affairs and senior governmental advisor, and Han Kongsŏ 韓功敘 as right vice director of state affairs.

The Censorate submitted a memorial.

> In the organization plan for government officials, there is only one left vice director and one right vice director in the State Affairs Department.

---

8. Koryŏ law stated that the mandatory retirement age for officials was seventy. However, the king could ceremonially grant an armchair and walking staff to indicate that an official should continue in office.

Im Chongil is currently serving as the right vice director of state affairs. Appointing Han Kongsŏ to the same position will increase the number of right vice directors of state affairs by one, a distortion of the bureaucratic system. Please rescind Han Kongsŏ's appointment.

The king did not approve.

Munjong Twelfth Year (1058)

Second Month, Spring

Sinhae (10th day). The Military and War Council submitted a petition.

Iron paid as tribute under the jurisdiction of the Western Military Command has been used to manufacture weapons. Recently, to support the construction of Hŭngwang monastery, an increase in taxes was ordered, which has had the effect of multiplying the hardships that people must endure, some to the point of breaking. We propose that the tribute iron paid from the districts of Yŏmju, Haeju, and Anju for the production of weapons in the years *chŏngyu* (1057) and *musul* (1058) be entirely credited to Hŭngwang monastery so that the people's present difficulties can be reduced.

The king approved. Learned men commented:

In *The History of Tang* 唐史, it is said: "Although temples standing in a row filled the street, they could not save the country from crisis and collapse. Although monks filled the street, they could not protect the king." In regard to this case, how is this not wrong?

Muo (17th day). Ch'oe Sang, the administrator of the crown prince's readers-in-waiting (*chi tonggung sidoksa* 知東宮侍讀事) and an Imperial Secretariat drafter, submitted a memorial.

When we reached Kŭmgyo station to send off the Khitan envoy Wang Chongnyang, he saw a line of torches in the night and remarked, "I'm ashamed to see servants in thin clothing holding torches and shivering with cold, but it's easy to violate curfew when one gets drunk at a farewell banquet outside the city. Next time, I will depart early in the morning. I was told before I came that your court would pour wine until late in the evening for envoys. I was deeply impressed by the rituals and music I saw here, which resemble those of our country. However, I went to the court three times and the lights were lit at each banquet. At our court, the laws only allow the lighting of candles on wedding nights. When officials receive envoys, candles cannot be lit even if it is the middle of the night." I share the opinion that it would be proper to receive envoys after the sun rises, just as a king faces brightness to rule over the country, and I also fear that the virtue of frugality may be harmed through excessive consumption of the candlelight and lamplight that are purchased by the hard work of the people. In ancient times, when Chen Wan 陳完 (706–? BCE) was offered wine by the Duke of Huan, who called for light so that the banquet could continue, Chen said, "I have divinations for you concerning the day, but nothing about the night." Please have official farewells take place during the morning assembly and hold the banquets during the day.

The king approved.

Sinyu (20th day). The Khitans sent the acting right vice director of state affairs So Hŭi 蕭禧 with news about the death of the grand dowager empress. The king received the envoy wearing a black hat and white mourning clothes.

Fourth Month, Summer

Imja (12th day). There was an earthquake.

Pyŏngjin (16th day). A party of Eastern Jurchens, led by General Soothing Faraway Lands Taro, were granted an audience and made an offering of good horses.

Fifth Month

Kyŏngjin (11th day). Thirty-three Eastern Jurchens, led by General Submitting to Virtue Sanggon 霜昆, were granted an audience and made an offering of good horses. The king gave them vessels and articles of clothing in accordance with their rank.

Muja (19th day). The king went to Pongŭn monastery, where he appointed the monks Haerin and Nanwŏn 爛圓 (999–1066) as state preceptor and royal preceptor, respectively.

Imjin (23rd day). The king issued a decree.

> It is now the busy farming season, but we have not had rain. I fear that this calamity will get worse because prisoners have been falsely accused.

The king released all those convicted of minor crimes.

Sixth Month

Imin (3rd day). The Khitans sent the generalissimo of the Left Metropolitan Guard (*chwa yŏnggunwi sangjanggun* 左領軍衛上將軍) So Kan 蕭侃 with items left by the late dowager empress.

Musin (9th day). The Secretariat-Chancellery (*chungsŏ munhasŏng* 中書門下省) submitted a memorial.

> The royal decree concerning the astronomical observer Yi Sinhwang 李神貺 stated that there have been no errors in his observations and predictions regarding natural calamities, and it awarded him a title of the eighth rank. Regardless of his performance, Yi Sinhwang's family lineage is unknown, and he was impeached twice at the start of his career. Moreover, taking observations is his duty and not a suitable reason to award a promotion.

The king responded: "For excellence in astronomy, there is no one like Yi Sinhwang. Proceed with the previous decree."

Kyech'uk (14th day). Twenty-three Eastern Jurchens, led by the Chŏngjo Pundae 分大, were granted an audience and made an offering of their native products. The king gave them gifts in accordance with their rank.

Kabin (15th day). The king received the bodhisattva ordination in Kŏndŏk Hall.

Seventh Month, Autumn

Kimyo (11th day). The Secretariat-Chancellery submitted a petition.

> The imperial decree ordered that the stipendiary land[9] belonging to Kyŏngch'ang Hall 景昌院 be transferred to Hŭngwang monastery, and that its slaves, ships, and fishing nets 魚梁 revert to the government. Kings in earlier times bestowed land and servants to palaces and halls so that they would be passed down from one generation to the next, ensuring sufficient incomes for each. In these times, with the increasing number of royal family members, we already have reason for concern that the stipendiary lands bestowed to palaces and halls may not be enough to support them—how can land now be transferred from a palace to a monastery? Although respecting the Three Treasures 三寶[10] is said to produce wonders, one should not neglect the country's foundation. We request that the land, people, ships, and fishing nets be returned to Kyŏngch'ang Hall.

The king's decree:

> Returning stipendiary land that has already been offered to the Three Treasures can be difficult. Bestow public land (*kongjŏn* 公田)[11] as much as was originally promised, and proceed with the request for the other things.

Kyŏngin (22nd day). The king issued a decree.

> For the past few years, the weather has been irregular and natural calamities have come repeatedly. This is a result of the anger over unjust trials. To respond to Heaven's reprimand and attend to the wishes of the people, I shall impose lenient punishments while reflecting on my own cultivation of virtue. Those who committed a crime and were demoted

---

9. *Ch'ŏnsik* 田柴 in the original text, referring to the Field and Woodland Rank system for assigning tax revenues generated by plots of land to officials, government institutions, or other designated recipients.
10. The Buddha, Buddhist scriptures, and Buddhist monks.
11. Lands designated for general tax collection.

or expelled among civil and military officials, including palace clerks (*namban* 南班),[12] in both capitals, and among senior local leaders and military officers 將校 in *chus*, districts, prefectures, and garrisons, shall have the gravity of their crimes reviewed by the relevant officials and their previous positions restored. Those who were sentenced to penal servitude or less for public malfeasance and flogging or less for private malfeasance shall be excluded.

Eighth Month

Ŭlsa (7th day). A party from Song led by the merchant Huang Wenjing 黃文景 came with an offering of their native products.

The king expressed a wish to cut timber in T'amna and Yŏngam prefecture 靈巖郡[13] to build large ships for future trade with Song. The Imperial Secretariat–Chancellery submitted a memorial in response.

> We established friendly relations with the Khitans so that there would be no danger of war at the border, allowing our people to live in comfort. This is the best way to preserve the country. The Khitans sent a letter in *kyŏngsul* (1010) that stated: "Your country conspires with the Jurchens to the east and carries on exchanges with Song to the west. Please let us know the scheme you are devising." Also, when the ministry director Yu Ch'am 柳叅 was sent to the Khitans as an envoy, the resident governor of the Eastern Capital asked why we had dispatched an envoy to Song. If the information in question leaks out, this will certainly cause a break in our relations with the Khitans. Furthermore, T'amna has barren land and its people are poor. They can barely earn a livelihood by fishing. Last autumn, they suffered the hardship of building a new Buddhist monastery by having to cut their timber and ship it across the sea. We fear there will be trouble if they are additionally burdened by having to cut timber to build ships. Our country is blessed with a culture and institutions that have flourished for a long time, and merchant ships

---

12. Palace clerks were lower-ranking clerical officials who were responsible for various menial duties in the palaces.
13. Present-day Yŏngam, South Chŏlla.

are lining up to bring in rare and precious treasures. Consequently, we can see no practical benefit to building larger ships for trade with Song. Unless we intend to permanently sever our relations with the Khitans, it would not be appropriate to establish relations with Song.

The king approved.

Ninth Month

Kisa (1st day). Ch'ungju *mok* 忠州牧 submitted ninety-nine new woodblock plates for printing medical books, including *Hwangje P'alsibil Nangyŏng* 黃帝八十一難經, *Ch'ŏnokchip* 川玉集, *Sanghallon* 傷寒論, *Ponch'o Kwalyo* 本草括要, *Soa Sossi Pyŏngwŏn* 小兒巢氏病源, *Soa Yakchung Pyŏngwŏn* 小兒藥證病源, *Isip P'alron* 一十八論, and *Chang Chung Kyŏng Ojangnon* 張仲卿五臟論. The king ordered the Imperial Archives library to store them.

Ŭrhae (7th day). The Khitans sent their acting left cavalier attendant-in-ordinary Yayul Yŏnnyŏng 耶律延寧 as a response envoy from the Eastern Capital.

Eleventh Month, Winter

Kyŏngo (3rd day). The king issued a decree

> We have condolences from the Khitans in the form of silken cloth and gold and silver bowls in Chŏngjong's memorial hall. Look in the Buddhist canon for prayers to foster the repose of his spirit.

Ŭryu (18th day). Twenty-two Eastern Jurchens, led by General Soothing Faraway Lands Taro, were granted an audience and made an offering of their native products.

Twelfth Month

Chŏngyu (1st day). The Khitans sent the Yŏnju regional inspector 筵州刺史 Kwak Chaegwi 郭在貴 with a letter of congratulations on the king's birthday.

Twenty-six Eastern Jurchens, led by General Embracing Transformation Yidonghwa 尼冬火, were granted an audience and made an offering of their native products. The king gave them promotions and gifts in accordance with their rank.

Intercalary Month

Pyŏngja (10th day). Fifty Eastern Jurchens, led by General Comforting the Frontier Kododal, were granted an audience and made an offering of excellent horses.

Pyŏngsin (30th day). There was a solar eclipse.

THIRTEENTH YEAR OF MUNJONG (1059)

First Month, Spring

Chŏngyu (1st day). The king went to Kŏndŏk Hall to receive the New Year Congratulations of his officials. He hosted a banquet for the royal family and his royal aides and invited the retired affairs manager Kim Chŏngjun to attend. During the banquet the king bestowed a horse raised in the palace to each of the guests, and the party lasted until late at night.

Ŭlsa (9th day). Eighteen Eastern Jurchens, led by the Chŏngwi Morŏgŭm 沒於金, were granted an audience and made an offering of excellent horses.

Chŏngmi (11th day). Thirty-five Eastern Jurchens, led by the Chungyun Yasiro 耶施老, were granted an audience and made an offering of good horses.

Second Month

Chŏngmyo (2nd day). Twenty-two Eastern Jurchens, led by the Chŏngbo Osa, were granted an audience and made an offering of excellent horses.

Kapsul (9th day). A group headed by Yi Sŏnjŏng 異善貞, a commander in the Western Regional Military Command (*ansŏ tohobusa* 安西都護府使) and a Slave Bureau assistant executive (*togwan wŏnoerang* 都官員外郎), presented seventy-three new woodblock plates for *Prescriptions for Elbow Pain* (*Zhouhoufang* 肘後方), eleven woodblock plates for *Collection of Doubtful Cases* (*Yiyuji* 疑獄集), and ten woodblock plates for *Chuanyuji* 川玉集. The Kyŏngsan district administrator (*chi kyŏngsanbusa* 知京山府使) and Palace Administration assistant executive (*chŏnjung naegŭpsa* 殿中內給事) Yi Sŏngmi 李成美 presented 680 new woodblock plates for the *Book of Sui* (*Suishu* 隋書). The king ordered the Imperial Archives library to store the printing plates and gave articles of clothing to the donors.

The king sent the Public Works assistant executive (*sangsŏ kongbu wŏnoerang* 尚書工部員外郎) Ch'oe Sŏkchin 崔奭珍 to the Khitans as a memorial envoy.

Ŭrhae (10th day). General Comforting the Frontier Kŏdabul 居多弗 of the Eastern Jurchens was granted an audience and made an offering of his native products.

The king went to Kŏndŏk Hall to retest the examination candidates. Yang Sillin 楊信麟 and others passed the examination.

Third Month

Imsul (28th day). The king ordered the imperial diary keeper (*kigŏju* 起居注) Yi Yujŏk, the investigating censor Yi Pyŏngyang 李秉陽, and the Capital Garrison Division general (*kŭmowi changgun* 金吾衛將軍) Pang Hyŏn 邦賢 to review the cases of those who had been imprisoned. He then ordered the release of sixty-three people convicted of minor crimes.

Fourth Month, Summer

Pyŏngja (12th day). The king personally conducted an ancestral rite at the Imperial Ancestral Shrine.

The Song merchant Xiao Zongming and others requested permission to watch the king's procession on the street. The king granted the request.

On this day, the king declared an amnesty.

Kyŏngjin (16th day). The Namwŏn district administrator (*chi namwŏnbusa* 知南原府事) and de facto assistant executive of the Rites Ministry (*si yebu wŏnoerang* 試禮部員外郎) Yi Chŏnggong 李靖恭 (d. 1099) presented fifty-four new woodblock plates for the *Illustrations of the Three Ritual Classics* (*Sanlitu* 三禮圖) and ninety-two woodblock plates for the *Writings of Sun Qing* (*Sun Qing zishu* 孫卿子書). The king gave him articles of clothing and ordered the Imperial Archives library to store the printing plates.

Fifth Month

Ŭlmi (2nd day). A burial chamber in Hyŏn Tomb was robbed by a thief. The king ordered the imprisonment of Ŭn Chŏng 殷貞, the grand general guarding imperial tombs (*nŭngsil siwi taejanggun* 陵室侍衛大將軍), as well as others, and ordered their punishment.

Pyŏngjin (23rd day). The king decreed: "The woodlands for collecting firewood should be limited for all officials in both capitals up to Masuryŏng 馬首嶺.[14] Also, set up signs that prohibit logging and harshly punish those who violate the order."

Sixth Month

Ŭryu (23rd day). The king decreed: "The court ladies of King Chŏngjong, Lady Han 韓, Lady of Lesser Han,[15] and Lady Wi 韋, should be given thirty *sŏk* of nonglutinous rice from the Royal Land Office (*naejangt'aek* 內莊宅) every year."

---

14. Literally, the peak of Masu mountain.
15. Han Cho 韓祚 had two daughters, the elder of whom was known as Lady Han, and the younger, Lady of Lesser Han 小韓.

Eighth Month, Autumn

Mujin (6th day). When it was time for the Song merchants from Quanzhou, including Huang Wenjing, Xiao Zongming, and the physician Jiang Chaodong 江朝東 among others, to return to Song, the king issued a decree: "Xiao Zongming, Jiang Chaodong, and one other person from Song shall be allowed to remain in Koryŏ."

Kyeyu (11th day). The king hosted a banquet for the director of public works Hong Hae 洪措 and the supreme general Ha Hŭnghyu, both of whom were at least eighty, in the garden inside the Audience gate. The king entertained them throughout the day, personally pouring a wine made from flowers and bestowing articles of clothing.

The king also provided food and wine at the Polo Field for 1,280 people, including elders, men and women suffering from a serious illness or disability, filial sons and grandsons, and virtuous husbands and wives. The king authorized grants of food and wine to the Western Capital and the provinces on the same day.

Ŭryu (23rd day). A group led by the Song merchant Fu Nan 傅男 came with an offering of their native products.

Chŏnghae (25th day). The king issued a decree: "In the two capitals and southeastern regions, households with three sons may allow one son who has reached the age of fifteen to leave home to become a Buddhist monk."

Ninth Month

Pyŏngsin (4th day). The Khitans sent the acting right cavalier attendant-in-ordinary Yayul Yŏnnyŏng 耶律延寧 as a response envoy from the Eastern Capital (*tonggyŏng hoesasa* 東京回謝使).

Tenth Month, Winter

Kapsin (23rd day). Two Khitans, Taui 多于伊 and Namurŭng 男于陵, came to submit.

Eleventh Month

Ŭlsa (14th day). The king went to Pŏbwang monastery to hold the Assembly of the Eight Prohibitions.

Kabin (23rd day). Twenty-four Eastern Jurchens, led by General Submitting to Virtue Moha 毛下, were joined by twenty-three others, led by the Chŏngbo Kosa 高史, and were granted an audience. They made offerings of excellent horses.

Twelfth Month

Sinyu (1st day). There was a solar eclipse.

The Khitans sent the acting minister of education Yayul Tŏk 耶律德 with a letter of congratulations on the king's birthday.

The king ordered the retrial of criminals.

Fourteenth Year of Munjong (1060)

First Month, Spring

Sinmyo (1st day). The king canceled the New Year Congratulations.

Kyech'uk (23rd day). The king held the Śakra Devānām-Indra ritual (*Ch'ŏnjesŏk toryang* 天帝釋道場)[16] in Mundŏk Hall for seven days.

Second Month

Kyehae (4th day). The king went to Changwŏn Pavilion.

Kapsul (15th day). The king went to Pongŭn monastery to hold the Lantern Festival.

---

16. A Buddhist assembly with prayers to Heaven (Śakra Devānām-Indra) for relief from countrywide crises such as war.

Third Month

Chŏngsa (28th day). The king appointed Yi Chŏnggong as general censor.

Fourth Month, Summer

Kimi (1st day). The king appointed Wang Ch'ongji as high grand marshal, Kim Wŏnjŏng as high minister of education, and Kim Hyŏn as high minister of works.

Fifth Month

Kabo (7th day). The king himself conducted the Daoist Ch'o ritual at the Polo Field.

Sixth Month

Kyŏngo (13th day). The king appointed Kim Ŭijin as administrator of the Civil Personnel Ministry (*chi sangsŏ ibusa* 知尙書吏部事), and Yang Kukchŏng 楊國楨 as administrator of the Censorate.

Seventh Month, Autumn

Kyŏngo (19th day). Thirty-six people from Song, led by the merchant Huang Zhu, came with an offering of their native products.
Kyech'uk (27th day). The Naval Administration Office of the Southeastern Sea (*tongnamhae sŏnbyŏng tobusŏ* 東南海船兵都部署) submitted a report: "Wi Hyonam 位孝男 from the Yesŏng River, who had drifted to Tsushima island, has been repatriated." The king rewarded the envoy from Tsushima with generous gifts.

Eighth Month

Muo (2nd day). The king issued a decree.

> The rainy season has not ended since the summer and it is now well into autumn. I fear that the harmony of the seasons may have been disrupted by improper punishments. I therefore order the vice director of the Censorate Pak Ch'ung 朴忠, the left deputy recipient of edicts (*chwa pu sŭngsŏn* 左副承宣) Kang Wŏn'gwang 姜源廣 (d. 1070), the left reminder Ch'oe Sŏk, and the grand general of the Envoy Escort Division Cho Ok 曹玉 to retry criminals.

Kyehae (7th day). Thirty-nine people from Song, led by the merchant Xu Yi 徐意, came with an offering of their native products.

Ŭrhae (19th day). Forty-nine people from Song, led by the merchant Huang Yuanzai 黃元載, came with an offering of their native products.

Ninth Month

Musul (12th day). Nineteen Eastern Jurchens, led by General Embracing Transformation Arin 阿藺, were granted an audience and made an offering of their native products.

Kyemyo (17th day). The king appointed the Song literary licentiate candidate No In (Ch. Lu Yin) 盧寅 to the position of collator in the Imperial Archives because of his literary talent.

Ŭlsa (19th day). The king appointed Yi Yuch'ung as commissioner of the Palace Secretariat.

Kyech'uk (27th day). The king ordered the retrial of criminals.

Eleventh Month, Winter

Kyŏngin (5th day). The Khitans sent the Koju district surveillance commissioner (*Koju kwannae kwanch'alsa* 高州管內觀察使) So O 蕭奧 as their edict envoy (*sŏnsasa* 宣賜使).

Musul (13th day). The king went to Pŏbwang monastery to hold the Assembly of the Eight Prohibitions.

Thirty-seven Eastern Jurchens, led by Grand General Submitting to Virtue Agaju 阿家主, were granted an audience and made an offering of their native products.

Twelfth Month

Pyŏngjin (1st day). The Khitans sent the Yŏngju district surveillance commissioner (*Yŏngju kwannae kwanch'alsa* 永州管內觀察使) Yayul Nyŏl 耶律烈 with a letter of congratulations on the king's birthday.

Kapsa (9th day). A fire in the Imperial Secretariat–Chancellery burned down an attached house on the southeast side of Hoegyŏng Hall.

Fifteenth Year of Munjong (1061)

First Month, Spring

Muja (4th day). Venus was visible during the day.

Kyech'uk (29th day). The king appointed Yi Yuch'ung as director of punishments, Kim Hwasung as Hallim academician, Wang Musung as superintendent of the Censorate and director of revenue, and Kim Wŏnhwang as director of military affairs.

Second Month

Sinyu (7th day). The king appointed Im Chongil as left vice director of state affairs and commissioner of the Palace Secretariat.

Kyemi (29th day). The king issued a decree.

> How punishments are implemented is crucial to kingly rule. If they are too strict, the people will become impoverished. If they are too lenient, the people will become slack. If they are applied fairly, then yin and yang come into balance and there is good weather. If, however, the legal

system loses fairness, then resentment builds until a disaster occurs. Now, dismal officials have existed in every age, and although I have urged prudence in the enforcement of our laws, I fear that we constantly fall short of the sages' wise example, due to the atrocious behavior of mediocre officials and clerks. From now on, officials appointed to the Ministry of Punishments[17] must be carefully selected so that no one receives unfair punishment.

Third Month

Imjin (9th day). The king appointed Ch'oe Sunhan 崔順漢 as director of revenue and Chŏng Ch'ŭng 鄭層 as acting director of public works.
Chŏngyu (14th day). Due to last year's fire in the Chancellery, which occurred while the right scholarly counselor-in-ordinary Ch'oe Wŏnjun and the senior governmental advisor Kim Hyŏn were on night duty, Ch'oe and Kim were demoted to the positions of superintendent of imperial manufactories (*p'an sobugamsa* 判少府監事) and left vice director of state affairs, respectively.
Kiyu (26th day). Na Kyeham 羅繼含 and others passed the state examination.

Fourth Month, Summer

Pyŏngjin (3rd day). The Khitans sent the acting minister of works So Susa 蕭嗽思 as a response envoy from the Eastern Capital.
Kapsul (21st day). The king appointed Chang Chungyŏng 張仲英 as director of public works.

Sixth Month

Kyech'uk (2nd day). The king went to Pongŭn monastery and visited the National Academy (*kukchagam* 國子監). The king said to the royal attendants, "Confucius is the teacher of all rulers. How dare I not pay respect?" and bowed twice.

---

17. *Ch'unbu* 秋部 in the original text, a cognomen of the Ministry of Punishments (*hyŏngbu* 刑部).

Chŏngsa (6th day). The king appointed several Song literary licentiate candidates to government office. Chin Wi (Ch. Chen Wei) 陳渭 was appointed collator in the Imperial Archives, So Chŏng (Ch. Xiao Ding) 蕭鼎 and So Ch'ŏn (Ch. Xiao Qian) 蕭遷 became recipients of edicts in the Audience Ceremonies and Presentations Office (*hammun sŭngji* 閤門承旨), and Sŏp Sŏng (Ch. Sheng Cheng) 葉盛 became palace recipient of edicts (*chŏnjŏn sŭngji* 殿前丞旨). Chin Wi was good at composition, and the other three, especially So Chŏng, were good at music.

Kimyo (28th day). The king changed the government position held by his brother Wang Ki from director of the Imperial Secretariat to director of the Secretariat (*chungsŏryŏng* 中書令). At the same time, all the other positions and offices in the former Imperial Secretariat 內史 were renamed as belonging to the Secretariat 中書.

Eighth Month, Autumn

Imja (2nd day). The military commissioner of the Eastern Frontier Circuit submitted a petition.

> A major in Chŏngju named Kyŏngbo 耿甫 led a group of twenty on a reconnaissance of the enemy. They suddenly encountered an enemy unit of two hundred soldiers, led by Ahabi 阿下費, and fought hard to defeat them, beheading around ten. Please reward them for their meritorious military service.

The king approved.

The king appointed Kim Haenggyŏng 金行瓊 as Hallim academician.

Mujin (18th day). The king appointed Ch'oe Yusŏn as superintendent of the Rites Ministry.

Pyŏngja (26th day). A party of Song merchants led by Guo Man 郭滿 came with an offering of their native products.

Intercalary Month

Sinsa (1st day). The king performed the rite for Distributing the Calendar in the Imperial Ancestral Shrine.

Ninth Month

Chŏngmyo (18th day). The Military and War Council submitted a petition.

> An enemy unit led by Arabul 阿羅弗 crossed the border and plundered frontier villages. The military chief registrar of P'yŏngno Garrison (*P'yŏngnojin pyŏngma noksa* 平虜鎭兵馬錄事) Kang Young 康瑩 and the chief registrar of the Northwestern Frontier District Military Commission (*sŏbungmyŏn pyŏngma noksa* 西北面兵馬錄事) Ko Kyŏngin 高慶仁 led their soldiers out and pursued the enemy until they reached Hangma Garrison 降魔鎭, beheading several tens and capturing numerous weapons. Please reward them.

The king approved.

Muin (29th day). The king appointed Im Chongil as senior governmental advisor and Wang Musung as managing administrator of the Palace Secretariat.

Tenth Month, Winter

Chŏngmi (28th day). The king appointed Han Kongsŏ as eminent minister of works and high left vice director of state affairs (*su sangsŏ chwa pogya* 守尙書左僕射).

Eleventh Month

Kyŏngsul (1st day). The king appointed Ch'oe Yubu 崔有孚 as left mentor to the crown prince (*t'aeja chwa sŏja* 太子左庶子), Kim Yang 金陽 as right mentor to the crown prince, Ch'oe Sang as left proclaimer to the crown prince (*chwa yudŏk* 左諭德), Yi Yujŏk as right proclaimer to the crown prince, Pak

Ch'ung as companion of the crown prince (*chungyun* 中允), Chŏng Kongji 鄭功志 as left grand master admonisher (*chwa ch'ansŏn taebu* 左贊善大夫), and Hwang Hangji as right grand master admonisher.

Sinmi (22nd day). The king appointed Ch'oe Yusŏn as senior governmental advisor and provisional superintendent of the Hallim Academy (*kwŏnp'an hallimwŏnsa* 權判翰林院事).

Twelfth Month

Kyŏngjin (1st day). The Khitans sent the acting grand mentor and Yŏngju regional inspector So Sul 蕭述 with a letter of congratulations on the king's birthday.

Pyŏngsin (17th day). The king appointed Wang Ch'ongji as superintendent of civil personnel and director of the Chancellery, Kim Wŏnjŏng as vice director of the Chancellery with a concurrent assignment as Secretariat-Chancellery joint affairs manager (*tong chungsŏ munha p'yŏngjangsa* 同中書門下平章事), Ch'oe Yusŏn as vice director of the Secretariat (*chungsŏ sirang* 中書侍郎) with a concurrent assignment as Secretariat-Chancellery joint affairs manager, Yi Yuch'ung as senior governmental advisor and pillar of the state, Kim Wŏnhwang as commissioner of the Palace Secretariat, Kim Ŭijin as left scholarly counselor-in-ordinary and deputy administrator of the Palace Secretariat, and Kim Yangji as director of the Censorate.

Pyŏngo (27th day). The king appointed Xiao Zongming from Song as provisional audience usher (*kwŏnji hammun chihu* 權知閣門祇侯).

Sixteenth Year of Munjong (1062)

First Month, Spring

Imsul (14th day). The Khitans sent the acting right vice director of state affairs Yayul Chang 耶律章 as a response envoy from the Eastern Capital.

The king dismissed Kim Wŏnjŏng from his post in the capital and appointed him as commissioner of the Western Capital.

Second Month

Kihae (21st day). The king invested Prince Wang To 王燾 (d. 1099) as Eminent Director of State Affairs (*kŏmgyo sangsŏryŏng* 檢校尙書令) and High Minister of Education.

Ŭlsa (27th day). Ko Hyŏp 高叶 and a party from T'amna were granted an audience and made an offering of their native products.

Sixth Month, Summer

Pyŏngja (1st day). A party of Eastern Jurchens, led by General Submitting to Virtue Pundae, were granted an audience with the court.

Ŭlsa (30th day). The king appointed the Foreign Relations director and Censorate administrator Ch'oe Sang 崔賞 as vice director of rites and administrator of the Military Commission of the Northwestern Frontier District in autumn and winter (*chi sŏbungmyŏn ch'udongbŏn pyŏngmasa* 知西北面秋冬番兵馬事), and the left grand master of remonstrance Hong Tŏgwi as vice military commissioner of the Northeastern Frontier District in autumn and winter (*tongbungmyŏn ch'udongbŏn pyŏngma pusa* 東北面秋冬番兵馬副使).

Seventh Month, Autumn

Kyŏngsin (15th day). The Palace Secretariat commissioner and Military Affairs director Kim Wŏnhwang died. The king awarded him the posthumous title of Strong Respect (*ŭigyŏng* 毅敬) and gave one of his sons a protected appointment to a government position.

Imsin (27th day). A party of Eastern Jurchens, led by Monae 毛乃, were granted an audience with the court.

Eighth Month

Muin (4th day). A party of Eastern Jurchens, led by Nŭgŏŭl 勒於乙 and Umonae 亐毛乃, were granted an audience with the court.

Ŭryu (11th day). The king went to Hŭngwang monastery and issued a decree.

> Many people have worked hard for a long time to build this monastery. Today the main building is near completion, as I have seen, and I am moved to bestow a special grace on my subjects. Those deserving of severe punishments across the country shall have their sentence reduced to exile. Those sentenced to penal servitude or less for public malfeasance, together with those sentenced to flogging or less for private malfeasance, shall be pardoned. The officials who supervised the construction shall be rewarded and given additional titles.

Imin (28th day). The marquis of Kaesŏng 開城侯, Wang Kae, died.

Tenth Month, Winter

Kimyo (6th day). The ruler of T'amna, Ko Il 高逸, was granted an audience and made an offering of his native products.

Kyŏngja (27th day). A party of Eastern Jurchens, led by Grand Generals Submitting to Virtue Marihae 摩里害 and Agaju, were granted an audience with the court.

Twelfth Month

Kapsul (1st day). The Khitans sent the T'aeju district surveillance commissioner (*T'aeju kwannae kwanch'alsa* 泰州管內觀察使) Ko Sujŏng 高守正 with a letter of congratulations on the king's birthday.

Seventeenth Year of Munjong (1063)

First Month, Spring

Kyemyo (1st day). The king hosted a banquet for officials in Kŏndŏk Hall and bestowed silks in accordance with their rank.

Musin (6th day). The State Finance Commission submitted a petition: "Gold is produced in Ingnyŏng county and Sujŏnjang 簹田場[18] in Sŏngju 成州[19] in the Northwestern Frontier District. Please add them to the tribute register."

Second Month

Kapsul (2nd day). The king appointed the vice director of punishments and right grand master of remonstrance Yi Yujŏk as vice military commissioner of the Northwestern Frontier District in spring and summer (*sŏbungmyŏn ch'unhabŏn pyŏngma pusa* 西北面春夏番兵馬副使), and the vice director of imperial manufactories Yi Tŭngno as vice military commissioner of the Northeastern Frontier District in spring and summer (*tongbungmyŏn ch'uhabŏn pyŏngma pusa* 東北面春夏番兵馬副使).

Chŏngch'uk (5th day). A party of Eastern Jurchens, led by General Submitting to Virtue Hŏehwa 懷化, were granted an audience and made an offering of excellent horses.

Kich'uk (17th day). A party of Eastern Jurchens, led by General Submitting to Virtue Sanggon, were granted an audience and made an offering of good horses.

Kyŏngin (18th day). The king appointed Chang Yŏng 蔣英 as general censor and Yun Chomyŏng 尹祚明 (d. 1070) as palace censor.

---

18. A location in Sujŏn for people who had special abilities and/or produced special goods.
19. Present-day Sŏngch'ŏn, South P'yŏngan.

Third Month

Pyŏngo (4th day). The Khitans sent a copy of the Tripitaka. The king proceeded to the western outskirts of the capital to receive it with the requisite courtesies.

Sinhae (9th day). The new ruler of T'amna, Turyang 豆良, was granted an audience with the court. The king graciously conferred on him the title of Myŏngwi changgun 明威將軍.[20]

Fourth Month, Summer

Ŭrhae (4th day). The king gave the Nine Classics 九經 and the histories 史, commentaries 傳, and texts of the Hundred Schools 百家書 that had been kept in the library of the Imperial Archives to the crown prince.

Sinch'uk (30th day). The king appointed Yi Hwang 李璜 as director of revenue and Pak Hŭijung 朴希仲 as acting director of public works.

Fifth Month

Kapchin (3rd day). The king went to Mundŏk Hall to retest the examination candidates. Hong Ki 洪器 and others passed the state examination.

Seventh Month, Autumn

Kyŏngsin (21st day). The king appointed the Imperial Stables director Min Ch'angso 閔昌素 as administrator of the Military Commission of the Northwestern Frontier District in autumn and winter, and the State Affairs right office chief Kim Sŏkcho 金錫祚 as vice military commissioner of the Northeastern Frontier District in autumn and winter.

Mujin (29th day). The king appointed Kim Wŏnjŏng as high grand marshal and director of the Chancellery. Kim died soon after.

---

20. A rank 4b2 title for military officials.

Eighth Month

Sinmyo (22nd day). The king appointed Wang Musung as military commissioner of the Mobile Headquarters of the Northeastern Frontier District, and Yi Yuch'ung as superintendent of the State Finance Commission and Middle Military commander of the Northwestern Frontier District (*sŏbungmyŏn chunggun pyŏngmasa* 西北面中軍兵馬使). The king ordered Wang Ibo to serve concurrently as commissioner of the Western Capital.

Ninth Month

Kyŏngja (2nd day). The king issued a decree: "Since there has been little rain this year, we cannot expect a good harvest. Local officials are ordered to prepare a plan for famine relief."

Imin (4th day). The Song merchant Guo Man came with a party bringing an offering of their native products.

Kyŏngsul (12th day). Following precedent, the king conferred the additional titles of Eminent Grand Marshal and Director of the Chancellery on Pak Sŏnggŏl, and Executive of the Secretariat (*chungsŏ sirang p'yŏngjangsa* 中書侍郎平章事) and Pillar of the State on Im Chongil before allowing them to retire.

Tenth Month, Winter

Kyŏngo (3rd day). The Song merchants Lin Ning 林寧 and Huang Wenjing came with an offering of their native products.

Imjin (25th day). The king went to Changwŏn Pavilion.

Eleventh Month

Kyemyo (6th day). The Khitans sent the Ikchu regional inspector So Kyŏk 蕭格 to pay respects to the king.

Kapcha (27th day). A party of Eastern Jurchens, led by General Submitting to Virtue Marihae 摩離害 and General Comforting Faraway Lands Tarodae 多老大, were granted an audience with the court.

Twelfth Month

Mujin (1st day). The Khitans sent their right grand master of remonstrance Yi Ilsuk 李日肅 with a letter of congratulations on the king's birthday.
Pyŏngsul (19th day). The king appointed the vice director of military affairs Chŏng Tongjo 鄭同祚 as deputy resident governor of the Western Capital and the vice director of palace revenues Pak Kŏhu 朴臣厚 as deputy resident governor of the Eastern Capital.

Eighteenth Year of Munjong (1064)

First Month, Spring

Chŏngyu (1st day). The king canceled the New Year Congratulations.
Sinyu (25th day). The military commissioner of the Northwestern Frontier Circuit submitted a petition.

> Last *imin* (1062), enemies from Mongp'o village 蒙浦村 infiltrated the territory of P'yŏngno Garrison and hid between the Chŏlch'ung guard post 折衝戍 and Hangma guard post 降魔戍 to prepare an invasion. The tribal chief Chejunna 齊俊那, who resides within our territory after submitting to Koryŏ, discovered their plan and came to inform the commander of P'yŏngno Garrison. With our troops lying in wait and concealed in the grass, the enemy launched their attack. We counter-attacked and captured or killed most of them. Please reward Chejunna generously with gold and silks.

The king approved.

Second Month

Kyeyu (7th day). The king issued a decree.

> Following precedent, the commissioner of sacrifices to local mountains (*oesan chegosa* 外山祭告使) visits all ten provinces during the spring and fall seasons. These tours, together with others like it, occur with such frequency that the post-road stations 驛路 are becoming impoverished. From now on, the royal commissioner of warehouse inspection (*kamch'angsa* 監倉使) for the Northern and Eastern Frontier Circuits and the pacification commissioner (*anch'alsa* 按察使) of P'aesŏdo province will serve as the commissioner of sacrifices to local mountains in their areas. In the other southern provinces, the commissioner of sacrifices to local mountains will fulfill his duties as before. This shall become the custom hereafter.

Third Month

Kabin (18th day). The king held the three-day ritual for the recitation of the *Humane Kings Sutra* in Hoegyŏng Hall. He also fed ten thousand Buddhist monks at the Polo Field.

Fourth Month, Summer

Kyŏngo (4th day). The king issued a decree.

> Taeun monastery was founded by the late king to offer prayers for the country's good fortune. Yet the public land designated for its use is so barren that the tax revenue produced is insufficient to support the requisite Buddhist ceremonies. One hundred *kyŏng* of fertile fields shall be bestowed to the monastery.

Kyŏngin (24th day). The king issued a decree.

> From the fifteenth day of the fifth month to the fifteenth day of the seventh month, porridge and vegetables shall be prepared at Pot'ong monastery 普通院 in Imjin county 臨津縣 and given to travelers.

Fifth Month

Ŭlsa (10th day). The king ordered his senior governmental advisor Yi Yuch'ung to give food and other gifts to a party of thirteen Western Jurchens, led by the Yŏngwŏn changgun 寧遠將軍[21] Kojiji, at the Foreign Relations Court (*yebinsi* 禮賓寺).

Intercalary Month

Mujin (3rd day). A party of one hundred Eastern Jurchens, under the command of Majilgae 麻叱盖, sailed along the waterway to Namp'o 南浦 in P'yŏnghae prefecture, setting fire to houses and capturing nine men and women.

Sinmi (6th day). The Military Affairs Ministry submitted a petition.

> The registry of hereditary soldier families (*kunban ssijok* 軍班氏族)[22] was compiled a long time ago, and it has been severely damaged. The number of troops under our command is therefore unclear. Let us recompile the registry in accordance with the former practice.

The king approved.

Sixth Month

Sinch'uk (7th day). The Military and War Council submitted a petition.

> When the tribesman leader Majilgae and his war party plundered P'yŏnghae prefecture, the generals and officials of our defense force failed to pursue and capture them. They should be impeached by the Censorate and punished.

The king approved.

---

21. A rank 5a2 title for military officials.
22. *Kunban* 軍班 were ordinary soldiers whereas *muban* 武班 were officers.

Seventh Month, Autumn

Chŏngmyo (4th day). The military commander of the Northeastern Frontier District submitted a petition.

> Last *muja* (1048), Hwan'ga county 豢猳縣[23] was plundered by eastern tribesmen and more than a hundred of men and women were hurt or killed. Even more, a substantial fire there, this spring, burned the fortress, many warehouses, and villagers' homes. With two such disasters, the residents can no longer live in peace. The people should be relocated, and a new fortress built to defend against further pirate attacks.

The king ordered: "Relocate them to Yang village 陽村." Yang village was located about two thousand *po* south of the old fortress.

Pyŏngsul (23rd day). A party of Song merchants led by Chen Gong 陳鞏 came with an offering of their native products.

Kyŏngin (27th day). The Imperial Stables Court (*t'aebokshi* 太僕寺) submitted a petition: "Please follow precedent and continue to send the horse selection commissioner (*sŏnmasa* 選馬使) to six provinces." The king approved.

Eighth Month

Kabo (1st day). A party of Song merchants led by Lin Ning came with an offering of their native products.

Tenth Month, Winter

Pyŏngjin (25th day). The Khitans sent the acting right cavalier attendant-in-ordinary Yayul Kŭng 耶律亘 with an edict from the emperor.

> Since we acceded to the throne due to the great achievements of previous sage kings, we have strived to follow the practice of ruling with discretion. After ten years, we have now pacified territories in every

---

23. Present-day Kosŏng-gun, Kangwŏn.

direction under Heaven, and to aid our country's fortunes, Heaven continues to send auspicious signs in this time of prosperity. In particular, our officials have been submitting memorials requesting permission to present an honorable title to my meritless self, and with the passage of time, these requests have become so heartfelt that we cannot bear to keep turning them aside. We have therefore decided to meet the high expectations of our people by accepting the honorable title, and the ceremony will be held on the first day of the first month of next year. As a tributary state in our court, you have served us with unswerving loyalty, and we believe you will share our joy when you hear this magnificent news. We now dispatch our protocol envoy (*yebinsa* 禮賓使) Yayul Kŭng to bring you this edict. We trust you will understand it well.

Eleventh Month

Kimyo (18th day). The king informed the Imperial Portrait Hall of the crown prince's marriage.

Imo (21st day). The Revenue Ministry submitted a petition.

> There was no rain in Kwangju *mok* 廣州牧 from spring well into the fall this year, and after the long drought, they suffered from hail so badly there was no grain to reap. Also, Pongju suffered a massive flood last *kyŏngja* (1060), inundating fields and houses and causing people to lose their homes. We suggest that the land survey by officials in these two regions be ceased.

The king approved.

Twelfth Month

Imjin (1st day). The Khitans sent the minister of imperial granaries Ho Chung 胡仲 with a letter of congratulations on the king's birthday.

Three Khitans, led by Kono 高奴, and eight Hŭksu Malgals, led by P'ogi 包棄, came to submit.

Nineteenth Year of Munjong (1065)

First Month, Spring

Sinyu (1st day). The king canceled the New Year Congratulations.

Kapsin (24th day). Sixteen Eastern Jurchens, led by Nijidal 尼之達, were granted an audience and made an offering of excellent horses.

Second Month, Spring

Sinmyo (1st day). Twenty-two Eastern Jurchen, led by Sanggon, were granted an audience and made an offering of their native products.

Sinch'uk (11th day). Twenty-seven Eastern Jurchens, led by General Abuhan 阿符漢 and O Hwamun 吳火文, were granted an audience and made an offering of good horses.

Kabin (24th day). Prince Wang Hŭi 王熙[24] was invested with the titles of Merit Subject for Maintaining Benevolence (*suin* 守仁), Preserving Righteousness, Kaebu ŭidong samsa, High Minister of Works, Director of State Affairs, Supreme Pillar of the State, and Marquis of Kyerim 雞林侯. He was given a fief of one thousand households.

Kimi (29th day). The resident governor of the Khitans' Eastern Capital sent an official document stating that the dowager empress[25] had been invested with the titles of Benevolent Virtuousness 慈懿, Humane Harmony 仁和, Brilliant Generosity 文惠, Filial Respect 孝敬, Manifesting Sacredness 顯聖, Shining Virtue 昭德, Broadening Affection 廣愛, and Venerating Heaven 宗天. The emperor had been given the additional titles of Holy Brilliance 聖文, Supernatural Valor 神武, Complete Achievement 全功, Grand Reign 大略, Sagacious Benevolence 聰仁, Sapient Filiality 睿孝, and Heavenly Blessing 天祐.

---

24. Wang Hŭi became King Sukchong (r. 1095–1105).
25. The wife of Emperor Xingzong (r. 1031–1055).

Fourth Month, Summer

Kyesa (4th day). The Khitans sent Yayul Yŏng 耶律寧 and Chŏng Munt'ong 丁文通 as investiture envoys bearing the emperor's edict.

> Given your faithful and diligent allegiance to our country, we have entered into a safe and peaceful time. The Office of Protocol was following its regulations when it conferred additional titles on us. So too, we would like to share the happy occasion by extending our grace to distant areas. We therefore will bestow on you a special investiture ceremony and thereby spread the news of your favor.
>
> Thus we will display our grace for all the world to see. Accept the deep consideration we now extend to you and act accordingly. The Yŏngwŏn district military commissioner (*Yŏngwŏn'gun chŏltosa* 寧遠軍節度使) Yayul Yŏng has been appointed our lead investiture envoy, and the Ikchu district surveillance commissioner 益州管內觀察使 Chŏng Munt'ong has been appointed our deputy investiture envoy to present you with the letter of investiture and gifts including official robes, carriages, silverware, rolls of silk, saddled horses, bows and arrows, wine, and assorted other items as specified in the accompanying list. You may accept them when they arrive.

The letter of investiture stated:

> Upon receiving the mandate of Heaven, we ascended the throne and inherited the great enterprise of our ancestors, which consists of developing the country, keeping our vassal lords close, and increasing the number of vassal states. In acceding to the throne of Chumong, you have broadened the territory of Hyŏnt'o 玄菟, expanded royal authority for future generations, and faithfully assisted the imperial court. Coincidentally, an age of peace and abundance has arrived, and we have assumed additional titles in a resplendent ceremony attended by all the court officials.[26] We wish to share this especially felicitous occasion widely, and thus have composed the official document giving you special privileges through imperial investiture.

---

26. *Chŏl* 綎 in the original text, meaning the sash or belt worn by officials to indicate their rank and grade in the morning assembly of the court. Here, *chŏl* can be translated as the whole court or all the officials of the court.

Ah! We invest you with the proud titles of Rectifying the Age, Serving Governance, Completing Integrity, Offering Loyalty, Merit Subject for Dedication to Superiors, Commander Unequaled in Honor, Acting Grand Preceptor, Director of the Secretariat, Director of the State Affairs Department, Supreme Pillar of the State, and King of Koryŏ with a fief of twenty thousand households and an actual fief of two thousand households. In receiving such a bountiful fortune, your virtue is unparalleled.

All the energy of the universe flows to you, so you were venerated as a hero from the time of your birth. You received virtue from Heaven when you were born, so you were gentle and benevolent from childhood. From the time of your accession as king of Koryŏ, you have faithfully maintained your fief and titles, and you have ruled well, your moral influence spreading into the lands of Chinhan 辰韓 and Pyŏnhan 弁韓.[27] You have also served our country faithfully as a feudal lord, requesting our calendar and performing deeds comparable to the exploits of Duke Huan of Qi and Duke Wen of Jin. You should continue to respect our imperial court even as you undertake the task of conserving and defending your country. Given your accomplishments, we add to your status the merit titles of Maintaining Justice (*sujŏng* 守正) and Preserving Righteousness and bestow an additional fief of three thousand households and an actual fief of three hundred households, with the rest remaining unchanged as before.

Ah! The higher one ascends, the humbler one should behave. This upstanding lesson is a remedy for immoderate behavior, just as serving the great is the surest plan for preserving your country. Koryŏ is a model country, and the Koryŏ king, an example for feudal lords. Do not depart from the duty of constant prudence. Do not deviate from sincere compliance and emulation so that you can maintain the heritage left you by preceding generations. If you treasure my words and constitute yourself a guardian of our imperial court, you shall reside in bliss forever.

Kyŏngja (11th day). The king received the investiture decree in the southern outskirts of the capital. The official bestowal included an imperial crown, imperial robes, a jade scepter, jade strips, an ivory carriage, royal garments, rolls of silk, bows and arrows, saddled horses, and other items.

---

27. Two of the Three Han, or Samhan, referring to Koryŏ.

Also, the Khitans sent Yayul Chŏk 耶律迪 and Maanyŏ 麻晏如 as investiture envoys to deliver the emperor's edict to the crown prince.

> Engraving your ancestors' lessons on your heart, you have occupied the glorious position of prince from a young age. Upon being invested as crown prince, you held the rank of an archduke. When all the court officials gathered for the performance of a magnificent ceremony, the imperial title we received gave us the thought of an edict that would disseminate our grace and demonstrate our affection for Koryŏ by bestowing high titles and munificent gifts. We have now appointed the Iju district surveillance commissioner Yayul Chŏk and the chief minister of imperial regalia (*wiwigyŏng* 衛尉卿) Maanyŏ appointed as lead investiture envoy and deputy investiture envoy, respectively. They will convey to you our gifts of official robes, carriages, silverware, rolls of silk, saddled horses, bows and arrows, wine, and other items, as specified in the accompanying list. You may accept them when they arrive.

The letter of investiture stated:

> Upon receiving the mandate of Heaven, we resumed the felicitous plan of the preceding reigns. Looking within, we sought harmony, mindful of the prosperity of the imperial family. Looking out, our caring heart grew more generous when we beheld the crown prince of a neighboring country on our border. Radiant as jade and pure as pearl, you have grown in the realm to the east and have learned to treat the imperial court with complete sincerity. Coincidentally, the number of titles we possess increased still further in conjunction with the arrival of a period of stability, and we would like to promulgate the happiness of this occasion by granting you the special privilege of receiving additional titles as well.
>
> Earlier, we invested you as Military Commissioner of the Obeying Justice Army, Supervisory Surveillance Commissioner of Sangju and Muju Provinces, Grand Master of Imperial Entertainments, Acting Grand Marshal, Secretariat-Chancellery Joint Affairs Manager, Commissioned with Extraordinary Military Powers in Sakchu, Acting Regional Inspector of Sakchu, Supreme Pillar of the State, and Duke of Samhan with a fief of three thousand households and an actual fief of five hundred households.

Wang Hun 王勳 is a pillar of the country as well as a man of heavenly ability with special talents. You have learned the lessons of decorum, music, poetry, and literature. You are well aware of the rituals that shape relations between a king and his subjects, and a father and his son, and the brilliance of your clever plan to use military resources to support the running of government is outstanding.

Even more, you were recommended to occupy a glorious position early on and you have already received special favor from this court. The rank of your position is that of archduke, which almost brings you into the company of feudal lords. You hold the authority of a military commissioner when giving orders to the troops[28] under your command. When dealing with issues of statecraft at the highest level of government,[29] your duties are those of a manager of affairs. You embrace others with tolerance while adhering to principle, which affords room for your gifts of cleverness and shrewdness. Accordingly, we will bestow on you special titles that raise your official rank and disclose at the same time the kindness in our shining reign of peace.

Therefore, we send Yayul Chŏk, our lead investiture envoy and Iju District surveillance commissioner, and Maanyŏ, our deputy investiture envoy and acting chief minister of the Imperial Regalia Court (*su wiwigyŏng* 守衛尉卿), with a fully verified official document investing you as Affiliated Director of the Chancellery and Specially Advanced Lord (*t'ŭkchin* 特進). Your other titles will remain unchanged.

Ah! Meeting with an opportune time comes only rarely. In view of the long and distinguished service that has been provided to us for generations, we dare not forget that which is most agreeable. As you tackle the affairs of state, you must do your best to marshal your energy. Do not become prideful because of the favors heaped on you, but do everything in your power to fix your mind and heart on what you are here to serve. By following these regal teachings, you will be empowered to preserve absolute purity and brilliance forever.

---

28. *Bi zhuang* 碧幢 or *bi you zhuang* 碧油幢 in the original text, referring to military barracks or badges. Here the term is translated in a more general sense.

29. *Hwanggak* 黃閣 in the original text, referring to the highest office of the central government, and translated here as the highest level of government.

Kyemyo (14th day). The crown prince received the investiture decree in the southern outskirts of the capital. The official bestowal included an imperial crown, imperial robes, an ivory scepter, bamboo books, carriages, royal garments, rolls of silk, saddled horses, bows and arrows, wines, and other items.

Fifth Month, Summer

Kyeyu (14th day). The king went to the Imperial Portrait Hall and called on the royal preceptor Nanwŏn to tonsure Prince Wang Hu 王煦 (1055–1101) and let him become a monk [named Ŭich'ŏn 義天].

Kimyo (20th day). The king went to Yŏngt'ong monastery.

Sixth Month, Summer

Kabo (6th day). The king went to Mundok Hall to retest the examination candidates but found that the general censor No Tan 盧旦 (d. 1091) had submitted a petition in defiance of the king's purpose. Indignant, the king decided not to retest the examination candidates and made a special point of passing those who had taken the examination more than ten times, including Yi Wŏnjang 李元長 among others.

Sinhae (23rd day). Seventeen Eastern Jurchens, led by General Embracing Transformation Ingul 仍蔚, were granted an audience and made an offering of excellent horses.

Autumn, Seventh Month

After insufficient rainfall all spring and summer, torrents of welcome rain finally came. The king ordered his royal attendants to compose poems celebrating the rain.

Ŭrhae (17th day). The king went to the Eastern Pond, boarded a Dragon Ship, and hosted a reception with libations at which the crown prince and royal family were also in attendance. The party continued until midnight.

Eighth Month, Autumn

Pyŏngo (19th day). The king sent the right vice director of state affairs Kim Yangji and the vice director of palace administration Sŏ Chŏng 徐靖 to the Khitans with a letter of gratitude for the investiture of the king.

Ninth Month, Autumn

Kyemi (26th day). Song merchants led by Guo Man and Huang Zong 黃宗 came with an offering of their native products.

The king sent the director of rites Ch'oe Sang and the vice director of construction and maintenance Kim Sŏngjŏm to the Khitans with a letter of gratitude for the investiture of the crown prince.

Twelfth Month, Winter

Pyŏngsul (1st day). The Khitans sent the left grand master of remonstrance (*chwa kanŭi taebu* 左諫議大夫) Pu P'yŏng 傅平 with a letter of congratulations on the king's birthday.

TWENTIETH YEAR OF MUNJONG (1066)

First Month, Spring

Pyŏngjin (1st day). The king canceled the New Year Congratulations.
Ŭrhae (20th day). The king issued a decree: "Beginning this year, the butchering of livestock shall be prohibited across the country for three years."
Kimyo (24th day). The king appointed Kim Yanggŏm 金良儉 as administrator of the Military Commission of the Northwestern Frontier District in spring and summer (*ch'unhabŏn chi sŏbungmyŏn pyŏngmasa* 春夏番知西北面兵馬事).

Second Month

Kihae (15th day). A fire broke out at Unhŭng granary 雲興倉.
Sinhae (27th day). The king issued a decree.

> The Unhŭng granary fire occurred because of the negligence of the officials in carrying out their duty. To lose overnight in a sudden blaze the value of many years of grain—how shameful! From henceforth, all granaries and treasuries will employ officials and clerks assigned specifically to fire prevention. The Censorate will conduct inspections periodically, and in the event of a fire, those who were on day duty [during non-working days like holidays] will be the first to be detained, regardless of their rank, and questioned.

Third Month

Muo (4th day). The king himself conducted the Daoist Ch'o ritual at the Polo Field.
Chŏngch'uk (23rd day). A star appeared in the northwestern sky. It seemed to be the same size as the moon and then turned into a comet.

The Khitans renamed their country, reverting to its previous name of Great Liao 大遼.

Fourth Month, Summer

Kyŏngin (7th day). An earthquake occurred in Kaegyŏng.
Kyesa (10th day). The king again prayed for rain.
Imin (19th day). The king issued a decree.

> The royal attendants shall be appointed as adjunct inspectors of the left granary (*chwach'ang pyŏlgam* 左倉別監) and adjunct inspectors of the right granary (*uch'ang pyŏlgam* 右倉別監) in Kaegyŏng, and also as adjunct inspectors of the Yongmun granary 龍門倉別監 and adjunct inspectors of the Unhŭng granary 雲興倉別監.

Kyemyo (20th day). The king conducted his ancestral rites at the Imperial Ancestral Shrine and at a separate shrine.

Ko Chungsin 高仲臣 and others passed the state examination.

Kapchin (21st day). The king sent the director of water control Ko Pokchang 高復昌 to Liao with a letter of congratulations on the country's renaming.

Pyŏngo (23rd day). The acting director of the imperial stables (*sŏp t'aebokkyŏng* 攝太僕卿) Yi Ch'onghyŏn 李聰顯 was dismissed from his position for being lazy and careless in his work.

Fifth Month

Ŭlmyo (2nd day). The king issued a decree: "The Marquis of Kugwŏn 國原侯 shall have his name changed from Wang Chŭng to Wang Ki 王祁."

The king prayed for rain on the riverside.

Seventh Month, Autumn

Kabin (2nd day). The king issued an imperial edict.

> With the seventh lunar month comes autumn and the time for grains to ripen. But the weather is still extremely hot and the drought is severe. This must be due to the people's resentment over unjust punishments, causing my days and nights to be filled with worry. I cannot feel at ease under these circumstances, and I order all offices across the country to evaluate punishments to eliminate injustice and resentment.

Ninth Month

Ŭlch'uk (14th day). The king went to Wangnyun monastery.

Kyŏngjin (29th day). The king went to Myot'ong monastery for the Maricī ritual (*Marijich'ŏn toryang* 摩利支天道場).[30]

---

30. A Buddhist ritual with prayers for the prevention of military invasions.

Eleventh Month, Winter

Imja (2nd day). Liao sent the Kwiju regional inspector 歸州刺史 Yayul Ha 耶律賀 as a special envoy with an imperial edict to deliver.

Twelfth Month

Sinsa (1st day). Liao sent its minister of imperial entertainments Wang Kŏhok 王去惑 with a letter of congratulations on the king's birthday.

Twenty-First Year of Munjong (1067)

First Month, Spring

Kyŏngsul (1st day). The king canceled the New Year Congratulations.
Kyŏngsin (11th day). The construction of Hŭngwang monastery was completed after twelve years. The scale of the monastery was approximately 2,800 *kan*. As innumerable monks from all regions began to gather for the assembly to commemorate the monastery's completion, the king ordered the director of military affairs Kim Yang and the Central Buddhist Registry's right roster clerk (*uga sŭngnok* 右街僧錄) Towŏn 道元 to select one thousand clerics for participation in the assembly and subsequent assignment to Hŭngwang monastery.
Mujin (19th day). The king held a special convocation of the Grand Assembly of the Lantern Festival 燃燈大會 for five days and nights at Hŭngwang monastery.[31] The king had issued an imperial edict ordering all authorities, the Western Regional Military Command, the Kaesŏng district 開城 府, Kwangju, Suju 水州,[32] Yangju 楊州, Tongju, Suju 樹州,[33] and Kangwha

---

31. This was a special Lantern Festival for two reasons. First, it was held on *mujin*, the nineteenth day of the first month, whereas the Lantern Festival was usually held on the fifteenth day of the second month. Second, the Grand Assembly (*taehoe* 大會) of the Lantern Festival usually occupied the second day of the two-day Lantern Festival. In this case, however, the king ordered the grand assembly to last for five days.

32. Present-day Suwŏn city, Kyŏnggi.

33. Present-day Puch'ŏn city, Kyŏnggi.

county and Changdan county 長湍縣³⁴ to erect multicolored stages and position them in an unbroken sequence leading from the gardens of the royal palace to the gates of Hŭngwang monastery, creating a wall made of lantern light. Lanterns had also been hung on the trees lining both sides of the king's path, so that the night was as bright as day.

On this day, the king led the government officials in a formal ceremony. The king burned incense and gave away precious items and articles of clothing. The grandness of all the ceremonies and events had never been seen before.

Sinmi (22nd day). The king went to a temporary pavilion located east of Sinbong Pavilion to host a banquet for his officials.

Pyŏngja (27th day). The king worshiped at Ch'ang Tomb.³⁵ He raised the rank of the officials in charge of the ritual by one grade and gave assorted gifts to the attending soldiers in accordance with their rank.

Intercalary Month

Chŏnghae (8th day). Twenty-two Eastern Jurchens, led by General Embracing Transformation Ing'ul, were granted an audience and made an offering of their native products.

Second Month

Kiyu (1st day). The king went to Sinbong Pavilion and issued an amnesty decree to commemorate the completion of Hŭngwang monastery.

Kyŏngo (22nd day). The king issued a decree: "Henceforth, all regions shall make no further offerings of dried fish."

---

34. The area between present-day Paju city in Kyŏnggi and Changdan-gun, Kaesŏng city.
35. The tomb of King Taejo's father.

Third Month

Kich'uk (11th day). The retired Secretariat director Wang Ch'ongchi died.

Kyesa (15th day). The king issued a decree.

> The deceased Chancellery directors Ch'oe Hang and Kang Kamch'an and the senior governmental advisor Kim Maeng served several kings with upright integrity and unimpeachable morality, and their merit will be written down in history. The whole world is at peace today because of their merit, and our people also enjoy this peace. I therefore award to Ch'oe Hang and Kang Kamch'an the posthumous titles of High Grand Preceptor and Director of the Secretariat, and to Kim Maeng the posthumous titles of Grand Preceptor to the Crown Prince and Director of the Chancellery.

Musul (20th day). The king went to Changwŏn Pavilion.

Ulsa (27th day). The king issued a decree: "A total of 49,400 *sŏk* of various grains shall be transported by ship to the northern border regions and distributed to the people of the frontier."

Fifth Month, Summer

Musul (21st day). The king hosted a banquet for elder statesmen in the garden inside the Audience gate and gave them gifts of clothing and assorted goods.

Sixth Month

Sinyu (15th day). The king received the bodhisattva ordination in Kŏndŏk Hall.

Seventh Month, Autumn

Kyesa (17th day). Venus was visible during the day.

Ninth Month

Ŭryu (10th day). The king went to Songak Pavilion 松岳亭 to host a reception with libations. He ordered the officials charged with literary composition to write poems and pieces of rhythmic prose.

Chŏngyu (22nd day). The state preceptor Haerin requested permission to retire to the mountains due to his advanced age. The king personally escorted him to Hyŏnhwa monastery and gave him gifts of tea, medicine, gold and silver flatware, silks, and other treasures.

Twelfth Month, Winter

Ulsa (1st day). Liao sent the Yŏngch'ŏn district surveillance commissioner (*Yŏngch'ŏn kwannae kwanch'alsa* 寧川管內觀察使) Ho P'yŏng 胡平 with a letter of congratulations on the king's birthday.

Twenty-Second Year of Munjong (1068)

First Month, Spring

Kapsul (1st day). There was a solar eclipse.

Chŏngch'uk (4th day). A party of Eastern Jurchens, led by General Submitting to Virtue Sanggon 霜鯀, were granted an audience with the court.

Kyesa (20th day). The king went to Hŭngwang monastery to hold an assembly celebrating the monastery's completion (*kyŏngsŏnghoe* 慶成會). The king stayed for two nights and then returned to the palace.

Chŏngyu (24th day). The king appointed Ch'oe Yusŏn as superintendent of the Civil Personnel Ministry, Wang Musung as superintendent of the Punishments Ministry, and Kim Ŭijin as superintendent of the Military Affairs Ministry. The other ministries remained as before.

Musul (25th day). The king appointed Kim Haenggyŏng as director of the Military Affairs Ministry and Yi Chŏng 李頲 (1025–1077) as right scholarly counselor-in-ordinary.

Second Month

Sinhae (8th day). The king appointed the Construction and Maintenance director Chŏn Sŏkcho 全錫祚 as managing military commissioner of the Northwestern Frontier District in spring and summer, and the Palace Revenues vice director Yi Chingmang 李徵望 (d. 1081) as vice military commissioner of the Northeastern Frontier District in spring and summer.

Third Month

Chŏngmyo. The Yugyŏk changgun Kayaying 加也仍, ruler of T'amna, was granted an audience and made an offering of his native products.

Fourth Month, Summer

Kapcha (23rd day). The king appointed Ch'oe Sang as deputy administrator of the Palace Secretariat.
Pyŏngin (25th day). The king went to Mundŏk Hall to retest the examination candidates. Ch'oe Yin 崔駰 and others passed the state examination.

Fifth Month

Kabo (23rd day). The king issued a decree.

> From spring into the summer, rain has still not come at the appropriate time, and with the weather so hot, the crops have withered. All of this is due to my lack of virtue and must be considered evidence of my shortcomings. With trepidation, I will follow the instructions of Heaven and release, as of today, all those guilty of small crimes across the country, together with those sentenced to a punishment of exile or less for public malfeasance as well as those sentenced to penal servitude or less for private malfeasance.

Sixth Month

Imin (2nd day). A party of Eastern Jurchens, led by General Submitting to Virtue An Ku 安矩, were granted an audience with the court.

Kyŏngsin (20th day). The military commissioner of the Eastern Frontier (*tonggye pyŏngmasa* 東界兵馬使) submitted a report.

> The Military Commission executive Im Hŭiyŏl 任希悅 and chief registrar Chŏng Sin 鄭申, together with General Kŏhŭng 巨興, were surveying Cho island 椒島[36] in warships when they encountered and fought an enemy fleet. They seized seven of the ten enemy ships and captured or killed many of their soldiers.

The king was greatly pleased and gave a set of ordinary dress and a silver belt inscribed with gold to Im Hŭiyŏl and each of the other leaders. He also awarded government posts and other items to the meritorious troops.

Seventh Month, Autumn

Sinsa (11th day). Huang Shen 黃愼 from Song was granted an audience with the king. In it Huang explained:

> Our emperor summoned the military and chief supply commissioner for Jianghu, Liangzhe, and the Jinghu area (*Jianghuai liangzhe jinghu nanbeilu duda zhizhi fayunshi* 江淮兩浙荊湖南北路都大制置發運使) Luo Zheng 羅拯 and declared to him: "Koryŏ has long been known as a land of noble men whose ancestors were wholeheartedly dedicated to hard work. However, their descendants have been cut off from us for a long time. As I now hear that they are ruled by a wise king, I believe it would be worthwhile to send someone there to obtain good counsel." Because of Luo Zheng's recommendation to the emperor, I have come to convey to you the will of the emperor.

---

36. This island is off the coast of present-day South Hwanghae province.

The king was pleased and treated his guests with solicitude and lavish abundance.

The Song merchant Lin Ning and others came with an offering of their native products.

Chŏngyu (27th day). The military commissioner of the Eastern Frontier submitted a report.

> The Military Commission executive Im Hŭiyŏl and the Naval Administration Office vice commissioner (*tobusŏ pusa* 都部署副使) Pae Haengji 裴行之, acting with the Wŏnhŭng Garrison vice commissioner 元興鎭副使 Sŏk Sugyu 石秀珪 and others, were again patrolling Cho island when they reached Yŏmnap'o 閻羅浦 just at nightfall. They encountered eight enemy ships there and destroyed three of them. Some of the enemy soldiers managed to reach the shore, and about thirty of them were killed before the rest dispersed.

The king gave out government posts and other generous rewards.

Eighth Month

Chŏngsa (17th day). The king ordered the crown prince to summon the Song examination candidates to Okch'ŭk Pavilion 玉燭亭, where he tested Sin Su (Ch. Shen Xiu) 慎修, Chin Chamgo (Ch. Chen Qiangu) 陳潛古, Chŏ Wŏnbin (Ch. Chu Yuanbin) 儲元賓,[37] and others on poetic and rhythmic prose composition.

Kimi (19th day). The king appointed Kang Wŏn'gwang as director of the Censorate.

Kyŏngsin (20th day). The king appointed the director of imperial regalia Mun Yangnyŏl as administrator of the Military Commission of the Northwestern Frontier District in autumn and winter, and the vice director of punishments Hong Tŏgwi as vice military commissioner of the Northeastern Frontier District in autumn and winter.

---

37. Sin Su, Chin Chamgo, and Chŏ Wŏnbin were scholars from China who had sworn allegiance to Koryŏ.

Ninth Month

Kapsin (15th day). The retired high grand preceptor and Secretariat director Ch'oe Ch'ung died.

Tenth Month, Winter

Ŭlmyo (16th day). A party of Eastern Jurchens, led by General Embracing Transformation Arin 阿隣, were granted an audience with the court.

Twelfth Month

Kihae (1st day). Liao sent the Ikchu district surveillance commissioner Wi Sŏng 魏成 with a letter of congratulations on the king's birthday.
Musin (10th day). The left vice director of state affairs Wang Hyŏn 王顯 submitted a memorial three times to request permission to retire.
This year, a new royal palace was established in the Southern Capital 南京.[38]

Twenty-Third Year of Munjong (1069)

First Month, Spring

Muja (20th day). A party of Eastern Jurchens, led by General Embracing Transformation Saŏhwa 沙於賀, were granted an audience with the court.

Second Month

Muo (21st day). The king appointed the Imperial Stables director Ha Churyŏ as administrator of the Military Commission of the Northeastern Frontier District in spring and summer (*chi tongbungmyŏn ch'unhabŏn pyŏngmasa* 知東北面春夏番兵馬事), and the vice director of palace revenues Pak Yangdan

---

38. Present-day Seoul.

朴陽旦 as vice military commissioner of the Northwestern Frontier District in spring and summer.

Third Month

Kisa (2nd day). The king went to Hŭngwang monastery and ascended a south-facing peak to conduct the Kyeŭm ceremony 禊飲.³⁹ After it, he composed a poem for the Double Third 上巳⁴⁰ and commanded his royal attendants to write poems in response.

Fourth Month, Summer

A drought was declared.
Kyemyo (7th day). The king went to Chin'gwan monastery.

Fifth Month

Kyŏngjin (15th day). The king went to Changwŏn Pavilion, where he discovered a stone with propitious markings in a pond below the pavilion. He ordered all civil officials to compose a song or poem to mark the occasion.
Kapsin (19th day). The king prayed for rain.
Kyesa (28th day). The king appointed Chŏng Yusan 鄭惟產 (d. 1091) as left office chief of the State Affairs Department and right grand master of remonstrance, Yang Ch'ich'un 楊稚春 as general censor, Han Ŏk 韓億 and Yi Tŏksŭng 李德昇 as palace censors, Son Kwan 孫冠 (1024–1109) as left rectifier of omissions, and Cho Yun'gan 趙倫簡 and Sim Chuch'an 沈周贊 as investigating censors.

---

39. A Chinese ceremony to wash away all undesirable things. It originated in the ancient capital of Luoyang, where people would bathe in the river on the third day of the third month and consume wine and spirits.

40. The third day of the third month commemorated the annual return of the swallows that had flown south of the Yangtze River for the winter.

Sixth Month

Imin (7th day). A party from Song led by the merchant Yang Congsheng 楊從盛 came with an offering of their native products.

Seventh Month, Autumn

Ŭlch'uk (1st day). There was a solar eclipse.
Chŏngch'uk (13th day). A party from Song led by the merchant Wang Ning 王寧 came with an offering of their native products.
Kyesa (29th day). The king appointed the left office chief of the State Affairs Department and right grand master of remonstrance Chŏng Yusan as vice military commissioner of the Northwestern Frontier District in autumn and winter (*sŏbungmyŏn ch'udongbŏn pyŏngma pusa* 西北面秋冬番兵馬副使), and the vice director of military affairs Yi Chingmang 李澄望 as vice military commissioner of the Northeastern Frontier District in autumn and winter.

Winter, Intercalary Eleventh Month

Chŏngyu (4th day). The king's younger brother Wang Ki, the duke of P'yŏngyang, died.

Twelfth Month

Kyehae (1st day). Liao sent the Censorate vice director Ko Yong 高聳 with a letter of congratulations on the king's birthday.

The acting right vice director of state affairs Yayul Kŭngniga 耶律極里哥 came as a response envoy from the Liao Eastern Capital.

Twenty-Fourth Year of Munjong (1070)

First Month, Spring

Kyesa (1st day). The king canceled the New Year Congratulations.

Kyŏngja (8th day). A meteorite fell to earth in Taegu county 大丘縣[41] and turned to stone.

Kiyu (17th day). The king appointed Kim Yanggam 金良鑑 as right office chief of the State Affairs Department and left grand master of remonstrance, Yi Chŏnggong as Hallim academician, Kim Kong 金珙 as right deputy recipient of edicts (*u pu sŭngsŏn* 右副承宣), Pak Tŏgyŏng 朴德英 as right rectifier of omissions, Kang Ansŏ 康安庶 as palace censor, and Kim Ye 金銳 and Kim Sanggi 金上琦 (b. 1031) as left and right rectifier of omissions, respectively.

Second Month

Pyŏngin (5th day). The king went to Hŭngwang monastery and held a grand assembly to celebrate the completion of the newly founded Chassi [Maitreya] Hall 慈氏殿 in the monastery. He rested for the night and returned to the palace.

Imsin (11th day). The king went to Pongŭn monastery to hold the Lantern Festival.

Kyeyu (12th day). It had been decided that the Lantern Festival would be held on the twelfth day this year since the Royal Memorial Day fell on the thirteenth and the fifteenth was the day for Cold Food. During the festival's Grand Assembly, the king hosted a banquet in Chunggwang Hall for the crown prince, the royal family, and his royal attendants, which lasted until dawn.

---

41. Present-day Taegu, North Kyŏngsang.

Third Month

Kimi (28th day). The king appointed Kim Tŏkpu 金德符 (d. 1082) as advisor to the crown prince.

Fourth Month, Summer

Sinyu (1st day). The king hosted a small banquet in Sangch'un Pavilion 賞春亭. During the festivities, he ordered the crown prince, the royal family, and his royal attendants to each compose a piece of rhythmic prose on the theme of the blossoming flowers.

Sinmi (11th day). The king prayed for rain on the riverside.

Imsin (12th day). The king appointed the vice director of military affairs and left grand master of remonstrance Mun Chŏng 文正 (d. 1093) as vice military commissioner of the Northwestern Frontier Circuit (*sŏbungno pyŏngma pusa* 西北路兵馬副使), and the Imperial Archives vice director Ko Yu as vice military commissioner of the Northeastern Frontier Circuit (*tongbungno pyŏngma pusa* 東北路兵馬副使).

Pyŏngja (16th day). The king went to Mundŏk Hall to retest the examination candidates. Ch'oe Iksin 崔翼臣 and others passed the state examination.

Fifth Month

Imin (13th day). The king ordered Prince Wang T'aeng 王竀 to receive ordination at Hyŏnhwa monastery. The prince shaved his head and became a monk.

Sixth Month

Walls were built at Hŭngwang monastery.

Seventh Month, Autumn

Ŭlmi (7th day). The king appointed the right office chief of the State Affairs Department and grand master of remonstrance Kim Yanggam as vice military commissioner of the Northwestern Frontier Circuit, and the vice director of revenue Kim Yakchin as vice military commissioner of the Northeastern Frontier Circuit.

Eighth Month

Sinmi (14th day). The retired affairs manager Kim Ŭijin died.
Kimyo (22nd day). The Censorate director Kang Wŏn'gwang died.

Luo Zheng, the Song supply commissioner for Hunan, Jinghu, and Liangzhe, sent Huang Shen to the court again.

The king issued a decree.

> Yiubul, the father of the Western Jurchen chief Hoedŏk 懷德, has contributed to the safety of our frontier since the reign of the previous king. I therefore award Hoedŏk the rank of General Supporting the State.

Ninth Month

Pyŏngsin (9th day). The king hosted a banquet in Sangch'un Pavilion and ordered his royal attendants to each compose a poem or piece of rhythmic prose. The party ended late at night.

Tenth Month, Winter

Kyŏngo (13th day). The king went to Hyŏnhwa monastery.

Eleventh Month

Kabo (7th day). The king established charcoal and iron storehouses (*t'anch'ŏlgo* 炭鐵庫) on all four sides of Kaegyŏng for defense.

Twelfth Month

Chŏngsa (1st day). Liao sent the chief minister of imperial regalia Hwauk 和勗 with a letter of congratulations on the king's birthday.

Twenty-Fifth Year of Munjong (1071)

First Month, Spring

Chŏnghae (1st day). The king canceled the New Year Congratulations.

Kihae (13th day). The king appointed Kim Haenggyŏng as superintendent of the Punishments Ministry and left vice director of state affairs, Ch'oe Yubu as right vice director of state affairs, Hong Tŏgwi as director of the Military Affairs Ministry, and Chŏng Yusan as Hallim academician.

Sinch'uk (15th day). The king appointed Kim Yanggam as left office chief of the State Affairs Department and administrator of the Censorate, and Noh In as right office chief of the State Affairs Department and left grand master of remonstrance.

Imin (16th day). The king invested Prince Wang Su 王琇 (d. 1095) with the titles of Eminent Director of State Affairs and High Minister of Works. He appointed Ch'oe Yusŏn as high minister of education, and Yi Yuch'ung as high minister of works.

Imja (26th day). The king appointed Kim Haenggyŏng as senior governmental advisor.

Kyech'uk (27th day). A party of Western Jurchens, led by General Embracing Transformation Punt'ae 紛泰, were granted an audience and made an offering of their native products.

Second Month

Sinmi (15th day). The king went to Pongŭn monastery to hold the Lantern Festival.

Muin (22nd day). The king held a special convocation of the Lantern Festival [again]. He worshiped at the Imperial Portrait Hall.

Third Month

Kyŏngin (5th day). The king sent the vice director of public finance Kim Che 金悌 as an envoy to Song bearing a memorial and gifts. Previously, when Huang Shen returned to Song, the king had sent through Fujian 福建 his request for permission to send tribute offerings to Song. On this occasion, however, Kim Che was sent through Dengzhou to offer tribute.

Musul (13th day). Kang Wŏn'gwang was posthumously awarded the title of Grand Preceptor to the Crown Prince.

Sinch'uk (16th day). Twenty-two Eastern Jurchens, led by General Submitting to Virtue Sanggon, paid the ransom for our countrymen who had been taken captive and returned them home.

Musin (23rd day). The king went to Taean monastery.

Fourth Month, Summer

Imsul (7th day). The king prayed for rain.

Chŏngmyo (12th day). Ten Western Jurchens, led by Chief Noudal 奴亐達, were granted an audience and made an offering of their native products. The king gave them government posts.

Kyeyu (18th day). The king himself conducted the Daoist Ch'o ritual at the Polo Field.

Muin (23rd day). The king went to Wangnyun monastery.

Imo (27th day). Eighteen Western Jurchens, led by Chief Mahodal 麻胡達, were granted an audience and made an offering of their native products. The king promoted Mahodal to the rank of General Submitting to Virtue and gave him other gifts as well.

Fifth Month

Ŭryu (1st day). The king appointed Wang Musung as superintendent of the Military Affairs Ministry and vice director of the Secretariat with a concurrent assignment as Secretariat-Chancellery joint affairs manager.
Chŏnghae (3rd day). The king prayed for rain on the riverside.
Kyesa (9th day). A party of Western Jurchens, led by Yoyŏn 裛演, were granted an audience with the court. The king gave them official positions and other rewards.
Musul (14th day). The Law Office submitted a petition.

> The Foreign Relations assistant executive (*yebinsŏng chubu* 禮賓省注簿) Zhou Hang 周沆 from Song was appointed for his talent in writing. However, since he has committed the crime of accepting bribes, he should be returned to his home country and the office land he had been granted should be revoked.

The king approved.
Sinhae (27th day). The king went to Hyŏnhwa monastery.

Sixth Month

Kyŏngsin (7th day). Song Yu 宋由, a craftsman of saddles 鞍工, was recognized as a descendant of the grand mentor and merit subject for unification So Kyŏktal 蘇格達. The king gave him a special exemption from required labor and allowed him to become an official.
Kapcha (11th day). The king prayed for rain on the riverside.

Seventh Month, Autumn

Kapsin (1st day). The king went to Wangnyun monastery.

Eighth Month

Sinyu (9th day). Fifteen Eastern Jurchens, led by General Submitting to Virtue Kosa, were granted an audience and made an offering of their native products.

Pyŏngja (24th day). Twenty Eastern Jurchens, led by General Embracing Transformation Saŏha, were granted an audience and made an offering of good horses.

Chŏngch'uk (25th day). Thirty-three people from Song, led by the merchant Guo Man, came with an offering of their native products.

Ninth Month

Ŭryu (4th day). Thirty-six people from Song, led by the merchant Yuan Ji 元積, came with an offering of their native products.

Kyŏngin (9th day). In honor of the Double Nine, the king went to Sangch'un Pavilion to host a banquet for the crown prince, the marquis of Kyerim, the marquis of P'yŏngyang 平壤侯, the state councillors Yi Yuch'ung and Wang Musung, and several others. He gave a horse to each of them.

Chŏngyu (16th day). Thirty people from Song, led by the merchant Wang Hua 王華, came with an offering of their native products.

Tenth Month, Winter

Ŭlmyo (4th day). Sixty-one people from Song, led by the merchant Xu Man 許滿, came with an offering of their native products.

Eleventh Month

Ŭlmi (14th day). The king went to Pŏbwang monastery to hold the Assembly of the Eight Prohibitions.

Sinch'uk (20th day). A group of Western Jurchens, led by Chief Mandubul 漫頭弗, came to submit. The king gave them official positions and other rewards in accordance with their rank.

Imin (21st day). Ten Western Jurchens, led by Chief Inju 紉主, and fifty-eight Eastern Jurchens, led by the chiefs Tarogon 多盧昆 and Sanggon, were granted an audience and made offerings of their native products.

Pyŏngo (25th day). The high minister of education Yu Koman 庾高滿 died.

Twelfth Month

Sinhae (1st day). Liao sent the Ikchu regional inspector Ko Wŏngil 高元吉 with a letter of congratulations on the king's birthday.

Pyŏngja (26th day). The king appointed Yu Hong 柳洪 (d. 1091) as supervising secretary and left recipient of edicts, and Ŭn Chŏng 殷鼎 as vice director of the Imperial Archives and right deputy recipient of edicts.

VOLUME 9

Compiled by Chŏng Inji, Chŏnghŏn Grand Master, minister of works, director of the Hall of Worthies, deputy director of the Royal Lectures Office and State Records Office, headmaster of the Royal Confucian Academy.

MUNJONG (1072–1083)

Twenty-Sixth Year of Munjong (1072)

First Month, Spring

Sinhae (1st day). The king issued a royal decree commanding the Rites Ministry to revise the ceremonial dress code.

Chŏngsa (7th day). The king went to Hŭngwang monastery.

Pyŏngin (16th day). The king appointed the vice director of military affairs Mun Chŏng as vice military commissioner of the Northwestern Frontier, and the vice director of revenue Min Ch'angsu as vice military commissioner of the Northeastern Frontier.

Imsin (22nd day). Twenty-five Eastern Jurchens, led by Maduhan 麽豆漢, came to submit.

Kapsul (24th day). The king held a special convocation of the Lantern Festival in Chunggwang Hall.

Third Month

Kyesa (13th day). The king appointed Kim Tŏkpu as right vice director of state affairs, Yi Ch'onghyŏn as director of rites, and Kim Yang as director of public works.

Kabo (14th day). The king went to Chin'gwan monastery.

Kyŏngja (20th day). The king went to Mundŏk Hall to retest the examination candidates. Pak Yugak 朴維恪 and others passed the examination.

Fourth Month, Summer

Kapcha (15th day). There was heavy hail.

Kisa (20th day). The Secretariat executive Yi Yuch'ung died.

Fifth Month

Pyŏngsin (17th day). A party of Western Jurchens, led by General Submitting to Virtue Masanae 麼舍乃, were granted an audience and made an offering of their native products.

Sixth Month

Kyŏngsul (2nd day). Song sent the medical officials Wang Yu 王愉 and Xu Xian 徐先.

Kapsul (26th day). Kim Che returned from Song bearing five imperial edicts. The first said:

> After inheriting the kingdom of your forebears, you have kept in mind your wish to serve our imperial court. You have presented respectful words in tribute offerings to our throne, and then carried out your promise to remember each season's greetings. What can be compared to such sincere and earnest loyalty?

The second said:

> You have kept peace and tranquility in the Samhan for generation after generation while ruling over disparate areas as the predominant power. You have served the suzerain state with faithful loyalty, revering the imperial family with abiding sincerity, and remembering your devotion to our court day and night. As an exceptional lord, you have fully

inherited the noble designs of your forebears, and when we read your memorial, we could not help but admire you.

The third said:

Your pure loyalty and filial devotion can be felt even from far away, and your diligent dispatch of envoys will always find reward from our quarter. But as your sincere dedication to fulfilling your responsibility as the king of a tributary state is more than praiseworthy, it moves us to give you a sign of our favor. Your envoy Kim Che is returning to you with credentials and various goods in addition to the clothes, caps, silks, and the like listed in the accompanying document. When they arrive, you may accept them with a glad heart.

The fourth said:

We have examined the goods that your envoy Kim Che presented, and they are as follows:

Two royal robes and one yellow woolen gown 襴衫, wrapped in a double-layered red silk cloth. A red woolen *p'yŏnbok* 便服,[1] wrapped in a double-layered red silk cloth with gilt. They were inside a box lacquered in black with silver cresting. The lock on the box was plated with gold and silver. The clothes and the box were wrapped in a double-layered cloth embroidered with red plum blossoms.

One gold belt with a weight of forty *nyang*, wrapped in a double-layered red silk cloth with embroidery. The belt was inside a box of eighty *nyang* with silver cresting, and wrapped in a double-layered red silk cloth with embroidery.

One gold belt with a weight of thirty *nyang*, inside a box of sixty *nyang* with silver cresting, and wrapped in a piece of silk embroidered with red plum blossoms.

Two small gold boxes with a weight of sixty *nyang*, inside two woolen belts and a double-layered woolen sack, wrapped in a double-layered silk cloth embroidered with red plum blossoms, and wrapped again in a double-layered silk cloth embroidered with red plum blossoms.

---

1. A royal robe that the king wore on ordinary days.

Two sets of gold dishes 盤盞 with a weight of forty *nyang*, wrapped in a double-layered silk cloth embroidered with red plum blossoms, and wrapped again in a double-layered silk cloth embroidered with red plum blossoms.

One gold kettle with a weight of sixty-five *nyang*, wrapped in a double-layered silk cloth embroidered with red plum blossoms, and wrapped again in a double-layered silk cloth embroidered with red plum blossoms.

One gold gong with a weight of 150 *nyang*, wrapped in a double-layered silk cloth embroidered with red plum blossoms, and wrapped again in a double-layered silk cloth embroidered with red plum blossoms.

Six red woolen cushions with a backrest, wrapped in a double-layered silk cloth embroidered with red plum blossoms. Four yellow woolen cushions, wrapped in a double-layered silk cloth embroidered with red plum blossoms. Six red woolen mattresses, wrapped in a double-layered silk cloth embroidered with red plum blossoms. Four yellow woolen mattresses, wrapped in a double-layered silk cloth embroidered with red plum blossoms. All of these were inside a box lacquered in black with silver cresting, which itself was inside a box with a silver lock, wrapped in a double-layered silk cloth embroidered with red plum blossoms.

Four excellent bows 細弓, each in a double-layered silk sack embroidered with red plum blossoms. Twenty-four *hyoja* arrows 哮子 and eighty iron-tipped arrows 細鏃箭, and two weapons with gold and silver gilt, wrapped in woolen cloth, inside a double-layered sack embroidered with red plum blossoms.

A set of weapons with white silver gilt, wrapped in black leather, in a double-layered red silk sack. A set of weapons with gold and silver gilt, wrapped in white leather, in a double-layered red silk sack. Both sacks were wrapped in a double-layered red silk cloth.

Twenty knives ornamented with silver, inside sheaths lacquered in black with silver cresting, and wrapped with silver. Ten of the sheathed knives were in sacks made of white silk, and the other ten were in sacks made of blue silk. Each was again wrapped in a double-layered silk cloth embroidered with red plum blossoms.

Four excellent horses. Two saddles had ornaments with gold and silver gilt, small and big woolen saddle flaps, saddle clothes, and saddle cushions. All of them were covered with a double-layered red silk towel, and wrapped again with double-layered red silk with embroidery. The other two saddles had ornaments with silver gilt, big saddle flaps made of black leather, small saddle clothes made of red silk, and saddle cushions. All of them were covered with a double-layered red silk towel, and wrapped again with a double-layered red silk with embroidery.

In addition, there were twenty jars of aromatic oil, 2,200 *kŭn* of pine nuts, 1,000 *kŭn* of ginseng, 2,000 *p'il* of *saengjung* hemp cloth 生中布, and 2,000 *p'il* of *saengp'yŏng* hemp cloth 生平布.

You have ruled Liaodong over successive generations with true propriety and have turned your heart toward our court with the intention of introducing civilized institutions to your kingdom. Now you have sent an envoy over a great distance to offer tribute, and have shown filial devotion to your father by serving our court with continued loyalty and sincerity. As your actions combine the two virtues of loyalty and filial piety, we were most impressed when we read your memorial. Your envoy is returning to your country with a gifts of silverware as listed in the accompanying document. When they arrive, you may accept them with a glad heart.

The fifth said:

> We heard from your envoy Kim Che that he had offered silver to Posowang monastery 普炤王寺 and other temples and held a Buddhist rite to pray for the long life of the emperor. Originally, Qizi (K. Kija) received a fief in Liaodong where he established a country, and the Buddha propagated Buddhism near Surbaya. You sent your envoy there to pray for us, and your sincerity shines brightly.

The Song emperor was well aware that letters are held in high esteem in Koryŏ. Thus, whenever he issued an edict, he would surely have had officials charged with literary composition present him with alternative drafts so that he could select the best one. He would also have ensured that the literary talents of the document envoys (*shuzhuangguan* 書狀官) selected to accompany the imperial envoys were thoroughly tested by the Imperial Secretariat before their departure for Koryŏ.

Seventh Month, Autumn

Kyesa (16th day). The king appointed the chancellor of the National Academy and Hallim academician Chŏng Yusan as administrator of the Military Commission of the Northwestern Frontier District in autumn and winter, and the vice director of military affairs Yi Sŏk 李碩 as vice military commissioner of the Northeastern Frontier District in autumn and winter.

Pyŏngo (29th day). Lieutenant Kŏsin 巨身 was executed for plotting treason.

Intercalary Month

Kabin (7th day). The king appointed Ch'oe Yubu as superintendent of the Ministry of Punishments.

Ninth Month

Kapcha (19th day). A party of Eastern Jurchens, led by Sanggon, were granted an audience and made an offering of excellent horses.

Eleventh Month, Winter

Pyŏngo (1st day). Liao sent the Yongju regional inspector Yayul Chik 耶律直 as its triennial envoy.

Twelfth Month

Ŭrhae (1st day). Liao sent the acting grand marshal Chang Irhwa 張日華 with a letter of congratulations on the king's birthday.

Kyŏngin (16th day). A party of Eastern Jurchens, led by Saŏha, were granted an audience and made an offering of their native products.

Musul (24th day). The king appointed Yi Chingmang as director of military affairs.

Twenty-Seventh Year of Munjong (1073)

First Month, Spring

Ŭlsa (1st day). The king canceled the New Year Congratulations.
   There was an earthquake.
Mujin (24th day). The king went to Poje monastery.

Second Month

Ŭrhae (1st day). The king ordered the relevant authorities to build a pavilion at P'yŏngni station 平理驛 for use as a rest stop on his royal tour.
Muin (4th day). The king appointed Chŏng Yusan as acting director of punishments, No In as director of palace administration, and Yu Hong as vice director of military affairs and administrator of memorials.
Kapsin (10th day). The king went to Hŭngwang monastery.
Ŭlmi (21st day). A party of Eastern Jurchen officials came to submit, requesting that their territories be incorporated into the provinces of Koryŏ. Among them were the Taesang[2] Kodohwa, who was commandant (*toryŏng* 都領) of Kwiju and Sunju 順州, and his deputy commandant (*pu toryŏng* 副都領) Kosa. Also present were General Submitting to Virtue Kosa, commandant of Ikchu and Ch'angju 昌州; Commandant Kŭmbu 黔夫; General Supporting the State Yaho 耶好, commandant of Chŏnju 甂州 and Sŏngju 城州; General Submitting to Virtue Osabul 吳沙弗; General Supporting the State Taro 多老, commandant of Kongju 恭州; Commandant P'agabul 巴訶弗; the Wŏnbo Ahol, commandant of Ŭnju and Pokchu 服州; Nagŏsu 那居首, commandant of Onju 溫州; Sambin 三彬; Arodae 阿老大; and Yidabul, commandant of Sŏngju 誠州.

   The king thereupon awarded the title of Grand General Embracing Transformation to Kodohwa and General Kosa, giving them new names as well, Kodohwa becoming Son Posae 孫保塞 and Kosa, Chang Sŏch'ung 張誓忠. The king also awarded the title of Grand General Supporting the

---

2. Although the original text uses the characters Taesang 大常, it should have been Taesang 大相.

State to Yaho and Taro, giving them the names Pyŏn Ch'oe 邊最 and Yu Hambin 柳咸賓, respectively. The king gave to Osabul the title of General Embracing Transformation and the name Wi Pŏn 魏蕃, and to Ahol the title of General Submitting to Virtue and the name Yang Tongmu 楊東武. Finally, the king awarded the title of Taesang to Kosa, Kŭmbu, Pagabul, Nagŏsu, Sambin, Arodae, and Yidabul, giving them the names Mun Kyŏngmin 文格民, Kang Chŏk 康績, No Su 盧守, Chang Taewŏn 張大垣, Han Pangjin 韓方鎭, Ko Chonghwa 高從化, and Cho Changwi 趙長衛, respectively. Appropriate gifts were then given to all, in accordance with their rank.

Including Grand General Supporting the State So Tŏk 蘇德, commandant of Sŏngju 城州, fourteen Eastern Jurchens had attended the audience and offered fine horses.

Chŏngyu (23rd day). The king went to Pongŭn monastery to hold a special convocation of the Lantern Festival to celebrate the completion of a new Buddhist statue. He also ordered that Chunggwang Hall and all government buildings be specially decorated, that the streets of the capital be illuminated with thirty thousand lanterns for two nights, and that music be played for everyone's enjoyment.

Musul (24th day). The king went to the main throne hall, observed the Lantern Festival, and hosted a reception with libations attended by the crown prince, the state councilors, Secretariat-Chancellery and Censorate officials, drafters of imperial edicts and proclamations, and royal attendants, among others. The party continued until late in the evening.

Third Month

Kiyu (6th day). The king held the *Prajñāpāramitā-sūtra* ritual (*Panyagyŏng toryang* 般若經道場) for five days in Hoegyŏng Hall to avert natural disasters.

Chŏngsa (14th day). The king went to Kaeguk monastery.

Chŏngmyo (24th day). The king went to Honghwa monastery. Then he went to Hyŏnhwa monastery, where he hosted a reception with libations in Pongnae Pavilion 蓬萊亭. The king returned to his palace late at night.

Fourth Month, Summer

Kapsul (1st day). There was a solar eclipse.

Pyŏngja (3rd day). The king issued a decree.

> Tribesmen living outside the fifteen districts in the Northeastern Frontier region have continued to submit to the Koryŏ authorities and have requested the incorporation of their territories into the administrative districts of Koryŏ. This is due to the powerful spirits of the Imperial Ancestral Shrine and the Altar of the Gods of Earth and Grain. Let the senior state councilors inform the Imperial Ancestral Shrine and the Altar of the Gods of Earth and Grain. After tribesmen from near and far have completely submitted to the court and are incorporated into our districts, I will personally conduct a thanksgiving ceremony at the Imperial Ancestral Shrine and the Altar of the Gods of Earth and Grain. Let the relevant authorities discuss the order and rites for the ceremony, and whether the crown prince could represent me at the ceremony.

Imjin (19th day). The king went to Kusan monastery and hosted a reception with libations in Kwi Pavilion 龜臺 attended by the crown prince, the royal family, and the state councilors. The king returned to the palace late at night after the party was over.

Chŏngyu (24th day). The king went to the Outer Śakra monastery.

Fifth Month

Chŏngmi (5th day). The military commissioner of the Northwestern Frontier submitted a report.

> Chief Mandubul 曼豆弗 and other Western Jurchen tribesmen wish to have their territories incorporated into the districts and prefectures of Koryŏ, following the example of the eastern tribesmen. They promise that if their wish is granted, they will become loyal vassals and terminate relations with the Khitan tribes.

The king issued a decree, "Grant them an audience with the court." The king ordered that if there were people who came to submit in the future, they should be convinced to come to the court.

The military commissioner of the Northwestern Frontier submitted another report.

> From the areas adjacent to P'yŏngno Garrison, Jurchen chiefs and General Soothing Faraway Lands Korŏbu 骨於夫 and Yogyŏl 要結 of Myŏkhae village 覓害村 came and said, "We originally lived in Ije village 伊齊村 and received the title of Taewan 大完 from the Khitans. Recently, the Koryŏ court convinced us and granted us an audience in the eleventh month of the year *kiyu* (1069). His Majesty gave us a warm reception and graciously awarded us offices, and we cannot express how deeply we were touched by what the king did. However, our residences are four hundred *li* from here, too far to come and go. Please allow us to move the Jurchens who are currently under Khitan rule, along with five households including that of Chŏgyaho 狄耶好, to Myŏkhae village so that they can be registered and serve as frontier guards (*pyŏnbyŏng* 藩屏) for all time."
>
> According to our investigation, there are thirty-five households containing 252 people, and we ask you to incorporate them into the register of Koryŏ. A Jurchen chief also told me, "Tribal thieves, who are scattered around Samsan village 三山村 and valley and along the seaside, plunder and kill travelers passing through that area. They have become our enemies, and to take revenge we informed the Chungyun Yasŏro 夜西老 of Samsan village and the chiefs of the Samsipto 三十徒[3] of our plans. They responded with enthusiasm and now we will lead an army to attack the thieves. Please send your local Koryŏ officers to watch the battle."
>
> I sent Lieutenant Colonel Munsŏn 文選 with officers from Chŏngju along with translators dressed in Jurchen uniforms and Jurchen soldiers under the command of Sanggon, the commandant of Nabokki village 那復其村. Munsŏn sent me this report: "Commandants from a number of villages, including Kolmyŏn 骨面, led their men to Abangp'o 阿方浦 in Samsanch'on to reconnoiter the lair of the enemy. The enemy

---

3. The Hŭksu tribesmen were called Samsipto because they had thirty tribes.

had built stone walls on a coastal ridge and beside the streams in Yujŏn village 由戰村 and Nagal village 羅竭村, where there were 150 households. Around five hundred of them, on foot as well as on horseback, were preparing for the battle, having moved their families, the aged and the young, and their treasures into the fortress. The Jurchen army on our side launched a sudden attack with loud battle cries, which threw the enemy into disarray. The Jurchen army killed 220 of them in the first charge, and the rest retreated to take up defensive positions in the fortress. The army chased after them with great tenacity and destroyed the fortress by setting fire to it. Around 332 people surrendered and were taken captive, while those who still resisted burned to death in the fire. The army had planned to advance on Yujŏn village next, but with a heavy rain starting to fall and provisions running short, they turned back." After a few days, the army regrouped and Munsŏn and 2,030 of the Jurchens set up camp below the stone wall surrounding Yujŏn village. With the gate firmly shut, the enemy stoutly defended their fortress, and as the wall was too steep to climb and provisions were running short again, the army gave up the siege and reluctantly retreated.

In the battle of Nagalch'on, 680 Jurchen soldiers led by the Jurchen Taewan and commandants Taŏgae 多於皆 and Abanni 阿半尼 defeated the enemy with all their strength. Munsŏn and fifteen of his men earned merit in overseeing the battle. Please reward them to affirm what is right and wrong.

Thirteen officials, including the Chancellery director Ch'oe Yusŏn, submitted a memorial.

> The thieves of Samsan village have never invaded our borderland. However, they trusted in the strength of their military on the border and engaged in a private feud without permission from our government. Please do not reward them.

The king approved.

Kiyu (7th day). The king conducted the Daoist Ch'o ritual at the Polo Field, praying to all the gods to avert natural disasters.

Kyŏngo (28th day). The king went to Hyŏnhwa monastery.

Sixth Month

Kapsul (2nd day). The king went to Pongŭn monastery.

Muin (6th day). The military commissioner of the Northeastern Frontier District submitted a petition.

> We already have nine villages, including Samsan, Taeran 大蘭, and Chijŭl 支櫛, in our register. In addition, Yŏmhan, the chief of Soŭlp'o village 所乙浦村; Abani 阿反伊, the chief of Sojijŭl village 小支櫛村; and Soŭndu 所隱豆, the chief of Taejijŭl 大支櫛, Nagina 羅其那, Oan 烏安, Muiju 撫夷州, and Korai 骨阿伊 villages have come to us to request that their 1,238 households be included in our register. From Taejijŭl village to Yoŭngp'o 裏應浦 in Sojijŭl village, long walls stretch for seven hundred *li* along the coast. With households from the north coming one after another to submit to the court, we should not use our military fortifications to stop them. Please order the relevant authorities to report the names of new districts to the throne so that official documents can be issued with a seal.

The king approved.

Kimyo (7th day). In the Western Capital, General Yu Sŏp 柳涉 was responsible for defenses along the Amnok River. To patrol the river, he was using information from Khitans who had come over and submitted, causing the Khitan army to send out a war party to capture them. The Khitan soldiers breached the long wall facing the river and advanced toward Chŏngju. When Yu Sŏp was unable to stop them, the king ordered his dismissal from office.

Ŭlmi (23rd day). The military commissioner of the Eastern Frontier Circuit submitted a report.

> A party of eastern [Jurchen] tribesmen led by the chiefs Kondu and Koebal 魁拔, representing 1,970 households from twelve villages, including Taeje 大齊, Chago 者古, and Hasa 河舍, came to petition the court citing the precedent of Sanggon. Also, Chief Arohan 阿老漢, representing clans[4] such as the Turyong 豆龍, Kori 骨伊, and Yŏp'ahan 餘波漢, wishes

---

4. *Purak* 部落 in the original text, a term usually translated as village.

to have his territories annexed to the districts under Koryŏ's jurisdiction. As they live in remote areas, none of them has ever requested an audience with the court before. Yet they have now come to submit. The areas beyond the Yŏp'ahan pass,[5] such as Chaech'ago 齋遮古, Taesai 大史伊, Ch'inggyŏn 稱見, Konjun 昆俊, Tanjun 丹俊, Muŭlbi 無乙比, and Hwadu 化豆, are extensive and frequented by the northern tribesmen who inhabit the region, so even if we should decide to establish new fortifications and redraw the border, we would not be able to do it. I suggest that we first incorporate the northern tribesmen who live on this side of the Yŏp'ahan pass, and then only gradually annex the lands that are farther away.

The king approved.

Pyŏngsin (24th day). The military commissioner for the Eastern Frontier submitted a report.

Jurchen pirates from the eastern tribes attacked P'ajam *pugok* 波潛部曲,[6] an area under the jurisdiction of the Eastern Capital, and took many of the inhabitants captive. Warships commanded by soldiers from the Naval Administration Office of Wŏnhŭng Garrison pursued the pirates as far as Cho island, where they engaged in battle and succeeded in beheading twelve of the enemy and recovering sixteen captives.

The king was pleased and awarded a silver medicine vessel to each of the Military Commission administrators (*chi pyŏngmasa* 知兵馬事) and also to the Naval Administration Office general (*yŏnggun tobusŏ changgun* 領軍都部署將軍) Yŏm Han 廉漢, the Imperial Archives director Yi Sŏngmi, and others. He also gave government posts and suitable rewards to the meritorious officers in accordance with their rank.

Kyŏngja (28th day). The king went to a riverbank to perform a rite to stop the rain.

---

5. The Yŏp'ahan area was in the Mach'ŏn mountains, North Hamgyŏng.

6. A local administrative unit smaller than a county and similar in scale to a *hyang* 鄉, usually where the lowest class of people lived.

Seventh Month, Autumn

Imin (1st day). The relevant authorities submitted a memorial.

> The military commissioner of the Northeastern Frontier District has reported that the Jurchen chiefs of Chijŭl 支櫛, Nabal 那發, Yowarip 裏臥立, Taesin 大信, Sŏho 西好, and Mujugi 無主其 villages wish to offer fine horses along with their native products.

The king issued a decree indicating his approval.

Pyŏngo (5th day). The king issued a decree.

> The Hŭksu translator 譯語 Kasŏro 加西老 persuaded eastern Jurchen tribesmen to submit to the jurisdiction of our administrative districts. In recognition of his deeds, he shall be granted a new name, that of Ko Maeng 高孟, and the title of Executive Captain of the Capital Gate Division (*kammunwi sanwŏn* 監門衛散員).

> The Naval Administration Office of the Southeastern Sea (*tongnamhae tobusŏ* 東南海都部署) submitted a report.

> Forty-two Japanese, led by Ōsokutei 王則貞 and Matsunaga Toshi 松永年, have come with offerings they wish to present, including lacquer, a saddle bridge, knives, a mirror box, an inkstone case, a comb, a book table, a picture screen, an incense burner, a bow and arrows, mercury, and pearl shells. In addition, the manager 勾當官 of Iki island 壹岐島[7] has sent thirty-three Japanese, led by Fujii Yasukuni 藤井安國, who request permission to present their native products to the crown prince and government officials.

The king gave them permission to come to the capital by sea.

Eighth Month

Chŏngch'uk (6th day). Venus was visible during the day.

---

7. Present-day Iki city, Nagasaki prefecture.

Chŏnghae (16th day). The king sent the Imperial Stables director Kim Yanggam and the Secretariat drafter (*chungsŏ sain* 中書舍人) No Tan as envoys to Song bearing a letter of gratitude and an offering of native products.

The Song medical officials Wang Yu and Xu Xian returned to their homeland.

Ninth Month

Kapchin (4th day). The Hallim Academy submitted a petition.

> Eastern Jurchens who have submitted from Taeran and ten other villages request that their territories be called Pinju 濱州, Iju 利州, Pokchu 福州, Hangju 恒州, Sŏju 舒州, Sŭpchu 濕州, Minju 閩州, Taeju 戴州, Kyŏngju 敬州, Puju 付州, and Wanju 宛州. Please incorporate them into Kwisunju 歸順州[8] and issue official documents with a seal.

The king approved.

Mujin (28th day). The king held the five-day rite for Dispelling Calamities in Hoegyŏng Hall.

Tenth Month, Winter

Imo (13th day). The king held the formal investiture of Wang Su as the Marquis of P'yŏngyang. A magnificent ceremony with food and music had been prepared on a multicolored stage, and the king, who had entered the hall unobserved, watched while his queen and royal concubines, the crown prince, and the royal family enjoyed the performance.

---

8. Administrative unit created to oversee tribal peoples who lived at or beyond the official Koryŏ border. In China, a similar unit was known as Jimizhou 羈縻州.

Eleventh Month

Sinhae (12th day). The king held the Assembly of the Eight Prohibitions. He first went to Sinbong Pavilion and watched a music performance. At the Grand Assembly on the following day, visitors from Song, the Hŭksu tribe, the country of T'amna, and Japan offered fine horses and other gifts.

Twelfth Month

Kyŏngo (1st day). Liao sent the Yŏngju regional inspector Tae T'aek 大澤 with a letter of congratulations on the king's birthday.
Pyŏngsin (27th day). The king appointed Chŏng Yusan as director of rites, Ch'oe Yugil 崔惟吉 as director of revenue, and Min Ch'angsu as director of punishments.

Twenty-Eighth Year of Munjong (1074)

Second Month

Kyŏngo (2nd day). Thirty-nine Japanese, led by ship captain Shigetoshi 重利, came with an offering of their native products.
Kabo (26th day). The king invested his eldest daughter with the title of Princess.

Fourth Month, Summer

Mujin (1st day). The market was moved due to a long drought.
Kapsul (7th day). As torrential rains poured down, all the officials sent congratulatory memorials to the king.
Ŭryu (18th day). The king held the three-day Hundred Seat ritual for the recitation of the *Humane Kings Sutra* in the Inner Office.
Kabo (27th day). The king ordered the crown prince to retest the examination candidates. Yi Ha 李嘏 and others passed the state examination.

Sixth Month

Kyeyu (7th day). A party of Eastern Jurchens, led by General Embracing Transformation Choangin 祖仰仁, came with an offering of horses.

Pyŏngja (10th day). Eight people from Song, led by the Yangzhou 楊州 medical school instructor (*yizhujiao* 醫助敎) Ma Shian 馬世安, came.

Seventh Month, Autumn

Kihae (3rd day). The king appointed Yi Chingmang as right vice director of state affairs, Kim Yakchin as left scholarly counselor-in-ordinary, and No Tan as vice director of rites and right grand master of remonstrance.

Kyŏngja (4th day). The king held the Buddhist *munduru* rite (*munduru toryang* 文豆婁道場)⁹ at Sach'ŏnwang monastery 四天王寺 in the Eastern Capital for twenty-seven days. The king prayed for the defense of the northern frontier.

Eighth Month

Imsin (7th day). Twenty-eight Eastern Jurchens, led by General Submitting to Virtue Sora 所羅, came with an offering of fine horses. The king gave them gifts in accordance with their rank.

Sinmyo (26th day). The king appointed Yi Chŏng as provisional commissioner of the Western Capital (*kwŏn sŏgyŏng yususa* 權西京留守使).

Ninth Month

Pyŏngsin (1st day). The king appointed Ch'oe Sŏnji 崔善之, a fifth-generation descendant of the marquis of prospering writings Ch'oe Ch'iwŏn, as clerk of the Dyeing Office (*toyŏmsŏsa* 都染署史).

---

9. A ritual used in times of enemy invasion. While the esoteric *munduru* was recited, people prayed for the expulsion of enemy forces.

Ŭlmyŏ (20th day). Ten Western Jurchens, led by General Submitting to Virtue Kosu 古守, came with an offering of horses.

Twelfth Month, Winter

Kapcha (1st day). Liao sent its minister of imperial entertainments Ka Yŏng 賈詠 with a letter of congratulations on the king's birthday.

Twenty-Ninth Year of Munjong (1075)

First Month, Spring

Kabo (1st day). The king canceled the New Year Congratulations.
Imin (9th day). The Chancellery director Ch'oe Yusŏn died.
Pyŏngo (13th day). The king appointed Yi Chingmang as superintendent of the Military Affairs Ministry[10] and left vice director of state affairs, Chŏng Yusan as senior governmental advisor and chief editor of national history, and Yu Hŏng as vice commissioner of the Palace Secretariat.

Third Month

Kimi (27th day). The king appointed Chŏng Yusan as junior preceptor to the crown prince and Ch'oe Yugil as advisor to the crown prince.

Fourth Month, Summer

Pyŏngin (5th day). The king sent the vice director of punishments Ch'oe Sŏk 崔奭 (d. 1099) as an envoy to Liao with a letter of congratulations on the Day of Heavenly Peace. Also in the mission were the Palace Administration assistant executive Chŏn Hamjŏng 全咸正 with a letter of congratulations

---

10. *P'an pyŏngbusa* 判兵部事, a position rendered as *P'an pyŏngjosa* 判兵曹事 in the original text, evidently in error because the designation *jo* 曹, meaning "office," as in Military Affairs Office, had not yet been introduced in this period.

on the Day of Peaceful Land (*konnyŏngjŏl* 坤寧節),[11] the Slave Bureau assistant executive Cho Yubu 趙惟阜 with a letter of congratulations on the new year, and palace censor Hŏ Ch'ung 許忠 with an offering of native products.
Pyŏngsul (25th day). Due to the long drought, workers requisitioned for construction work in a number of locations were sent home.

Intercalary Month

Pyŏngsin (5th day). Eighteen Japanese merchants, led by Ōe 大江, came with an offering of their native products.

Fifth Month

Sinyu (1st day). The Astrological Service submitted a memorial to the throne indicating its fear that crops would be damaged by a continued drought from spring through the summer. It proposed praying for rain to the gods of the mountains and rivers. The king approved.
Ŭryu (25th day). Thirty-nine Song merchants, led by Wang Shunman 王舜滿, came with an offering of their native products.

Sixth Month

Imja (22nd day). Twelve Japanese, led by Asamoto Tokitsune 朝元時經, came with an offering of their native products.
Pyŏngjin (26th day). Thirty-five Song merchants, led by Lin Ning, came with an offering of their native products.

Seventh Month, Autumn

Ŭlch'uk (5th day). A messenger from the Military Administration headquarters in the Liao Eastern Capital (*tonggyŏng pyŏngma tobusŏ* 東京兵馬都

---

11. The birthday of the dowager empress in the time of Emperor Tojong 道宗 of Liao.

部署) arrived with notification that a new reign period had begun with the eleventh year of Hamong 咸擁 giving way to the first year of Taegang 大康.

Kyŏngo (10th day). Fifty-nine Japanese merchants came.

Kyeyu (13th day). Based on instructions received from the Liao Military Affairs Ministry (*ch'umilwŏn* 樞密院), the Military Administration headquarters in the Eastern Capital requested that the Koryŏ court resolve the remaining border issues on the east side of the Yalu [Amnok] River.

Kimyo (19th day). The king sent the Palace Secretariat administrator Yu Hong and the right office chief of the State Affairs Department Yi Tanggam 李唐鑑 to survey the border with the Liao envoy, but they returned without reaching agreement.

Kyŏngjin (20th day). The king appointed Yi Chŏng as vice director of the Secretariat with a concurrent assignment as Secretariat-Chancellery joint affairs manager; Chŏng Yusan as director of civil personnel; Kim Yakchin as provisional superintendent of the Finance Commission (*kwŏnp'an samsasa* 權判三司事), director of revenue, senior governmental advisor, and junior guardian of the crown prince; Mun Chŏng as director of punishments and administrator of the Palace Secretariat; Kim Che as director of foreign relations, deputy administrator of the Palace Secretariat, and joint administrator of the Security Council; Ch'oe Yugil as right vice director of state affairs; Yi Chŏnggong as director of rites and advisor to the crown prince; and Hong Tŏksŏng 洪德成 as director of the Imperial Archives, left grand master of remonstrance, and vice director of the Crown Prince's Household Management.

Eighth Month

Kyŏngin (1st day). There was a solar eclipse.

Kabin (25th day). The king appointed No Tan as Hallim academician, Pang Ogye 方吳桂 as director of revenue, and Cho Wiil[12] as acting director of public works.

---

12. Cho Wiil 曹爲一 is possibly Cho Il 曹一, mentioned as having come from the Khitans to submit to Koryŏ in the fourth year of Munjong (1050).

Tenth Month, Winter

Pyŏngsin (8th day). A comet over seven *ch'ŏk* in length was seen around the chariot mansion (*chinsŏng* 軫星) in the southern sky.[13]

Eleventh Month

Ŭrhae (17th day). Liao sent the Ikchu district surveillance commissioner Yayul Po 耶律甫 as a special envoy bearing an imperial edict.

Twelfth Month

Muja (1st day). Liao sent the grand mentor Mudal 武達 with a letter of congratulations on the king's birthday.

Chŏngmi (20th day). The king appointed Yi Chŏng as superintendent of the Northwestern Frontier District Military Commission (*p'an sŏbungmyŏn pyŏngmasa* 判西北面兵馬事); Kim Yakchin as superintendent of the Northeastern Frontier District Military Commission (*p'an tongbungmyŏn pyŏngmasa* 判東北面兵馬事); Ch'oe Yugil as left vice director of state affairs and Kim Yang as right vice director of state affairs; Yu Tŭkso as director of public works and superintendent of the Astrological Service and Astronomical Observation Institute (*p'an sach'ŏn t'aesaguksa* 判司天太史局事); No In as left scholarly counselor-in-ordinary; Kim Yanggam as right scholarly counselor-in-ordinary; Ch'oe Sŏk as director of the Palace Administration and administrator of the Censorate; Sin Su and No Sasang 盧師象 as general censors; Kim Sanggi as left rectifier of omissions and Chin Chamgo as right rectifier of omissions; Yi Chun as left reminder; and Hwang Sap'ae 黃師覇 and Hong Sŏk 洪奭 as general censors.

---

13. The chariot mansion is part of the Corvus constellation.

Thirtieth Year of Munjong (1076)

First Month, Spring

Mujin (11th day). Nineteen Eastern Jurchens, led by General Submitting to Virtue Changhyang 張向, were granted an audience and made an offering of excellent horses.

Kisa (12th day). Chŏ Wŏnbin was appointed the right reminder.

Kapsul (17th day). Ten Eastern Jurchens, led by General Submitting to Virtue Kaero, were granted an audience and made an offering of fine horses.

Second Month

Chŏnghae (1st day). There was a solar eclipse.

Kyŏngsul (24th day). Twenty Eastern Jurchens, led by Kabong 可封, were granted an audience and made an offering of their native products.

Third Month

Imsin (17th day). The king went to Mundŏk Hall to retest the examination candidates. Yi Uk 李昱 and others passed the state examination.

Fourth Month, Summer

Chŏngmi (22nd day). Liao sent the Yŏngju district surveillance commissioner So Yugang 蕭惟康 with an imperial edict reporting the death of the dowager empress.

> Forsaken by Heaven, we inform you that our mother, the dowager empress, has left this world, withdrawing her loving face from our sight forever. On whom may this insignificant person now lean? The grief and yearning that entangle our feelings lie so deep that the sorrow enveloping us can never be eased. As a vassal and bulwark of this imperial house, you too may know a heartfelt grief when you hear this sad news.

Kiyu (24th day). The king donned the white clothes of mourning and proceeded to the palace entrance, followed by his officials. He received the imperial edict there and conducted a mourning ceremony.

The king sent the director of revenue Wang Sŏk 王錫 (d. 1087) and the vice director of punishments Yi Chawi 李子威 to carry his letter of condolence to Liao and to attend the imperial funeral.

Sixth Month

Kihae (15th day). The king received the bodhisattva ordination in the Inner Office.

Eighth Month, Autumn

Chŏnghae (4th day). The king sent the vice director of public works Ch'oe Saryang 崔思諒 (d. 1092) to Song with an expression of gratitude and an offering of native products from Koryŏ.

Kyŏngsul (27th day). The relevant authorities submitted a petition: "The Khitans have erected military outposts near the Chŏngyung Garrison. Please send envoys to ask for their removal." The king approved.

Ninth Month

Kapcha (11th day). The king appointed Yi Chŏnggong as director of military affairs, Mun Hwang 文晃 as vice director of the Censorate, and Yang Huso 梁侯紹 as investigating censor.

Tenth Month, Winter

Kich'uk (6th day). The king appointed Pak Illyang 朴寅亮 (d. 1096) as right deputy recipient of edicts.

Musul (15th day). The relevant authorities submitted a report.

Twenty-five Japanese monks and laymen arrived in Yŏnggwang prefecture 靈光郡[14] and said: "We have made a Buddhist icon to be used for praying for the long life of the king." They wish to carry the statue to the capital and present it to the court.

The king approved.

Eleventh Month

Kyŏngo (18th day). With the onset of the winter solstice, the king issued a decree.

> Starting from today, yang will expand, and all things will come alive. If we leave them alone as they grow, they will fully develop according to their nature. Instructions shall be issued to regions [*chu*], districts, prefectures, and counties to ban fishing and hunting, and to punish those who violate the rule.

Liao sent the minister of imperial entertainments Sŏk Chonghoe 石宗回 to deliver articles that had belonged to the late dowager empress, including a royal dress, silks, and silver vessels. The emperor's edict stated: "As Heaven has not spared us from suffering, our sorrow knows no bounds after the loss of the dowager empress. By her august will, we bestow on you these precious relics."

Twelfth Month

Kyemi (1st day). Liao sent the minister of imperial entertainments Kwak Sŏlli 郭善利 with a letter of congratulations on the king's birthday. This year, the system of government offices was reformed.[15]

---

14. Present-day Yŏnggwanggun, South Chŏlla.
15. The Koryŏ political system achieved a stable configuration with the reforms indicated herein. When scholars discuss the Koryŏ political system, particularly during the early Koryŏ period, they are generally referring to the political system established in the thirtieth year of Munjong.

Thirty-First Year of Munjong (1077)

First Month, Spring

Imja (1st day). The king canceled the New Year Congratulations.

Imsul (10th day). The king appointed Yi Sŏk 李石 as director of public works.

Second Month

Ŭlmi (14th day). Lantern Festival. The king went to Chunggwang Hall and watched music performances.

Imin (21st day). Prince Wang Ki, the duke of Kugwŏn 國原公, was married. The king gave saddled horses, gold vessels, rolls of silk, and other cloth as wedding gifts.

Kyemyo (22nd day). The king held a special convocation of the Lantern Festival in Chunggwang Hall for three days.

Pyŏngo (25th day). Twenty Eastern Jurchens, led by General Embracing Transformation Pangjin 方鎭, were granted an audience and made an offering of excellent horses.

Third Month

Kabin (4th day). The king went to Hŭngwang monastery to hear a reading of the newly compiled *Avataṃsaka-sūtra,* written in gold letters. Sections were skipped.

Ŭlmyo (5th day). The king promoted Wang To, the marquis of Chosŏn 朝鮮侯, and Wang Hŭi, the marquis of Kyerim, to the rank of duke 公. The king also appointed Wang Pi 王伾 (d. 1092) as the marquis of Kŭmgwan 金官侯 and eminent minister of works, and Wang Ŭm 王愔 (d. 1086) as the marquis of Pyŏnhan 卞韓侯 and eminent minister of works.

Sinmi (21st day). The king went to the northwestern sector of Kaegyŏng, where he inspected repairs to the city wall. Then he hosted a reception with libations on the west-facing slope of Irwŏl monastery.

Chŏngch'uk (27th day). The king went to the southeastern sector of the capital and hosted a reception with libations on Manghae mountain 望海山.

Fifth Month, Summer

Imsul (13th day). The king gave Yi Chŏng appointments as high grand preceptor and director of the Chancellery, but he died on the same day.
Kapsul (25th day). To honor the anniversary of his father's death, the king donned white clothing and avoided the main throne hall. He also ordered a suspension of all music performances and prohibited hunting across the country for an entire month.

Sixth Month

Chŏngmi (29th day). To honor the anniversary of the late queen mother's death, the senior state councilors submitted a memorial of comfort to the throne and suspended music performances across the country.

Seventh Month, Autumn

Kiyu (1st day). Twenty-eight people, led by the Song merchant Lin Qing 林慶, came with an offering of their native products.

Eighth Month

Sinmyo (14th day). The king went to the riverside to pray for the rain to stop.

The commissioner of sacrifices in Naju province (*Najudo chegosa* 羅州道祭告使) and vice director of palace revenues Yi Tanggam submitted a petition.

Envoys from Song find it inconvenient to route their travel through the pavilion on Koman island 高巒島,[16] which is far from the waterway. A new pavilion in Chŏnghae county 貞海縣,[17] under the jurisdiction of Hongju, would be a welcome place to receive and send off envoys.

The king approved and named the new site Anhŭng Pavilion 安興亭.

Ninth Month

Sinhae (4th day). Forty-nine people, led by the Song merchant Yang Congsheng, came with an offering of their native products.

Eleventh Month, Winter

Pyŏngjin (9th day). The king appointed Chŏng Yusan as superintendent of the Rites Ministry, Kim Haenggyŏng as superintendent of the Military Affairs Ministry, Mun Chŏng as commissioner of the Western Capital and senior governmental advisor, Ch'oe Yugil as superintendent of the Finance Commission and high minister of works, Kim Che as left scholarly counselor-in-ordinary and administrator of the Palace Secretariat, Kim Yanggam as deputy administrator of the Palace Secretariat, and No In as director of rites.

Ŭlch'uk (18th day). Fifty Eastern Jurchens, led by General Submitting to Virtue Kang Su 康守, were granted an audience and made an offering of fine horses.

Twelfth Month

Chŏngch'uk (1st day). Liao sent the acting grand mentor Yang Sanggil 楊祥吉 with a letter of congratulations on the king's birthday.

The country of T'amna presented an offering of their native products.

---

16. Koman is one of the islands in present-day Poryŏng-gun, South Chungchŏng.
17. Present-day Haemi-myŏn, Sŏsan-gun, South Ch'ungch'ŏng.

Ŭlsa (29th day). The king appointed Kim Yakchin as grand guardian of the crown prince, Mun Chŏng as junior guardian of the crown prince, No Tan as Chancellery attendant, Ch'oe Sŏk as left grand master of remonstrance, O Yŏngp'ae 吳英覇 as miscellaneous affairs investigator, Kim Wihyŏn 金爲鉉 as general censor, Hong Ki as right rectifier of omissions, and Yang Sillin as right reminder.

Thirty-Second Year of Munjong (1078)

Second Month, Spring

Pyŏngjin (11th day). The Lantern Festival was held three days early to avoid overlapping with the Cold Food day.

Fourth Month, Summer

Ŭlsa (2nd day). U Wŏllyŏng 禹元齡 and others passed the state examination.
Kapcha (21st day). In honor of the Song emperor's birthday, the king requested that Buddhist services to pray for long life 祝壽齋 be held at two monasteries, Tongnim 東林 and Taeun.
Sinmi (28th day). Gu Yungong 顧允恭, a Song military instructor (*jiaolianshi* 教練使) from Mingzhou arrived with an official document stating the Song emperor's intention to send an envoy to re-establish formal relations. The king said:

> Could we ever have dared to expect the dispatch of an envoy from the Great [Song] Dynasty? With surprise, I rejoice, and command all officials to do their utmost to avoid mistakes when we receive the imperial envoys. Those who perform their assigned services with diligence and competence will be promoted regardless of the order of precedence. Negligent officials who make mistakes will be dismissed from their office and punished.

Fifth Month

Kyŏngja (27th day). The king sent the director of public works Mun Hwang and the vice director of revenue Ch'oe Sahun 崔思訓 to welcome the Song envoys at Anhŭng Pavilion.

Sixth Month

Kabin (12th day). The Song mission, led by the grand master of remonstrance (*zuo jianyi dafu* 左諫議大夫) An Tao 安燾, who had been designated the state envoy and courier (*guoxinshi* 國信使), and the imperial diarist (*qiju sheren* 起居舍人) Chen Mu 陳睦, arrived at Yesŏng River. The king appointed the director of military affairs No Tan as commissioner of envoy reception (*yŏnbansa* 筵伴使) and bade him welcome the Song envoys at Sŏgyo Pavilion 西郊亭. The king then appointed the Palace Secretariat commissioner and director of punishments Kim Che as a second commissioner of envoy reception and had him wait at Sunch'ŏn guesthouse 順天館. Finally, the Palace Secretariat administrator and director of revenue Kim Yanggam and the vice director of rites Yi Yangsin 李梁臣 were both appointed as commissioners of envoy entertainment (*kwanbansa* 館伴使).

Chŏngmyo (25th day). The king ordered the crown prince to go to Sunch'ŏn guesthouse to escort the envoys to the palace. The envoys dismounted at Ch'anghap gate 閶闔門 and entered the courtyard of Hoegyŏng Hall. Although the king was ill, he came out supported by his courtiers to receive the imperial edict.

> You inherited the throne from your ancestors and have governed the Samhan. You hold righteousness and benevolent rule in the highest esteem. You respect the imperial family and send tribute offerings across the sea to to give voice to your loyal heart. You are more than deserving of our imperial rewards. We hereby dispatch the left grand master of remonstrance An Tao and the imperial diarist Chen Mu as envoys to deliver the imperial gifts specified in the accompanying list. You may accept them when they arrive.

The gifts include: Two sets of royal robes in lacquer boxes decorated with gold and silver leaves, respectively, each set of robes comprising one suit of official dress woven of two-layered plum-colored silk with a floral pattern; one suit of ramie cloth woven of light-colored silk with a floral pattern; one dress of three-layered red-colored silk with a floral pattern; one vest of red-colored silk with a floral pattern; one belt of red-colored silk with a floral pattern; one pair of pants woven of white silk; one pair of leather shoes in a diaphanous red pocket wrapped in a two-layered embroidered red silk cloth; and two belts, each in a diaphanous red pocket wrapped in an embroidered silk cloth inside a silver box plated with gold. One belt is set with sixteen pieces of jade inscribed with ten figures of children playing various games, winding all around; it is decorated with turtle shell and hammered into red leather with a gold sash. The other belt has seventeen ornaments made of clear rhino horn inscribed with ten figures of children playing various games, winding all around; it is decorated with turtle shell and hammered into red leather with a gold sash.

There are four horses. One horse has a bridle adorned with gold and silver embossed with a mandarava flower, and a saddle made of purple embroidered silk, a leather saddle blanket, and a breast collar. The second horse has a bridle adorned with gold and silver embossed with rosettes, and a saddle made of blue embroidered silk, a leather saddle blanket, and a breast collar. The third horse has a bridle adorned with gold and silver embossed with a mandarava flower, a breast collar ornamented with knots, and reins and stirrups woven of red silk. The fourth horse has a bridle decorated with gold and silver embossed with rosette patterns, a breast collar ornamented with knots, and reins and stirrups woven of blue silk.

Two whips are in purple embroidered silk pockets. One is made of turtle shell, and the other is made of blue ivory.

There are 2,000 *nyang* of silver plates engraved with gold floral patterns. There are 10 bowls. There are 10 sets of plates with lids, each set containing 2 plates with lids.

There are 100 *p'il* of colored brocade called *ch'ŏngŭm* (川錦): 5 *p'il* of thinly woven silk with a pattern consisting of different fairies; 5 *p'il* of silk with a pattern consisting of figures playing instruments; 5 *p'il* of silk with a pattern consisting of various flowers; 5 *p'il* of thinly woven silk with a pattern consisting of clouds and geese; 10 *p'il* of thinly woven silk with a pattern consisting of round clouds and geese; 10 *p'il* of thinly woven silk with a pattern consisting of geese, clouds, and land; 10 *p'il* of roughly woven silk with a pattern consisting of four golden birds; 10 *p'il* of roughly woven silk with a pattern consisting of a blue lion; 20 *p'il* of roughly woven silk with a pattern consisting of a yellow lion; and 20 *p'il* of roughly woven silk with a pattern consisting of rolls of beads.

There are 100 *p'il* of colored brocade with floral patterns: 10 *p'il* of vivid yellow silk, 10 *p'il* of topaz-colored silk, 10 *p'il* of light pink silk, 10 *p'il* of dark pink silk, 10 *p'il* of apricot-colored silk, 10 *p'il* of orange silk, 10 *p'il* of light plum-colored silk, 10 *p'il* of dark plum-colored silk, 10 *p'il* of purple silk, and 10 *p'il* of cloud-colored silk.

There are 120 *p'il* of large-sized colored brocade: 10 *p'il* of vivid yellow silk, twenty *p'il* of topaz-colored silk, 10 *p'il* of light pink silk, 10 *p'il* of dark pink silk, 10 *p'il* of peach-colored silk, 10 *p'il* of orange silk, 10 *p'il* of light plum-colored silk, twenty *p'il* of dark plum-colored silk, 10 *p'il* of purple silk, and 10 *p'il* of cloud-colored silk.

There are 200 *p'il* of small-sized colored brocade: 20 *p'il* of vivid yellow silk, 20 *p'il* of topaz-colored silk, 20 *p'il* of light pink silk, 20 *p'il* of dark pink silk, 20 *p'il* of apricot-colored silk, 20 *p'il* of orange silk, 20 *p'il* of light plum-colored silk, 20 *p'il* of dark plum-colored silk, 20 *p'il* of purple silk, and 20 *p'il* of cloud-colored silk.

There are 500 *p'il* of colored silk gauze with floral patterns: 50 *p'il* of vivid yellow silk, 50 *p'il* of topaz-colored silk, 50 *p'il* of light pink silk, 50 *p'il* of dark pink silk, 50 *p'il* of apricot-colored silk, 50 *p'il* of orange silk, 50 *p'il* of light plum-colored silk, 50 *p'il* of dark plum-colored silk, 50 *p'il* of purple silk, and 50 *p'il* of cloud-colored silk.

There are 2,000 *p'il* of white raw silk.

Additional bestowals include the following: 10 *kŭn* of dragon and phoenix tea,[18] each *kŭn* inside a bamboo-shaped box with gold and silver plating. The box is decorated with bright gold and put inside a red lacquered box with a floral pattern, which is wrapped in red silk with a floral pattern. There are 5 *kŭn* of dragon tea and 5 *kŭn* of phoenix tea.

There are 10 bottles of ritual wine made from apricot seed. Each bottle has floral patterns plated with gold and silver. It is decorated with

---

18. Tea molded into balls resembling the shape of dragons or phoenixes, usually reserved for use in diplomatic exchanges.

bright gold and put inside a box with a floral pattern, which is wrapped in red silk with a floral pattern.

There are 10 clappers made with red and blue ivory engraved with gold. Each clapper is ornamented with red blossom–colored knots made into the shape of antlers to which silver bells with gold plating are attached, and is inside a vivid gold-colored pocket placed inside two nested red lacquered boxes with a floral pattern decorated with bright gold. There are 10 large red and yellow pipes. Each pipe is wrapped with silver thread plated with gold, and is inside a vivid gold-colored pocket placed inside two nested red lacquered boxes with a floral pattern decorated with bright gold. There are 10 small red and yellow pipes. Each pipe is wrapped with silver thread plated with gold, and is inside a vivid gold-colored pocket placed inside two nested red lacquered boxes with a floral pattern decorated with bright gold. There are 20 candlesticks, with 10 dragon candlesticks and 10 phoenix candlesticks. Each candlestick is inside a red silk pocket placed inside four nested red lacquered boxes with a floral pattern decorated with bright gold.

Upon receiving the imperial edict, the king spoke to the officials aligned behind him on his left and his right. "How could we have known that the emperor, far from neglecting a small country, would dispatch his envoy to bestow such generous gifts! We are exceedingly honored and appreciative of his beneficence, and I am personally overwhelmed."

The crown prince said that he and the head officials in the Eastern and Western capitals, the military commissioners for the eastern and northern frontiers, the administrators of the eight *moks*, and the four regional military commissioners would plan a countrywide congratulatory ceremony with suitable memorials to celebrate the occasion. The king ordered the crown prince to also host a banquet for the Song envoys in Kŏndŏk Hall.

Kisa (27th day). The king ordered the Palace Secretariat administrator and Civil Personnel director Yu Hong to hold a banquet for the Song envoys in the guesthouse where they were staying to recover from their travel.

Seventh Month, Autumn

Ŭlmi (23rd day). The Song envoy An Tao and the other members of his mission returned to Song. The king sent with them a memorial to the emperor expressing his gratitude and requesting medicine from a physician who could relieve his palsy.

At that time, as diplomatic ties with Song had long been interrupted, the king and people of Koryŏ rejoiced at the arrival of the Song mission led by An Tao. The king therefore showered them with innumerable goods, such as gold, silver, jewels, rice, and other grains in addition to the customary gifts of clothing and saddled horses. There were so many gifts that the envoys could not load them all on the ships designated for their return voyage. When they requested that these acquisitions be exchanged for silver, the king ordered the relevant authorities to grant their request. In reality, the Song envoys An Tao and Chen Mu were grasping misers by nature, so they bartered to reduce the number of side dishes offered to them at daily meals in exchange for silver, which they accumulated in large amounts. The people who dealt with them were critical at the time: "We had not seen any Chinese envoys since the vice minister (*shilang* 侍郎) named Lü Tan 呂端 came as an envoy and returned. When we heard about this visit, we thought we would see models of virtue. No one expected they would behave this way."

This month, the gold pagoda of Hŭngwang monastery was completed. The interior of the pagoda was filled with silver, and the exterior was coated with gold. For it, 427 *kŭn* of silver and 144 *kŭn* of gold were used.

Ninth Month

Kyeyu (1st day). Japan returned eighteen shipwrecked people from T'amna to Koryŏ.

Kabo (22nd day). The Military and War Council submitted a petition.

The fortress of P'alchoŭm Pugok 八助音部曲 was built on a plain near the sea, but its inhabitants cannot live in peace due to the frequent raids by pirates along the eastern seacoast. The walled city should be moved.

The king approved and issued a decree.

Fourteen Jurchens, led by Komasu 高麻秀, came to submit. The king had them settle in the south.

Tenth Month, Winter

Kapchin (3rd day). Twenty-three Eastern Jurchens, led by Marihae 麻里害, were granted an audience with the court. The king gave them government positions and new names.

Eleventh Month

Chŏngyu (27th day). The Ikchu district surveillance commissioner Yayul On 耶律溫 arrived as an edict envoy from Liao.

Twelfth Month

Sinch'uk (1st day). Liao sent the chief minister of imperial regalia Yŏ Saan 呂士安 with a letter of congratulations on the king's birthday.

THIRTY-THIRD YEAR OF MUNJONG (1079)

First Month, Spring

Sinmi (1st day). The king canceled the New Year Congratulations.

Second Month

Kyŏngsul (11th day). The king proceeded to Kŏndŏk Hall, where he summoned all the government officials and made several high-level appointments, including Kim Che as director of civil personnel, senior governmental advisor, and junior guardian of the crown prince.

Kyehae (24th day). A party of Eastern Jurchens, led by Chief Nura 厲羅, were granted an audience and made an offering of excellent horses.

Fourth Month, Summer

Kapchin (6th day). The king awarded the additional title of Prophet (*chigi* 知幾) to the gods of famous mountains and rivers across the country.

Kiyu (11th day). The military commissioner of the Northeastern Frontier District submitted a petition.

> The Jurchen Yaŭpkan 耶邑幹 came from Honghwa guard post 弘化戍 in Chŏngju. He said, "Six Jurchens including my father Arabul, my mother Osoae 吳曬, and my brother Chejuna 齊主那, came to submit in the year *chŏngsa* (1077). I ask to be allowed to live with them."

The king ordered: "Although tribesmen are the same as animals, he is devoted to his parents. Let him move to Yŏngnam 嶺南 and settle with his family."

Seven Western Jurchens, led by Suuna 須于那, were granted an audience with the court. Suuna offered to Koryŏ the letter of appointment he had received from the [Khitan] Northern Dynasty. The relevant authorities memorialized the throne to promote him to the rank of Wŏnbo. The king approved and awarded him gold and silk.

Fifth Month

Mujin (1st day). Northern tribesmen came through P'yŏngno pass 平虜關[19] on a raid. Waiting in the grassland to ambush them were troops led by Sublieutenants Kang Kŭm 康金 and Chongbo 從甫. Two of the enemy vanguard were shot, causing the others to scatter and flee. The military

---

19. Present-day Pyŏngwŏn, Pyŏngwŏn prefecture, South P'yŏngan.

commissioner requested that the troops be rewarded according to their rank. The king approved.

Sixth Month

Chŏngyu (1st day). There was a solar eclipse.

Kyehae (27th day). Twenty Western Jurchens, led by General Submitting to Virtue Koran 高亂, were granted an audience and made an offering of camels.

Seventh Month, Autumn

Sinmi (5th day). A mission of eighty-eight people arrived from Song, including Wang Shunfeng 王舜封, Xing Zao 邢慥, Zhu Daoneng 朱道能, Chen Shen 沈紳, and Shao Huaji 邵化及. The edict they brought from the emperor said:

> Your memorial gave us this account: "Due to the weight of my years, I have suffered a stroke. But my country has few physicians, and the ones we have offer ineffectual medicines and are unable to treat this condition. In supplication, I ask you to consider whether you could extend your imperial grace to a weakened person by procuring effective medicines like those of Shennong, and sending them to me with a worthy physician from the Zhou court to advise on how the medicines should be taken. I entreat you with all sincerity, and await your consent." From this, we have formed an idea about your plight. We know that while you rule a land on our eastern frontier, your heart has always felt at home in China, and since your ancestors sent tribute to our court for generations, we decided to send envoys with our edicts to lend due ceremony to our relations. When they returned, they delivered your memorial, which we found praiseworthy for its loyalty and sincerity. Moreover, after learning how you have suffered from your long illness and have been unable to find adequate medicine and physicians, we could not help but feel endless sympathy after your earnest request.
>
> We have therefore given a special order to send to your country across the sea a delegation of envoys accompanied by fine physicians with herbs collected from far and wide to treat your illness. You will

regain your health soon after they arrive. Indeed, know that there is help from Heaven wherever there is a loyal heart. Hereafter, you must take care of your health at all times to comport with the consideration we have shown you.

We now dispatch our secretarial receptionist (*gemen tongshi sheren* 閤門通事舍人) Wang Shunfeng and the Artisans Institute physician (*hanlin yiguan* 翰林醫官) Xing Zao, along with others, to cure your illness. They are bringing you one hundred different medicines, as specified in the accompanying list. You may accept them when they arrive.

The medicines are as follows: aloeswoods from Qiongzhou 瓊州, elecampanes from Guangzhou, iron powder from Kangningfu 康寧府, cloves from Guangzhou, lead powder from Dongjing 東京, native copper from Yongzhou 邕州, dragon's blood from Guangzhou, orpiment from Jiezhou 階州, tabasheer (*Concretio silicea bambusae*) from Xirong 西戎, plaster from Bingzhou 幷州, gastonia from Yunzhou 鄆州, Parthian fragrance (or bdellium) from Xirong, dendrobium from Shouzhou 壽州, chaff flower (*Achyranthes bidentata*) from Huaizhou 懷州, Jack-in-the-pulpits (*Arisaema heterophyllum*) from Qizhou 齊州, glue from Yunzhou, Sichuan lovage (*Ligusticum striatum*) from Yizhou 益州, nutmeg from Guangzhou, pinellia from Qizhou, thorowax root (*Bupleurum chinense*) from Yinzhou 銀州, broomrapes from Xiazhou 夏州, rhubarb from Shuzhou 蜀州, myrrh from Guangzhou, deer antler glue from Daizhou 代州, licorice from Yuanzhou 原州, gastrodia from Yunzhou, adlay from Zhendingfu 真定府, lindera root from Taizhou 台州, betal palm (*Areca catechu*) from Guangzhou, dwarf lilyturf tuber from Suzhou 蘇州, goji berry (*Lycium barbarum*) from Dingzhou 定州, bitter orange 枳殼 from Shangzhou 商州, Indian gooseberry from Guangzhou, Chinese yam from Beijing 北京, long pepper from Guangzhou, mountain cherry seeds from Dongjing, cinnamon from Liuzhou 柳州, sweet flag (*Acorus calamus*) from Xijing 西京, white turmeric (or zedoary) 蓬莪茂 from Guangzhou, red sage from Caizhou 蔡州, pagoda tree's sap from Xijing, bark of the silk-cotton tree (*Cortex Erythrinae*) from Haizhou 海州, milkwort from Dongjing, Sichuan pepper from Hanzhou 漢州, milk vetch root from Weishengjun 威勝軍, bugbane from Yizhou, siler root from Qizhou, asparagus from Yunzhou, Stephania root from Hanzhou, pubescent angelica root from Yizhou, oven-dried foxglove (*Rehmannia glutinosa*) from Tongzhou 同州, aconite root tubers from Shuzhou, teasel root from Dingzhou, silkworm larva from Chenzhou 陳州, notopterygium root from Yizhou, aconiti root from Shuzhou, sour mountain dates from Chuzhou 滁州, black head (*Aconitum carmichaelli*) from Shuzhou, Cibotium fern from Dingzhou, evodia fruit from Suzhou, aconite rootlet from Shuzhou, patchouli (*Agatache rugosa*) from Guangzhou, Asiatic plantain from Zhendingfu, azalea from Xijing, ephedra from Zhengzhou 鄭州, red peony from Xijing, water plantain (*Alisma*) from Ruzhou 汝州, rubber tree (*Eucommia ulmoides*) from Luzhou 潞州, dried foxglove from Xijing, dried orange peel from Luzhou 廬州, root of the Holy Ghost (*Angelica dahurica*) from Caizhou, inula flower from Xijing, black-end swallow wort from Dezhou 德州, anemarrhena from Zezhou 澤州, jujube (*Ziziphus spinosa*) seed from Bingzhou 幷州, morning glory from Dongjing, pharbitis from Dingzhou, largeleaf gentian root from Jingzhou 涇州, puncturevine caltrop fruit from Dongjing, nothosmyrnium root from Dangzhou 宕州, female ginseng (*Angelica sinensis*) from Shuzhou, roundleaf chastetree (*Vitex rotundifolia*) fruit from Dongjing, dried lacquer tree sap from Yizhou, hog-fennel (*Peucedanum*) root from Luzhou, dodder (*Cuscuta*) seed from Dongjing, arrowroot from Sizhou 泗州, broadleaf evergreen (*Skimmia reevesiana*) from Zezhou, sesame seed from Luzhou, skullcaps (*Scutellaria*) root from Zezhou, garden burnet (*Sanguisorbae*) root from Caizhou, five nunimous fingers (dried excrement of flying squirrels) from Dingzhou, star anise from Xijing, spurge from Dingzhou, Siberian ginseng from Hanzhou, magnolia bark from Zizhou 梓州, Indian madder root from Dingzhou, epimedium from Xijing, matrimony vine (*Lycium chinense*) bark from Dingzhou, knotweed from Xijing, big-flower clematis root from Shangzhou 商州, and skin of peony root from Xijing.

Additional medicines are as follows: fifty *nyang* of ox bezoar, eighty *nyang* of camphor, three hundred *nyang* of cinnabar, and fifty *che* 臍 of musk.

Each of these medicines is in a box engraved with floral patterns with gold and silver plating, the total weight of which is 400 *nyang*. These boxes have each been placed inside a red lacquered box wrapped in silk. Ten bottles of ritual wine made from apricot stone, which is to be used when taking medicine, have been placed in an eleven *ch'ŏk* bottle engraved with floral patterns with gold and silver plating, the weight of which is 1,000 *nyang*. This bottle is in a red lacquered box with floral patterns decorated with bright gold, and wrapped in silk.

Eighth Month

Chŏngsa (22nd day). Twenty-nine Song merchants, led by Lin Qing, came with an offering of their native products.

Ninth Month

Japan returned forty-four Koryŏ merchants, including An Kwang 安光, who had drifted to Japan.

Eleventh Month, Winter

Kisa (5th day). A party of Japanese led by the merchant Fujiwara 藤原 brought thirty wreath-shells and three hundred bundles of seaweed to offer to Hŭngwang monastery for prayers for the long life of the king.
Imsin (8th day). The T'amna manager (*T'amna kudangsa* 耽羅勾當使) Yun Ŭnggyun 尹應均 offered two pearls that shone like stars. They were quickly called the night-illuminating jewels (*yamyŏngju* 夜明珠).
Muin (14th day). The king ordered the crown prince to go to Pŏbwang monastery to hold the Assembly of the Eight Prohibitions. Then he went to watch music performances at the Polo Field.

Twelfth Month

Ŭlmi (1st day). Liao sent the imperial diarist Ma Kojun 馬高俊 with a letter of congratulations on the king's birthday.

THIRTY-FOURTH YEAR OF MUNJONG (1080)

Second Month, Spring

Pyŏngsin (2nd day). The king issued a decree.

The late Chancellery director Wang Ch'ongji and the Palace Secretariat commissioner and director of rites Chŏng Paegŏl were renowned for their peerless loyalty and outstanding abilities. Although they are long dead, how can I forget them? To express my wish to commemorate men of benevolence, I therefore bestow special favor on them by conferring the posthumous titles of High Grand Preceptor and General Secretary of the Royal Secretariat on Wang Ch'ongji; and on Chŏng Paegŏl, the titles of Expanding Literature (*hongmun* 弘文), Broadening Learning (*kwanghak* 廣學), Raising Sincerity, Merit Subject Supporting Edification (*ch'anhwa* 贊化), Kaebu Ŭidong Samsa, High Grand Marshal, Chancellor of the Chancellery, Supreme Pillar of the State, and Marquis of Glorifying Confucianism (*kwangyuhyu* 光儒侯).

Imin (8th day). Venus was visible during the day.

Third Month

Pyŏngin (3rd day). The king invested Prince Wang Su 王燧 with the titles of Eminent Minister of Works, High Director of State Affairs (*su sangsŏryŏng* 守尙書令), and Marquis of Puyŏ 扶餘侯.

Imsin (9th day). The Punishments Ministry submitted a petition: "Revenue Ministry officials arbitrarily gave Hŭngwang monastery lands to Mallyŏng Hall 萬齡殿, for which they should be punished." The king ordered a purge of Revenue Ministry officials and their clerks, exiling them to the countryside.

A party of Eastern Jurchens, led by General Embracing Transformation Yu Sin 劉信, were granted an audience with the court.

The king sent the director of revenue Yu Hong and the vice director of rites Pak Illyang to Song with a letter of gratitude for the medicinal goods and an offering of native products.

Fifth Month, Summer

Chŏngmyo (5th day). Kim Sangje 金尙磾 and others passed the state examination.

Sixth Month

A stone pagoda at Hŭngwang monastery was completed. The king issued an amnesty decree.

Seventh Month, Autumn

Kyehae (2nd day). Yu Hong and others returned from Song with eight imperial edicts. The first edict stated:

> You live in the land to the left of the Liao River, a land east of the sea (*haedong* 海東),[20] which you have governed in peace. Your cultivation of virtue has not violated any of our laws, and your performance of duty is admirably strict. When we read your memorial to the throne, we clearly saw your diligence and the depth of your sincerity. We praise you and send rewards as an expression of our deep favor.

The second edict stated:

> The gifts sent to express our gratitude are as follows: two suits of royal robes, two gold girdles, one gold vessel, a 2,000 *nyang* silver vessel with gold floral patterns, 100 *p'il* of colored silk, 100 *p'il* of colored brocade, 300 *p'il* of raw silk, 300 *p'il* of raw brocade, 40 festive costumes in satin, 20 pieces of satin head gear, one embroidered folding screen, two curtains with dragon drawings, 2,000 folds of large-sized paper, 400 ink sticks, two sets of ritual equipment and weapon with gold and silver plating wrapped in leather, four small bows, 24 *hyoja* arrows, 80 small arrows, two saddles and reins, two fine horses, and six wild horses. Recently, we sent envoys with gifts to repay your loyalty, and you sent tribute offerings and memorials to the throne again. Your courtesy and sincerity are highly praiseworthy.

---

20. Looking south from northeastern China, Koryŏ was to the left of the Liao River and east of the Bohai Sea, corresponding to the northern part of the Yellow Sea.

The third edict stated:

> The peace and order that prevail in your country have protected it, and you have faithfully fulfilled your duty to the throne. Because of this, we see your diligence and the strength of your endeavors, and we wish to present you with gifts to express our deep favor. Keep striving to exhibit your loyalty and your glory will be perpetuated. We send gifts and an imperial letter with your returning envoy Yu Hong, with official clothing and colored silks designated specifically for you.

The fourth edict stated:

> After striving to govern Samhan [Koryŏ] with steadfast virtue and courtesy for many years, you were attacked by illness. When we learned about your malady, we looked for fine physicians like Cang Gong 倉公 and efficacious medicines like the ones described in the writings of Tong Jun 桐君.[21] Now take the medicines that we have sent and use them to cure your body. As time passes, what illness cannot be cured? When we reflect on your suffering, our thoughts fly over the sea to your side, but the news that comes by royal messenger still arrives too slowly. You should only pursue tranquility and harmony, and this will bring you good fortune. Do not forget to cultivate your spirit so that you may live a long life.

The fifth edict stated:

> The tribute you sent is as follows: two sets of gold vessels, two sets of table cups, one set of kettles, ten back cushions woven with red wool, two mattresses made of red wool, 20 long swords, 2,000 *p'il* of mid-sized raw cloth, 1,000 *kŭn* of ginseng, 2,200 *kŭn* of pine nuts, 220 *kŭn* of aromatic oils, two saddles and reins, two fine horses, and one carriage inlaid with mother-of-pearl. You have ruled the country with a virtue cultivated over generations, and you have sent decorous tribute offerings in abundance. Since your envoys arrived just in time, we can send our gifts back with them, including clothes and silver vessels, to show you our special favor. May we both enjoy happiness and wealth in abundance, and many our amity last forever.

---

21. Cang Cong 倉公 was a famous physician during the Han dynasty. Tong Jun 桐君 was a highly reputed pharmacist in the time of the Yellow Emperor.

The sixth edict stated:

> We received the native products that you sent as gifts to the grand dowager empress. Your envoys asked after the health of the grand dowager empress, only to learn that she had already passed away. During this period of mourning, looking at the abundant gifts that were sent with your best wishes makes our grief grow even more. We wish to reward your good faith by showing you special mercy, and we bestow on you fine clothing and silver vessels.

The seventh edict stated:

> We received the native products that you sent as gifts to the dowager empress. Because we have maintained filial ties to the dowager empress even after we ascended the throne, you have sent her gifts from your distant land in the east and addressed a letter to the Changle Palace, where she is staying. The gifts are munificent and their deep intention to serve the imperial court is well founded. It is only natural that we should now demonstrate our benevolence by showing you mercy, and we bestow on you fine clothing and silver vessels through the returning envoys.

The eighth edict stated:

> You sent envoys from afar to present tribute offerings in a decorous manner. During the long voyage across the sea, they met such a violent storm that some fell into peril and their cargo was damaged. These accidents happened because the sailors were unskilled and not because of the carelessness of the envoys. You have long taken the lead in the respect shown to our court by establishing friendly relations with us. When your deep loyalty has already been clearly demonstrated, how can we be concerned about the quantity of the tributes? Heed our words and be guided by what we say.

When Yu Hong and others had set out to sea, their ship was caught in a typhoon and almost capsized. Upon their arrival in Song, they discovered that the tribute they were to deliver had mostly been lost. Taking to heart the emperor's message, the king pardoned them.

Chŏngmyo (6th day). Song sent the medical official Ma Shian.

Ninth Month

Sinyu (2nd day). The state councilor Chŏng Yusan memorialized the throne three times to request permission to retire. The king initially gave him an armchair and walking staff to allow him to continue serving the court, but released him from office after receiving repeated requests.

Pyŏngsul (27th day). The king went to the Western Capital.

Intercalary Month

Kyŏngja (11th day). Satsumashu 薩摩州 in Japan sent envoys with an offering of their native products.

Eleventh Month, Winter

Kich'uk (1st day). There was a solar eclipse.

Kihae (11th day). The king returned from the Western Capital and issued an amnesty decree.

Twelfth Month

Kimi (1st day). Liao sent the Yŏngju district surveillance commissioner Ko Sa 高嗣 with a letter of congratulations on the king's birthday.

The eastern [Jurchen] tribesmen rose in rebellion. The king appointed the Secretariat executive Mun Chŏng as superintendent of the Mobile Headquarters Military Commission (*p'an haengyŏng pyŏngmasa* 判行營兵馬事), the Palace Secretariat deputy administrator Ch'oe Sŏk and the director of military affairs Yŏm Han as military commissioners of the Mobile Headquarters, and the left recipient of edicts Yi Ŭi 李頠 as vice military commissioner of the Mobile Headquarters (*haengyŏng pyŏngma pusa* 行營兵馬副使). They led thirty thousand infantry and cavalry troops into battle, attacking the enemy from all directions, and took 431 heads.

Thirty-Fifth Year of Munjong (1081)

First Month, Spring

Ŭlmi (7th day). The king appointed Yŏm Han as director of the Military Affairs Ministry.

Chŏngyu (9th day). The king appointed Mun Chŏng as earl of Kaeguk in Changyŏn county 長淵縣開國伯, Ch'oe Sŏk as director of civil personnel and senior governmental advisor, Kim Yanggam as superintendent of the Military Affairs Ministry and senior governmental advisor, and Wang Sŏk as director of revenue and administrator of the Civil Personnel Ministry.

Chŏngmi (19th day). The Military Commission administrator of the Northwestern Frontier District (*chi sŏbungmyŏn pyŏngmasa* 知西北面兵馬事) Wang Chŏ 王佇 submitted a petition.

> Nine western [Jurchen] tribesmen, led by Chief Abuhwan 阿夫渙, have put all of their heart and strength into guarding the frontier. It is recommended that they be given titles and rewards.

The king ordered the promotion of three of the tribesmen, including Abuhwan, to the rank of General Soothing Faraway Lands. The other six, including Sandu 山豆, were promoted to General Embracing Transformation, and additional gifts were bestowed to all in accordance with their rank.

Second Month

Sinyu (4th day).[22] Six Western Jurchens, led by Chief Ch'adan 遮亶, were granted an audience and made an offering of weapons and ironclad armor. The king gave them robes and colored silks in accordance with their rank and seniority.

The king issued a decree: "If there are Eastern and Western Jurchen chiefs who wish to be granted an audience, the military commissioner

---

22. The term *sinyusak* 辛酉朔 appears in the original text, referring to the first day of the month. It was actually the fourth day of the second month.

(*pyŏngmasa* 兵馬使) should report to the court and obtain permission before granting entry to the palace. This shall be a permanent rule."

Pyŏngin (9th day). The king appointed Kim Che as grand guardian of the crown prince, Yu Hong and Yi Ŭi as advisors to the crown prince, and Yi Ilchŏng 李日禎 as executive of the Rites Ministry and miscellaneous affairs investigator.

Kapsul (17th day). Thirty Song merchants, led by Lin Qing, came with an offering of their native products.

Pyŏngja (19th day). The king issued a decree.

> Last winter, in the twelfth month, the Northeastern Frontier Circuit was cleared of tribesmen, ending the trouble in that region. This outcome was brought about by the spirits of our royal ancestors acting from above, and the grand strategies of a number of military commanders who worked in concert below. With their return in triumph, we must bring this news to the Imperial Ancestral Shrine and the six tombs. The relevant authorities shall select a date to conduct the ritual.

Third Month

Kabo (7th day). The king went to Changwŏn Pavilion.

Sinch'uk (14th day). The king appointed Kim Yanggam as provisional superintendent of the Palace Secretariat (*kwŏnp'an chungch'uwŏnsasa* 權判中樞院事).

Fourth Month, Summer

Kimi (2nd day). To celebrate the Song emperor's birthday, the king sent ceremonial gifts to the Song envoy Ma Shian's guesthouse, and held a banquet for him there.

Pyŏngja (19th day). The king prayed for rain.

Kyŏngjin (23rd day). The king sent the director of rites Ch'oe Saje 崔思齊 (d. 1091) and the vice director of civil personnel Yi Chawi as envoys to Song bearing gifts of native products and a letter of gratitude for the emperor's dispatch of physicians and precious medicines.

Imo (25th day). The Foreign Relations Office submitted a petition.

A Song man named Yang Zhen 楊震 arrived on a merchant ship claiming that he was an examination candidate (kŏja 擧子) but had not passed despite having taken the state examination repeatedly. Please allow him to return to his country as he wishes.

The king approved.

Fifth Month

Kich'uk (3rd day). Twenty-three Eastern Jurchens, led by Chief Chin Sun 陳順, were granted an audience with the court and made an offering of good horses.

The king issued a decree: "All Jurchens who come for an audience shall stay in the capital for no more than fifteen days and then leave the guesthouse. This shall be the rule hereafter."

Sinmyo (5th day). The king appointed Pak Illyang and O Yŏngsuk 吳英淑 as left recipient of edicts and right recipient of edicts, respectively, and Ch'oe Sahyŏn 崔思玄 as right deputy recipient of edicts.

Musul (12th day). The king sent the commissioner of audience ceremonies and presentations (*hammun injinsa* 閤門引進使) Ko Mongsin 高夢臣 to Liao with a letter of congratulations on the Day of Heavenly Peace. The king also charged the right rectifier of omissions Wi Kang 魏絳 with expressing his gratitude for the gifts he had received on his birthday, the Revenue Ministry executive Ha Ch'ungje 河忠濟 with making a tribute offering of native products, and the audience usher (*hammun chihu* 閤門祗侯) Ch'oe Chuji 崔周砥 with offering the New Year Congratulations.

Seventh Month, Autumn

Chŏngyu (12th day). The king issued a decree: "I fear that this untimely rain might damage the farm crops. The relevant authorities shall choose a day for praying for the rain to stop."

Kihae (14th day). The retired senior governmental advisor Yi Chingmang died. The king awarded him the posthumous title of Rectifying Wisely (*kwangjŏng* 匡靖) and suspended court business for ten days, ordering all the officials to attend his funeral.

Eighth Month

Kimi (5th day). Seventeen Western Jurchens, led by Mandu 漫豆, came to submit with their families. The Foreign Relations Office submitted a petition.

> According to the old law, only men of Song who possess abilities and our own people who had been taken captive by frontier tribesmen and seek to return to their homes shall be allowed entry into the country. As a Hŭksu Jurchen 黑水女眞, Mandu should be sent back under the terms of the old law.

The Rites Ministry director No Tan said:

> Although Mandu and the others belong to the ignorant, they should not be expelled since they have come to this country inspired by admiration for our ways and with a righteous spirit. We should allow them to settle in an administrative district in the south (*sannam* 山南) and add them to our household registers.

The king approved.

Sinyu (7th day). The king issued a decree.

> The palace in the Western Capital is old and dilapidated in many places. Craftsmen should be found to repair it. In addition, select two sites located ten *li* to the east and ten *li* to the west of the Western Capital, and build palaces on them. They shall be used as villas during royal inspection tours.

Mujin (14th day). Sixty-eight Song merchnts, led by Li Yuanji 李元績, were granted an audience and made an offering of their native products.
Kisa (15th day). It hailed, causing damage to the crops.
Imsin (18th day). General Submitting to Virtue Hogan 胡幹, an Eastern Jurchen, was granted an audience and made an offering of horses.

Ninth Month

Chŏngyu (14th day). Leader Ahae 阿亥 of the Northeastern tribesmen sent his son Sŏhae and others of his tribe, and they were granted an audience with the court.

Tenth Month, Winter

Kapcha (11th day). The king went to P'yŏngju for the hot springs.
Kyeyu (20th day). The king returned to the palace.
Pyŏngja (23rd day). The king issued an amnesty decree.

Eleventh Month

Chŏnghae (5th day). The king appointed Yi Chŏnggong as senior governmental advisor and editor of national history.
Imin (20th day). Liao sent the Iju district surveillance commissioner Yayul Tŏgyang 耶律德讓 as a special envoy bearing an imperial edict.
Chŏngmi (25th day). The director of military affairs Yŏm Han submitted a memorial requesting permission to retire. The king issued a decree rejecting his request.

Twelfth Month

Kyech'uk (1st day). Liao sent the minister of imperial entertainments Yang Ihyo 楊移孝 with a letter of congratulations on the king's birthday.
Kyehae (11th day). The Astrological Service administrator Yang Kwan'gong 梁冠公 submitted a petition.

> In response to the royal command, we corrected and now present the calendar for the coming year, *imsul* (1082). There are no outstanding questions except for the Nap Day (*nabil* 臘日).[23] Since the year *kimi*

---

23. *Nabil* was a ritual day for expelling bad spirits, held on the third dog day 戌日 after the winter solstice.

(1079), our court has followed the Song calendar in using the dog day. I, however, have some reservations. The *Book of Yin and Yang* that I read stated, "The dragon day that is closest before or after the Great Cold is marked as the ritual day." Our country has long followed this practice. Furthermore, the old histories state, "The Xia called the day Jiaping 嘉平, the Shang called it Jinxi 清祀, the Zhou called it Dazha 大蜡, and the Han called it La 臘." Their names were different, but all meant an event at the end of the year to offer sacrifices by hunting game and gathering the bounty to give thanks to all the gods. How could this not be important? We should not change the law arbitrarily. Please have the relevant authorities examine and decide, and then implement it.

The king approved.

Mujin (16th day). A lightning bolt struck the Buddha Hall at Yŏnghwa monastery 靈化寺 in Yŏngju 寧州,[24] hitting the earthen figure of the Heavenly King 天王塑像.

Imsin (20th day). The director of public works Hong Tŏngsŏng submitted repeated memorials requesting permission to retire. The king issued a decree rejecting his request.

Kyŏngjin (28th day). The king appointed Yu Hong as commissioner of the Palace Secretariat, Yi Ŭi as left scholarly counselor-in-ordinary and administrator of the Palace Secretariat, No Tan as right vice director of state affairs and Hallim academician recipient of edicts, Ch'oe Saje as right scholarly counselor-in-ordinary, Ch'oe Sahun as administrator of memorials, Im Kae 林槩 (d. 1107) as director of imperial regalia and administrator of the Censorate, Ch'oe Sahyŏn as executive of the Civil Personnel Ministry and miscellaneous affairs investigator, and Yi Chain 李資仁 (d. 1091) as general censor.

---

24. Present-day Anju city, South P'yŏngan.

Thirty-Sixth Year of Munjong (1082)

Second Month, Spring

Kyech'uk (1st day). The king appointed the National Academy chancellor Song Tŏgyŏn 宋德延 as administrator of the Military Commission of the Northwestern Frontier District, and the vice director of imperial regalia Kim Ŭich'ung as vice military commissioner of the Northeastern Frontier District.

Kapcha (12th day). A party of Eastern Jurchens, led by Yoŏgo 裹於古, were granted an audience with the court.

Third Month

Kyŏngja (19th day). The king ordered the relevant authorities to pray for rain to the gods of the mountains and rivers and at the Altar of the Gods of Earth and Grain.

Fourth Month, Summer

Kimyo (28th day). In Hoegyŏng Hall, the king conducted a Daoist Ch'o ritual invoking the North Star and the nine stars.[25]

A man of Hongwŏn county 洪原縣, under the jurisdiction of Naju *mok*, discovered one hundred *nyang* of gold and one hundred fifty *nyang* of silver while excavating the ground. He presented the gold and silver to the king, and the king returned them to the man, calling it a gift from Heaven.

Fifth Month

Kyemi (3rd day). The king ordered the retrial of criminals.

---

25. The nine stars are the sun and moon, the planets Mars, Mercury, Jupiter, Venus, and Saturn, and the Pleiades and Nahu star clusters.

Kyesa (13th day). The king conducted a Daoist Ch'o ritual in Nine Luminaries Hall (*kuyodang* 九曜堂)[26] and prayed for rain.
Kyŏngja (20th day). The king prayed for rain again at Hŭngguk monastery.
Chŏngmi (27th day). There was a heavy rain.

Sixth Month

Sinyu (11th day). The king issued an amnesty decree and gave one-grade promotions to all the officials in the two capitals.
Pyŏngin (16th day). The left vice director of state affairs and high minister of works Kim Tŏkpu died.

Seventh Month, Autumn

Musin (29th day). The lady of Sukkyŏng Palace 崇慶宮主, Lady Yi 李, died.

Eighth Month

Kabin (5th day). The king appointed Yi Chawi as right deputy recipient of edicts, Song Tŏgyŏn as administrator of the Censorate, Ko Kyŏng 高景 as general censor, and Yang Sillin as palace censor.
Muo (9th day). The king went to Mundŏk Hall to decide capital punishment cases. He ordered the Chancellery vice director Mun Chŏng and the left vice director of state affairs Yi Chŏnggong to carefully review them.
Ŭrhae (26th day). A party of Song merchants led by Chen Yi 陳儀 came with an offering of precious treasures.
This month, fourteen Eastern Jurchen bandits, including their leader Chief Changhyang, were exiled to a remote place in the south.

---

26. The Kuyodang was the shrine where Daoist Ch'o rituals were regularly held. The nine luminaries are the nine stars.

Ninth Month

Kyemi (5th day). The king made a tour of the south.

Chŏnghae (9th day). The king stayed in Pongsŏng county. He hosted a banquet to celebrate the Double Nine day and ordered the royal attendants and State Council officials in attendance to compose a piece of rhythmic prose to go with the title "Observing the Double Nine on the Road."

Kyemyo (25th day). The king stayed in Ch'ŏnan district.

Ŭlsa (27th day). The king arrived in Onsu prefecture 溫水郡.[27]

Tenth Month, Winter

Musin (1st day). The king presented to his officials a poem he had written entitled "A Tour of the South: Staying in Ch'ŏnan District in Late Autumn" and had each of them write a poem in response using proper rhyming words. These efforts he was pleased to rank, and the poem by the left scholarly counselor-in-ordinary Yi Ŭi was judged the most outstanding. Praising him, the king gave him a fine horse from the royal stable. He also gave silks to the other officials in accordance with the rank attained by their poems.

Sinhae (4th day). The senior state councilors congratulated the throne on the royal tour of the hot springs.

Kyŏngsin (13th day). The king left the hot springs.

Kyehae (16th day). The king stayed in Ch'ŏnan district.

Eleventh Month

Muin (1st day). At the king's temporary quarters, the crown prince submitted a memorial of congratulations on the first day of the lunar month. The king responded with a special royal decree.

Kapsin (7th day). The king returned to the capital and issued a decree.

---

27. Present-day Asan city, South Ch'ungch'ŏng.

Titles shall be given to the gods of the mountains and rivers that we passed by on this tour. Titles shall also be given, with rewards, to the attending officials, and gifts shall be presented to the petty officials and soldiers in accordance with their rank.

Pyŏngsul (9th day). Tsushima island of Japan sent envoys with an offering of their native products.

Twelfth Month

Chŏngmi (1st day). Liao sent the Yŏngju district surveillance commissioner Yi Kasu 李可遂 with a letter of congratulations on the king's birthday.
Chŏngsa (11th day). The Secretariat executive Kim Yakchin died. The king suspended court business for three days.

Thirty-Seventh Year of Munjong (1083)

First Month, Spring

Chŏngch'uk (1st day). The king canceled the New Year Congratulations.
Chŏnghae (11th day). The king hosted a banquet for the elderly at the Polo Field and bestowed gifts in accordance with their rank.
Muja (12th day). The king appointed Yi Chŏnggong and Ch'oe Sŏk as vice directors of the Secretariat with concurrent assignments as Secretariat-Chancellery joint affairs managers, and Kim Yanggam and Wang Sŏk as left and right vice directors of state affairs, respectively.

Second Month

Chŏngmi (1st day). The king gave stipend certificates to the officials.
Sinmi (25th day). A party of Eastern Jurchens, led by General Submitting to Virtue Yobin 姚彬 and the Yŏngwŏn changgun Pangjin, were granted an audience. They made an offering of horses, and the king gave them official positions and rewards.

Third Month

Chŏngch'uk (2nd day). Ŭm Chŏng 陰鼎 and others passed the state examination.

Kich'uk (14th day). The king ordered the crown prince to receive the Tripitaka sent from Song and place it in Kaeguk monastery with the proper ceremonies.

Sinmyo (16th day). The king went to Kaeguk monastery.

Fourth Month, Summer

Ŭlch'uk (20th day). Prince Wang Ch'im 王忱 died.

Kyeyu (28th day). The king issued a decree.

> The spring and summer months are busy seasons for agriculture. However, when recent frost and hail damaged the crops, I feared that it was owing to falsely charged prisoners. All prisoners shall therefore be given reduced punishments, and public works construction across the country shall cease for now.

Fifth Month

Pyŏngja (1st day). The king was ill.

Kyemyo (28th day). Venus was visible during the day.

Sixth Month

Chŏngmyo (23rd day). The king prayed for rain at the Royal Shrine and the Altar of the Gods of Earth and Grain.

Seventh Month, Autumn

Kyech'uk (10th day). All the officials attended the five-day *Avataṃsaka-sūtra* ritual at Hŭngguk monastery. They prayed for rain and for the wind to calm down.

Sinyu (18th day). Gravely ill, the king issued an imperial edict.

> Some time ago, I received the precious inheritance of our ancestors despite my lack of merit. Now, as I lie in my sick bed, my days dwindle as death draws near, and Heaven can sustain me no longer. The duty of administering the state cannot be left unattended for even a single day, so I pass the throne to Crown Prince Wang Hun and entrust all military and state affairs to his care. To you my officials, I leave the request that you constantly bear in mind my plain will and exert yourselves at all times to fulfill the duties of loyalty and filial devotion.

After these words, he died in Chunggwang Hall. His body was taken to the west side of Sŏndŏk Hall, where it lay in repose.

King Munjong was sixty-five and had reigned for thirty-seven years. The king was bright from childhood and fond of learning, with a talent for shooting arrows in his youth. He was tolerant, broad-minded, and benevolent. He never forgot his decisions. His posthumous title was Benevolent Filiality, and his temple name was Munjong. He was buried on the south-facing hill of Puril monastery. He received the additional posthumous titles of Determined Righteousness (*kangjŏng* 剛正) in the eighteenth year of Injong (1140), and Carrying Brightness (*myŏngdae* 明戴) in the fortieth year of Kojong (1253).

Yi Chehyŏn's evaluation of the king:

> The eighty years of succession from Hyŏnjong through Tŏkchong and Chŏngjong to Munjong were a golden age for Koryŏ because the throne went from father to son and thence from elder brother to younger brother. Munjong, in particular, being diligent and frugal by nature, nurtured his people with milder punishments, held learning in esteem, and promoted wise and talented men while always respecting the elders. He did not place unqualified people in office, nor delegate authority to favorites. He chose not to reward meritless relatives and refrained from pardoning intimates when they were guilty. His personal attendants numbered no more than ten, and with the eunuchs he employed, always chosen from well-qualified candidates, there were only twenty people around him. Consequently, his task became simplified, reducing the number of superfluous offices in the palace, saving expenses, and

allowing the country to become rich. State warehouses were filled with grain, every household thrived, and Munjong's reign was praised as an age of peace and prosperity.

A series of imperial messages came from Song giving generous recognition of his accomplishments, and Liao sent envoys annually to offer congratulations on each of the king's birthdays. Even the Japanese in the east offered rare treasures as tribute from across the sea, and tribesmen in the north, entering the border garrisons in increasing numbers, sought permission to settle in his domain as his subjects. Can it be a surprise that Yim Wan 林完 lauded him as the sage-king of our country? There was only one thing to criticize, and it occurred when the king removed a prefectural office to erect another Buddhist monastery. When its imposing walls grew higher than the city walls of the state capital, the monastery's tallest buildings likewise became more extravagant than a royal palace. With pagodas made from gold, it could be seen that all things were now being done for Buddhism. This was comparable to the unwise actions of Emperor Wu of Liang, yet the king did not know that those who would praise his virtues would lament over this matter.

SUNJONG

Sunjong 順宗, reigned 1083

Sunjong, the Great King of Manifest Grace (sŏnhye 宣惠), was named Hyu 烋 at birth, and this was later changed to Hun 勳. His courtesy name was Ŭigong 義恭. He was the eldest son of King Munjong, and his mother was Lady Yi 李, the dowager empress Inye 仁睿太后. He was born on kiyu (9th day) in the twelfth month of the first year of King Munjong (1047), and was invested as Crown Prince in the second month of the eighth year of Munjong (1054).

On sinyu (18th day) in the seventh month of the thirty-seventh year of Munjong (1083), the king passed away and Sunjong acceded to the throne in accordance with Munjong's regal will.

The king sent the left reminder and drafter of imperial edicts and proclamations O Injun 吳仁俊 to Liao to inform them of King Munjong's death.

Accession Year of Sunjong (1083)

Eighth Month

Kapsin (11th day). The king buried Munjong in Kyŏng Tomb 景陵.
Kyŏngja (27th day). The king went to Sinbong Pavilion and issued an amnesty decree.

Tenth Month, Winter

Kyeyu (1st day). The king held a three-day Buddhist ritual in Hoegyŏng Hall and fed thirty thousand monks.
Kapsin (12th day). The king issued a decree.

> My younger brother Prince Wang Un 王運 (1049–1094) shall be given the titles of High Grand Preceptor and Director of the Secretariat, and an actual fief of one thousand households.

The king had suffered from a chronic disease since his youth, and his illness worsened during his mourning for his late father.
Ŭlmi (23rd day). The king ordered his younger brother Wang Un, the duke of Kugwŏn, to handle all state affairs. The king issued an imperial edict.

> By the will of the last ruler, I inherited the arduous great task of my royal ancestors. However, the thought has been hanging over me that I, unqualified to rule, have presumptuously succeeded to the throne. I had hoped to discuss long-lasting policies with my officials to preserve the achievements of my royal ancestors and to illuminate the royal cause left unfinished by them. However, the overwhelming grief of mourning for my late father aggravated my disease, which worsened as the days went by. In early winter, it became acute, and

now my life flickers like a candle in the wind. How can I escape death? Because of this, I must leave to my successor the great task of conducting our state affairs.

My younger brother Wang Un, the duke of Kugwŏn, director of the Secretariat, and acting grand preceptor, has inherent talent and abilities, and his virtue ripens every day. He understands the toil of farming and has closely studied the consequences of punishing criminals. When he becomes the sovereign, he will fully meet the expectations of all the people. Let him ascend the throne without delay, while I am on my death bed. Ministers shall attend to the affairs of state by memorializing the throne, especially on matters concerning rewards and punishments. Officials charged with local administration shall mourn at their own seat of government and not leave their posts. For the period of mourning, the number of months shall be replaced by days, and the burial shall be kept as frugal as possible.

Life is limited, and we cannot evade causal law from beginning to end. Who is it that will not die? I only regret that my life is short. I leave everything with a few of my trusted attendants, and charge civil and military officials across the country to devote all their energy to upholding my brother with utmost loyalty. May the regal success of our throne endure forever! I leave this kingdom with my mind at ease, and if I close my eyes now, what regret can I have?

That day, the king died in his father's funeral hall. His body was moved to lie in repose in another room in Sŏndŏk Hall.
Sunjong died at the age of thirty-seven. His posthumous title was Manifest Grace, and his temple name was Sunjong. He was buried in the southern part of the capital, and his tomb was named Sŏng 成陵. He was awarded the posthumous titles of Beautiful Brightness (*yŏngmyŏng* 英明) in the eighteenth year of King Injong (1140), and Wise Legality (*chŏnghyŏn* 靖憲) in the fortieth year of King Kojong (1253).
Yi Chehyŏn's evaluation of the king:

> Three years of mourning are the prescribed rite for princes as well as for the people. However, since the time of Duke Wen, the crown prince of Teng, I have never heard of a case where someone wearing mourning clothes made of coarse hemp, eating gruel, and wailing piteously with

a haggard countenance so commanded the admiration of all those who came to pay their respects. At the death of his father, King Munjong, King Sunjong fell into deep grief, became ill, and died within four months. Even though he took it farther than any teaching of the sages, his devotion to his parents could reach no higher.

VOLUME 10

Compiled by Chŏng Inji, Chŏnghŏn grand master, minister of works, director of the Hall of Worthies, deputy director of the Royal Lectures Office and State Records Office, headmaster of the Royal Confucian Academy.

SŎNJONG

Sŏnjong 宣宗 (1083–1094)

Sŏnjong, the Great King of Achieving Peace (*ansŏng* 安成) and Filial Thoughtfulness (*sahyo* 思孝), was named Un 運, and his adult name was Kyech'ŏn 繼天. Originally, his given names were Chŭng 蒸 and Ki 祈. He was the second son of King Munjong and the younger brother of King Sunjong. He was born on *kyŏngja* (10th day) in the ninth month of the third year of Munjong (1049). Intelligent and perceptive from a young age, he grew to be modest, dutiful, and humble with a fund of knowledge that was deep and expansive. He was well read in the classics and histories, and he was a talented writer. He was installed as the Marquis of Kugwŏn 國原侯 in the third month of the tenth year of Munjong (1056) and soon rose to the rank of Director of State Affairs and Duke 公. When his brother Sunjong was crowned king in the seventh month of the thirty-seventh year of Munjong (1083), he received the additional titles of Acting Grand Preceptor and Director of the Secretariat.

Sunjong died on *ŭlmi* (23rd day) in the tenth month of the same year (1083). On *pyŏngsin*, in accordance with the late king's will, Sŏnjong acceded to the throne in Sŏnjŏng Hall wearing the mortarboard crown and royal robes. There he received the blessings and congratulations of his civil and military officials.

Accession Year of Sŏnjong (1083)

Tenth Month

Chŏngyu (25th day). The king held the *Golden Light Sutra* ritual in Kŏndŏk Hall.

Musul (26th day). The king led his officials, dressed in mourning clothes, to Sŏnjŏng Hall to perform the ancestral rites. After the ceremony, the officials walked to the west and entered the palace through the Audience gate to give consolation to the king. Then they went to Chasu Hall 慈壽殿 to console the dowager queen.

Eleventh Month

Kyŏngsin (19th day). King Sunjong was buried at Sŏng Tomb. The king himself presided at the funeral and expressed his great grief.

Chŏngmyo (26th day). The Hallim Academy submitted a petition.

> If any names contain the same characters and sounds as the name of the former king, those names—whether of *chus*, districts, counties, and prefectures across the country, or of monasteries, public or private gates, and guesthouses, or of any persons—should be changed.

The king approved.

Mujin (27th day). The king went to Sinbong Pavilion and declared an amnesty. He also promoted all civil and military officials by one grade. This month, the king sent the general censor Yi Chain to Liao to inform them of Sunjong's death.

Twelfth Month

Imsin (2nd day). The king held the five-day *Avataṃsaka-sūtra* ritual in Kŏndŏk Hall.

Chŏngch'uk (7th day). The king went to a dais in front of Sinbong Pavilion and received the congratulations of his officials. Then he went to Pŏbwang Monastery to hold the Assembly of the Eight Prohibitions, which was held this month because the previous month had been devoted to the royal funeral.[1]

Chŏnghae (17th day). The king presided over state affairs in Kŏndŏk Hall, and went to Sŏnjŏng Hall to receive reports on the moral considerations pertaining to current policies from the Chancellery executive Yi Chŏnggong, the Secretariat executive Kim Yanggam, and his senior governmental advisors Wang Sŏk and Yu Hong.

First Year of Sŏnjong (1084)

First Month, Spring

Sinch'uk (1st day). The king canceled the New Year Congratulations.

Kisa (29th day). Chŏngssang 貞雙, a monk at Poje monastery, submitted a petition:

> Following the model of the literary licentiate examination, monks pursuing learning in the Nine Mountains school 九山門 should be tested once every three years.

The king approved.

---

1. The Assembly of the Eight Prohibitions was normally held in the eleventh month of the year.

Third Month

Kyŏngja (1st day). Twenty Eastern Jurchens, led by General Punnaro 分那老, were granted an audience and made an offering of horses.

Fourth Month, Summer

Liao sent the Ikchu district surveillance commissioner Yayul Sin 耶律信 as a memorial service envoy (*ch'ikchesa* 勅祭使), and the Kwangju district surveillance commissioner (*Kwangju kwannae kwanch'alsa* 廣州管內觀察使) Yayul Ŏn 耶律彥 as a consolation envoy (*wimunsa* 慰問使).

Kapsul (5th day). The imperial edict written for King Munjong's memorial service said:

> King Munjong thoroughly understood the principles of courtesy and had truly mastered and embraced the art of living in equilibrium and harmony. Early blessed with the singular title of king, he found himself presented with a feudal domain to rule called the state. But the benevolent element of wood endowed him with the energy of the east, and he carried out his duties with faithful devotion, offering annual tributes as those duties dictated. He guided the emperor on the path of righteousness and the imperial court relied on his ability to perform feats of merit, with the people receiving the benefits. We regret that just as we sought to join our hands to his in a long reign, Heaven saw fit to take him from our side. The news of his death brought us great sadness, and cries of lamentation took the place of usual court business. Alas! Time does not linger and life is but a short interval, yet the thousand-year cycle did bring us together for fifty years as loyal lord and subject, and his sudden death moves us to utter these words of condolence. We intended to send an envoy to conduct your memorial rites, but your spirit knows this as you have already received our solemn intent.

Chŏngch'uk (8th day). The imperial edict written for King Sunjong's ancestral rites said:

King Sunjong inherited the pure spirit of stars and the energy in great mountains. He was the designated crown prince and used that ability when he became king. At a young age, he received the emperor's decree investing him as future king, and he dutifully learned to protect his land and what to aim for as vassal. He was capable of ruling his people. When he was about to take on the role of vassal, he was suddenly gripped by the death of his father. He inherited the position while we were still discussing his appointment. After our envoys departed for Koryŏ, they learned of his death at a post station and returned. The passing of another benevolent king compounded our shock, disbelief, and sadness. How could so unexpected a tragedy befall a people already in grief? We recall your presence and remember your devotion as we send our envoys to lift their cups at your memorial. Your spirit knows this as you have already received our solemn intent.

Fifth Month

Imsul (24th day). Ko Minik 高旻翼 and others passed the state examination.

Sixth Month

Imo (14th day). The Eastern Jurchens pillaged the farmlands of Mosan ferry 母山津 in Hŭnghae prefecture 興海郡.[2] Troops from the guard post vanquished them and took five captives.
Muja (20th day). The Japanese merchant Nobumichi 信通, from Chikuzenshū 筑前州, offered 250 *kŭn* of mercury.
Ŭlmi (27th day). A prince was born at Yŏnhwa Palace 延和宮.

Autumn, Eight Month

Imsin (5th day). The king issued a decree.

When King Hyŏnjong fled to the south, the Chancellery director Pak Sŏnggŏl escorted the royal procession. His service shall be recorded

---

2. Hŭnghae prefecture 興海郡 is present-day Hŭnghae-ŭp, P'ohang city, North Kyŏngsang province.

along with a certificate of merit (*nokkwŏn* 錄券) recognizing the Merit Subject for Later Unification 三韓後壁上功臣 Yang Kyu.

Kapsin (17th day). Song sent the left grand master of remonstrance Yang Jinglue 楊景略 as their memorial envoy (*jidianshi* 祭奠使), the Foreign Relations commissioner (*libinshi* 禮賓使) Wang Shunfeng as their deputy memorial envoy (*jidian fushi* 祭奠副使), the right grand master of remonstrance (*you jianyi dafu* 右諫議大夫) Qian Xie 錢勰 as their condolence envoy (*diaoweifushi* 弔慰使), and the vice commissioner of the Palace Audience Gate of the West (*sishang gemen fushi* 西上閣門副使) Song Qiu 宋球 as their deputy condolence envoy (*diaowei fushi* 弔慰副使).

Sinmyo (24th day). The Song memorial envoy convened an assembly of monks for the three-day Buddhist rite in Munjong's memorial hall.

Imjin (25th day). The memorial envoy initiated a second memorial rite in Sunjong's memorial hall.

Kyesa (26th day). The Song imperial edict related to King Munjong stated:

> Upon reflection, the king's inheritance of his feudal domain enabled him to become a proficient ruler whose sense of propriety and exceptional courtesy set an example for all his people. He was unwaveringly loyal to this court and had long displayed notable humility in his tribute offerings. He skillfully traversed the vast sea in a small boat, and his vigilance was rewarded with the pliant obedience of the wind and waves. Although countries in all directions have centered on this land of China, when we compare virtue and merit, who is higher than the king? Since we believed that he [Munjong] would live for a long time to guard China, how can we not feel an overwhelming bereavement after his death? We send our envoys to conduct the memorial rite in order to express our true sympathies.

The Song emperor's next edict stated:

> The deaths of father and brother are the greatest sadness known to man. The court extends its grace to you in order to convey its most respectful condolences. As a reverent and dutiful country, it is only right that Koryŏ should receive this honor, and we send our envoys with particular urgency as a means of lending our sympathy in your time of grief.

The Song emperor's letter of condolence stated:

> We have been apprised of the unwarranted tragedies of your father and your older brother's deaths, and wonder how anyone can withstand such suffering. What we have learned is truly painful and pitiable. You must now take the place of your father and older brother. We believe that your filial and fraternal love will fill you with quiet and steadfast comfort, enabling you to fulfill the expectations we have of you. We have sent envoys to convey to you our respectful condolences, along with gifts as specified in the accompanying list. You may accept them when they arrive.

Kabo (27th day). The imperial edict for King Sunjong's memorial rite stated:

> King Sunjong demonstrated great piety and loyalty from a young age. His particular virtue of adjusting his views while remaining steadfast to his beliefs was beautiful to behold. He was respectful in offering tribute and skilled at leading his country into alignment with his people's will. As he was so blessed, his health and success would have assured a pathway to receiving as much glory from the court as he offered in return. By what misfortune did he suddenly fall so ill? We believe that Heaven bestows its blessings and requires repayment like a scale weighing the balance of things. Who could have known the good accomplished in his life would result in such an untimely death? We send our envoys with haste so that they can arrive quickly and pay our humble respects while conveying our sincere sympathies.

The king's birthday was designated the Day of Heavenly Foundation (*ch'ŏnwŏnjŏl* 天元節).

Ninth Month

Kihae (2nd day). The king hosted a banquet for the Song envoys in Hoegyŏng Hall.
Imin (5th day). The king honored the Song envoys with another banquet.
Kapchin (7th day). The king attended a farewell send-off for the Song envoys, and sent memorials with them upon their departure.

Second Year of Sŏnjong (1085)

Second Month, Spring

Chŏngmyo (3rd day). The king held the Śakra Devānām-Indra ritual in Mundŏk Hall.

Sinmi (7th day). The king held the seven-day *Golden Light Sutra* ritual in Kŏndŏk Hall.

Kyeyu (9th day). We were informed by Liao that the era name had changed to Taean 大安. The king ordered the relevant authorities to report this to the Imperial Ancestral Shrine and the six tombs.

Ŭrhae (11th day). The king ordered that the *Humane Kings Sutra* would now be placed at the front of his procession, in accordance with Song custom.

Chŏngch'uk (13th day). The manager of Tsushima island sent envoys with an offering of tangerines.

Chŏnghae (23rd day). The king went to Kwibŏp monastery and fed the monks.

Third Month

Pyŏngsin (3rd day). Because the Cold Food day coincided with the Double Third,[3] the king declared his wish to hold a formal memorial rite in King Munjong's memorial hall. The relevant authorities informed him that the lack of adequate space would make it difficult. The king responded, "Ritual must bend to conditions," and proceeded with a reduced number of attendants.

Musul (5th day). Officials at Mizhou 密州 reported the death of the Song emperor and the accession of the crown prince.

Musin (15th day). The king held the Buddha's Topknot ritual (*pulchŏng toryang* 佛頂道場)[4] in Mundŏk Hall.

Kabin (21st day). The king went to Hŭngwang monastery and fed the monks.

---

3. The Cold Food day was determined by the solar calendar whereas the Double Third, held on the third day of the third month, followed the lunar calendar. Unusually, the two events co-occurred in 1085.

4. A Buddhist ceremony that invoked the power in the Buddha's *uṣṇīṣa* to dispel calamities.

Fourth Month

Kyŏngo (7th day). The king's younger brother, the monk Wang Hu, traveled to Song incognito.

Kim Chun 金晙 and others passed the state examinations.

Muin (15th day). The king went to the Outer Śakra monastery.

Kapsin (21st day). The king personally conducted the Daoist Ch'o ritual at the Polo Field.

Kyŏngin (27th day). Due to the ongoing drought, the king ordered the relevant authorities to lecture on the *Sutra for Rain and Snow* (*Unugyŏng* 雲雨經) in Imhae Hall for seven days. The king also offered prayers for rain to the mountain gods.

Imjin (29th day). The king ordered his royal attendants to conduct a review of criminal cases and release anyone convicted of a minor crime.

Fifth Month

Kabin (22nd day). The king held the seven-day *Golden Light Sutra* ritual in Kŏndŏk Hall to pray for rain.

Sixth Month

Chŏngch'uk (15th day). The king received the bodhisattva ordination in Kŏndŏk Hall.

Seventh Month, Autumn

Imin (10th day). The king hosted a banquet at the Polo Field for men and women who were eighty or older and gave them robes and other gifts in accordance with their rank.

Imja (20th day). On the second anniversary of King Munjong's death, the king went to Hŭngwang monastery to light incense.

Eighth Month

Sinmi (10th day). The king sent the director of revenue Kim Sanggi and the vice director of rites Ch'oe Samun 崔思文 as envoys to Song to express his condolences. The king also sent the director of public works Im Kae and the vice director of military affairs Yi Chain to offer congratulations on the new emperor's accession.

Chŏngch'uk (16th day). The king installed King Munjong's royal portrait in the Imperial Portrait Hall and personally conducted a memorial rite.

Muin (17th day). The king went to Sŏnjŏng Hall to authorize the execution of condemned criminals by the Punishments Ministry. He ordered that only simple foods should be served at his meals and no music played.

Ninth Month

Kiyu (18th day). The king released all those convicted of a minor crime.

Imja (21st day). The king himself conducted a memorial rite in King Sunjong's memorial hall.

Liao sent the vice censor-in-chief Yi Kagŭp 李可及 with a letter of congratulations on the king's birthday. However, the envoy's arrival was late, and people mocked him by saying, "His name is 'Arrive on Time' 可及, but he didn't arrive on time 何不及."

Tenth Month, Winter

Kyeyu (12th day). King Munjong was enshrined in the Imperial Ancestral Shrine.

Ŭrhae (14th day). The king held the three-day Hundred Seat Assembly for the recitation of the *Humane Kings Sutra* in Hoegyŏng Hall and fed thirty thousand monks.

Eleventh Month

Chŏngyu (7th day). King Sunjong was enshrined in the Imperial Ancestral Shrine.

Pyŏngo (16th day). Liao sent the Koju district surveillance commissioner Yayul Sŏng 耶律盛 as an envoy to end royal mourning 落起復使.

Kyech'uk (23rd day). Liao sent a mission led by the military commissioner of the Peacekeeping Army (*pojŏnggun chŏltosa* 保靜軍節度使) So Chang 蕭璋 and the minister of imperial entertainments On Kyo 溫嶠. They invested the king with the titles of Lord Specially Advanced, Acting Grand Preceptor, Director of the Secretariat, and Supreme Pillar of the State and presented him with a fief of ten thousand households and an actual fief of five hundred households. They also presented a number of gifts, including a mortarboard crown 冠冕, a carriage, a ritual jade tablet, a seal, articles of clothing, and patterned silk.

Kimi (29th day). The king received the Liao investiture decree in the southern outskirts of the capital.

Third Year of Sŏnjong (1086)

First Month, Spring

Kimi (30th day). The king bestowed the rank of Matron for Housekeeping to the wife of his father-in-law the vice director of rites Yi Ye 李預 and gave court positions serving the dowager empress to her and others. He also gave them stipends.

Second Month

Kyŏngsin (1st day). The king enshrined the director of the Secretariat and high grand preceptor Ch'oe Ch'ung and the Chancellery director and high grand marshal Kim Wŏnch'ung in the shrine of King Chŏngjong. He enshrined the Chancellery director and high grand marshal Ch'oe Chean and the director of the Secretariat and eminent grand preceptor Yi Chayŏn, the Chancellery director and eminent grand preceptor Wang Ch'ongchi, and the director of the Secretariat and high grand marshal Ch'oe Yusŏn in the shrine of King Munjong.

Pyŏngin (7th day). The king elevated his mother's rank to that of Dowager Empress.[5] The king went to Kŏndŏk Hall and received the congratulations of his officials, local as well as central. He also hosted a banquet for the officials.

The Yugyŏk changgun Kaŏnae 加於乃 from T'angna 乇羅[6] came with others to congratulate the king and present an offering of their native products.

Chŏngmyo (8th day). The lady of Chŏkkyŏng Palace 積慶宮主[7] married the marquis of Puyŏ, Wang Su.[8]

Mujin (9th day). The king went to Sinbong Pavilion and issued a general amnesty.

Kyŏngjin (21st day). The king gave the title of High Grand Guardian to the duke of Chosŏn 朝鮮公, Wang To, and the duke of Kyerim 雞林公, Wang Hŭi; and to the marquis of Sangan 常安侯, Wang Su 王琇, the marquis of Puyŏ, Wang Su 王燧, the marquis of Kŭmgwan, Wang Pi, and the marquis of Pyŏnhan, Wang Ŭm, he gave the title of High Minister of Education; and to the marquis of Chinhan 辰韓侯, Wang Yu, 王愉, the title of High Minister of Works.

---

5. This promotion was given to the dowager queen Lady Yi, King Munjong's first wife, who now became the dowager empress Inye 仁睿太后. In this case, the term *sangch'aek* 上冊 refers to the action of the king, who from a junior position in age was elevating his mother to a higher honorific position.

6. T'angna 乇羅 is present-day Cheju island.

7. The lady of Chŏkkyŏng Palace 積慶宮主 was the daughter of Munjong and the dowager empress Inye.

8. Wang Su was the son of Munjong and the worthy consort In'gyŏng 仁敬賢妃.

Intercalary Month

Kabin (26th day). The king sent the vice director of imperial regalia Ch'oe Sayŏl 崔思說 to Liao with a letter of congratulations on the Day of Heavenly Peace. He also sent the vice director of palace administration Kwak Sang 郭尙 with an offering of native products, and the vice director of revenue Kim Sajin 金士珍 with an expression of gratitude for the congratulations he had received from the emperor on his birthday.

Third Month

Sinyu (4th day). The king changed the posthumous title of the Chancellery director Ch'oe Suk from Benevolent Filiality (*inhyo* 仁孝) to Great Loyalty (*ch'ung' ŭi* 忠懿) to remove the conflict created when the former king [Munjong] received the same posthumous title.
Kimyo (22nd day). The manager of Tsushima island sent envoys with an offering of their native products.
Ŭryu (28th day). The king prayed for rain to the mountain and river gods.

Fourth Month, Summer

Kyesa (6th day). The king prayed again for rain.
Kabo (7th day). The king appointed No Sillyŏl 盧神烈 as director of the Revenue Ministry, Mun Han 文幹 as acting director of the Military Affairs Ministry, and Wang Kungmo 王國髦 (d. 1095) as director of the Imperial Regalia Court.
Sinch'uk (14th day). Due to the long drought, the relevant authorities moved the location of the city markets.
Kyŏngsul (23rd day). The king personally conducted a ritual at the Imperial Ancestral Shrine and awarded additional posthumous titles to all of the former kings and queens beginning with T'aejo.
Kyech'uk (26th day). The king appointed Yi Chŏnggong as director of the Chancellery and superintendent of the Civil Personnel Ministry, Ch'oe Sŏk

and Kim Yanggam as executives of the Chancellery, Yu Hong and Wang Sŏk as executives of the Secretariat, No Tan as left vice director of the State Affairs Department and senior governmental advisor, Ch'oe Saryang as commissioner of the Palace Secretariat, and Mun Hwang as administrator of the Palace Secretariat.

Kabin (27th day). The king conducted the ancestral rites and issued a special amnesty decree.

Fifth Month

Muo (2nd day). The king went to Kŏndŏk Hall to retest the examination candidates. Pak Kyŏngbaek 朴景伯 and others passed the state examination.

Pyŏngja (20th day). The king sent the vice director of rites Ch'oe Hongsa 崔洪嗣 to Liao with an expression of gratitude for granting an end to the period of royal mourning (*nakkibok* 落起復).[9] He also sent the director of foreign relations Yi Chaji 李資智 with New Year Congratulations, and the Palace Secretariat administrator Yi Chawi and State Affairs left office chief Hwang Chonggak 黃宗愨 (d. 1096) with an expression of gratitude for the investiture decree. In addition, the king sent the State Affairs right office chief Han Yŏng 韓瑩 as a memorial envoy with a request that Liao refrain from building their own border market (*kakchang* 榷場)[10] on the Amnok River.

Venus was visible during the day.

Sixth Month

Chŏnghae (1st day). The king went to Pongŭn monastery.
Kyemyo (17th day). The king issued an imperial edict.

---

9. The decree ending the mourning period for a king's predecessor authorized his return to state affairs.
10. *Kakchang* were border markets established by Koryŏ to trade with the Khitans and the Jurchens in Poju 保州 (present-day Ŭiju 義州) and Chŏngju 定州, respectively.

In accordance with the late king's regal will, my humble person was raised to the throne. Recently, misfortunes have been frequent and the drought has become disastrous. My desire to retain the faithful service of our many officials and to live under the Buddha's protection once meant that yin and yang were aligned and people's lives were harmonious. Although I have been dutiful in caring for this balance, and upon self-reflection, have issued several mass pardons, rain has still not fallen, and I fear this is the result of my own shortcomings. I also wonder if my officials too have been remiss, or if I have been unable to recruit outstanding people. I therefore order that all officials of the fifth rank and higher, retired senior officials, and currently inactive officials of the third rank and higher shall each submit a memorial within twenty-six days that frankly assesses my shortcomings, the rights and wrongs of current policies, and the wrongs and difficulties faced by my people. They shall also recommend at least one person possessing loyalty, talent, potential, and virtue. They shall report male and female monks who have demonstrated devoutness, persons who have failed to be properly filial or dutiful, and public officials who have failed to uphold common principles and bent the laws to interfere with the lives of the people.

Seventh Month, Autumn

Pyŏngin (11th day). The king issued an imperial edict.

In reading the memorials submitted by the officials, I found that many chose to mention an absence of regulations prohibiting excessive material extravagance. I therefore order the relevant authorities, the senior state councilors, scholars, and Censorate, to examine the models established by former kings and submit appropriate restrictions regarding our use of official dress and horses.

Muin (23rd day). King Tŏkchong's queen, Lady Kim 金, passed away.

Eighth Month

Pyŏngsul (1st day). The king appointed the director of punishments So T'aebo 邵台輔 (1034–1104) as military commissioner of the Northwestern

Frontier District, and the director of public works Yu Sŏk 柳奭 as military commissioner of the Northeastern Frontier District.

Kyemyo (18th day). The king held a banquet of consolation for the country's elders in the garden inside the Audience gate. He also went to the Polo Field to personally host a banquet for elderly commoners, to whom he distributed gifts. People who were seriously ill or disabled were served their food and wine separately.

Ninth Month

Muo (3rd day). The king issued a summons to the military officers of the capital and the Western Capital requiring them to undergo an archery inspection at the Eastern Pavilion, a process expected to last several months.

Kapcha (9th day). Liao sent the acting director of palace administration (*su chŏnjungkam* 守殿中監) Sa Sunjik 史洵直 with a letter of congratulations on the king's birthday.

Chŏngmyo (12th day). The marquis of Pyŏnhan, Wang Ŭm, died.

Tenth Month, Winter

Kapchin (20th day). The king ordered officials across the country to submit memorials in honor of the dowager empress's birthday. He further requested memorials for the new year, the summer and winter solstices, and the Assembly of the Eight Prohibitions, ordering that this become the ongoing custom.

Kiyu (25th day). The king prayed for snow.

Eleventh Month

Imsul (8th day). The king personally conducted the Daoist Ch'o ritual to pray for snow.

Mujin (14th day). The king went to Pŏbwang monastery to hold the Assembly of the Eight Prohibitions. Then he went to Sinjung monastery.
Kisa (15th day). Snow fell during the Grand Assembly and the clothes of the officials attending the banquet were soaked. When the king returned to the palace that night, the moon shone with special brightness, causing the king to halt his litter at Ch'angdŏk gate 昌德門. He had just ordered the royal family to raise a cup for a toast to the king's long life when the grand masters of remonstrance 諫議 Kim Sanggi and Yi Ch'ain, joined by the rectifier of omissions Wi Kyejŏng 魏繼廷 (d. 1107), said he should not do this, and so the king withdrew his order.

Twelfth Month

Musul (14th day). The king summoned the civil officials of the capital and the Western Capital to the Eastern Pavilion, where he inspected their archery technique.

Fourth Year of Sŏnjong (1087)

First Month, Spring

Kabin (1st day). The king canceled the New Year Congratulations.
Ŭlch'uk (12th day). The king sent the Imperial Archives director Im Ch'anggae 林昌槩 as a memorial envoy to Liao.
Kisa (16th day). The king ordered the relevant authorities to conduct rites at their ancestral shrines and also on the mountains to pray for heavenly assistance in the war.
Kapsul (21st day). The king personally conducted the Daoist Ch'o ritual in Hoegyŏng Hall.
Muin (25th day). Nineteen Eastern Jurchens, led by General Arohan 阿盧漢, were granted an audience and made an offering of their native products.
Kimyo (26th day). The king appointed So T'aebo as director of the Civil Personnel Ministry.

Kyŏngjin (27th day). The king sent the commissioner of audience ceremonies and presentations Kim Hanch'ung 金漢忠 as a special dispatch envoy (*milchinsa* 密進使) to Liao.

Second Month

Kyŏngin (7th day). The king appointed Im Kae as director of the Censorate, Ko Kyŏng as miscellaneous affairs investigator, and Ch'oe Sayŏl as general censor.
Kabo (11th day). The king went to Kaeguk monastery to celebrate the completion of the Tripitaka.
Chŏngyu (14th day). The king went to Pongŭn monastery to hold the Lantern Festival.
  Nineteen Eastern Jurchens, led by General Koep'al 恠八, were granted an audience and made an offering of horses.
Kyemyo (20th day). Venus was visible during the day.

Third Month

Pyŏngjin (4th day). The king went to Kwisan monastery and fed the monks.
Kimi (7th day). The king went to Hŭngwang monastery to celebrate the completion of Taejang Hall 大藏殿.
Sinyu (9th day). Thirteen Western Jurchens, led by Chief Soŭndu, were granted an audience and made an offering of their native products. The king gave them official titles.
Kyehae (11th day). The king appointed Ch'oe Sŏk as provisional superintendent of the Civil Personnel Ministry (*kwŏnp'an sangsŏ ibusa* 權判尚書吏部事).
Imsin (20th day). A group of thirty-two Japanese, led by the merchants Jūgen 重元 and Shinmune 親宗, came with an offering of their native products.
Kapsul (22nd day). A group of twenty people from Song, led by the merchant Xu Jian 徐戩, came with an offering of the newly annotated woodblocks of the *Avataṃsaka-sūtra*.

Pyŏngja (24th day). The king personally conducted the Daoist Ch'o ritual in Mundŏk Hall, praying to the North Star for agreeable winds and rain.
Muin (26th day). The king released all those convicted of minor crimes.
Kyŏngjin (28th day). The king went to Sŏnjŏng Hall to discuss state affairs. The Secretariat executive Yu Hong and the Chancellery executives Ch'oe Sŏk and Kim Yanggam reported on the moral considerations pertaining to current policies.

Fourth Month, Summer

Pyŏlsul (5th day). A group of twenty people from Song, led by the merchant Fu Gao 傅高, came with an offering of their native products.
Muja (7th day). Hearing that the Secretariat executive Wang Sŏk had died, the king suspended court business for three days.
Kyŏngja (19th day). The king went to Kwibŏp monastery to celebrate the completion of the Tripitaka.
Ulsa (24th day). The king held the seven-day *Golden Light Sutra* ritual in Kŏndŏk Hall and prayed for rain.
Musin (27th day). The king prayed for rain at Poje monastery.

Fifth Month

Chŏngsa (6th day). The king again prayed for rain.
Chŏngmyo (16th day). The king donned a white robe to worship at Hyŏn Tomb, where he presented a bamboo book exalting T'aejo Wang Kŏn's posthumous titles.
Mujin (17th day). The king held the *Humane Kings Sutra* recitation in Mundŏk Hall.
Kyŏngo (19th day). The king worshiped at Kyŏng Tomb.[11]
Imsin (21st day). The king worshiped at Ch'ang Tomb, where he presented a bamboo book that said:

---

11. The tomb of King Munjong.

The *Zhouyi* 周易 (*Changes of Zhou*) indicates that the solemnity with which we worship our ancestors is reflected in the majesty of the rites presented to them. The *Book of Classics* states that deceased spirits are most moved by expressions of utmost sincerity. It is fitting, then, for this rite to be offered out of a filial devotion born in genuine reverence. Although I received the throne easily and gladly at a young age, I have learned that the ceremonies of worship must be carried out properly to assuage the fears and worries of the present time. I have assigned services of great import to the officials tasked with such duties and offered ritual entreaties of my own to serve the needs of this land. I now request that you lend your unerring guidance to this humble and deeply respectful heart. I ask that you intercede with Heaven to impel the divine power to grant us good fortune, and that you will consent to guide us through generations of peace to come.

Kapsul (23rd day). The king appointed Ch'oe Sŏk as editor of national history, Kim Yanggam as superintendent of the Revenue Ministry, and Ch'oe Saryang as commissioner of the Western Capital and senior governmental advisor.

Ŭrhae (24th day). The king appointed Kim Haenggyŏng as vice director of the Chancellery with a concurrent assignment as Secretariat-Chancellery joint affairs manager.

Kimyo (28th day). The king personally conducted the Daoist Ch'o ritual in Hoegyŏng Hall and prayed for rain.

Sixth Month

Imo (2nd day). The king went to Pongŭn monastery.

Ŭryu (5th day). The king held the Dispelling Calamities rite in Hoegyŏng Hall for seven days.

Pyŏngsin (16th day). The king went to Pŏbwang monastery.

Sinch'uk (21st day). The king released all those convicted of minor crimes.

Seventh Month, Autumn

Kyech'uk (4th day). The king appointed Mun Hwang as military commissioner of the Northwestern Frontier Circuit and administrator of the Middle Military Command (*chi chunggun pyŏngmasa* 知中軍兵馬事), and Yi Chawi as military commissioner of the Northeastern Frontier District and administrator of the Mobile Headquarters (*chi haengyŏng pyŏngmasa* 知行營兵馬事).

Pyŏngjin (7th day). The king conducted the Daoist Ch'o ritual in the Inner Courtyard.

Kisa (20th day). The king went to Hŭngwang monastery.

Kyŏngo (21st day). The Naval Administration Office of the Southeastern Province (*tongnamdo tobusŏ* 東南道都部署) submitted a report: "A group of forty Japanese, led by Mototaira 元平 from Tsushima island, came with an offering of items including pearls, mercury, swords, and cattle and horses."

Imsin (23rd day). The king went to Sŏnjŏng Hall to discuss state affairs. Ch'oe Sŏk, Kim Yanggam, Yu Hong, and Ch'oe Saryang reported on the moral considerations pertaining to current policies.

Eighth Month

Kyemi (4th day). The king went to Sŏnjŏng Hall to render judgment on capital punishment cases.

Ŭryu (6th day). The king went to Wangnyun monastery.

Kihae (20th day). The king changed the name of Sunggyŏng Palace 崇慶宮 to Ponyŏng Palace 保寧宮, and Kyŏnghŭng Hall 慶興 to Wonhŭi Palace 元禧宮.

Pyŏngo (27th day). The king went to the Western Capital.

Chŏngmi (28th day). The king appointed the Censorate director Im Kae as military commissioner of the Northwestern Frontier Circuit, and the Water Control Court director Yun Iksang 尹翼商 as administrator of the Military Commission of the Northeastern Frontier Circuit (*chi tongbungno pyŏngmasa* 知東北路兵馬事).

Ninth Month

Kyŏngsul (1st day). The king was staying at Hoegyo station 懷蛟驛 when a night fire broke out in the guard barracks.

Sinhae (2nd day). The king hosted a banquet for his royal attendants aboard a floating pavilion 樓船 on the Taedong River.

Kyech'uk (4th day). The king proceeded to Changnak Hall to attend to state affairs.

Muo (9th day). Liao sent the Koju district surveillance commissioner Ko Hye 高惠 with a letter of congratulations on the king's birthday.

Kapcha (15th day). The king appointed Ch'oe Sŏk as eminent grand guardian, Ch'oe Saryang as eminent grand preceptor to the crown prince (*kŏmgyo t'aeja t'aesa* 檢校太子太師), Mun Hwang as eminent grand mentor to the crown prince (*kŏmgyo t'aeja t'aebu* 檢校太子太傅), and Yi Chawi as eminent minister of works.

Kyeyu (24th day). The king went to Hŭngbok monastery.

Pyŏngja (27th day). The king released all those convicted of minor crimes.

Muin (29th day). When the king held the Lantern ritual (*yŏndŭng toryang* 燃燈道場) at Hŭngguk monastery, lanterns were lit along the streets both inside and outside the palace.

Tenth Month, Winter

Kimyo (1st day). The king went to Hŭngguk monastery.

Kyemi (5th day). The king went to Chonghŭng monastery.

Ŭryu (7th day). The king personally conducted the Daoist Ch'o ritual in the Inner Office.

Chŏnghae (9th day). The king went to Kwanp'ung Pavilion 觀風亭 and Kuje Palace 九梯宮 before going to Yŏngmyŏng monastery 永明寺 to light incense. Then he sailed down the Taedong River on the Dragon Ship. It was already night when he returned to the palace.

Imjin (14th day). The king went to Yŏngbong Pavilion 靈鳳樓 and attended a performance by musicians playing on a temporary bridge 浮埃. Then he went to Hŭngguk monastery and held the Assembly of the Eight Prohibitions.

The king sent the vice director of foreign relations Yu Sin 柳伸 (d. 1104) as a memorial envoy to Liao.

Kyesa (15th day). The king held a banquet for the royal family and his royal attendants on a temporary bridge.

Ŭlmi (17th day). The king went to Hŭngbok monastery and Kŭmgang monastery 金剛寺.

Pyŏngsin (18th day). The king went to Hŭngbok monastery and Inwang monastery 仁王寺. He went to Che Pond 梯淵 and held a reception with libations on a floating pavilion. Then he sailed on the Taedong River and viewed an archery exhibition.

The king held the Hundred Seat ritual in Hoegyŏng Hall in the capital and fed thirty thousand monks at the Polo Field.

Musul (20th day). The king hosted a banquet for his officials in Changnak Hall.

Eleventh Month

Ŭlmyo (7th day). The king returned to the palace from the Western Capital.
Pyŏngjin (8th day). The king sent the vice director of imperial regalia Yu Sŏk 庾晳 to Liao with an expression of gratitude for the congratulations he had received from the emperor on his birthday.
Imsul (14th day). The king went to Pŏbwang monastery to hold the Assembly of the Eight Prohibitions.
Kisa (21st day). The king sent the vice director of palace administration Kim Tŏkkyun 金德均 to Liao with an offering of native products.
Sinmi (23rd day). The king appointed Yu Tan 維旦 as administrator of the Western Capital and director of the Military Affairs Ministry's branch office there (*punsa pyŏngbu sangsŏ* 分司兵部尙書), and Hwang Chonggak as deputy resident governor of the Western Capital and director of the Imperial Regalia Court.
Chŏngch'uk (29th day). The right vice director of state affairs Im Hŭiyŏl 任禧悅 died, and the king suspended court business for one day.

Twelfth Month

Kimyo (1st day). The king sent the general censor Ch'oe Sayŏl as a recruitment commissioner (*ch'ulch'usa* 出推使) to Chŏnju 全州, Chinju 晋州, and Naju 羅州 provinces. He also sent the Military Affairs assistant executive Yi Wi 李瑋 (1049–1133) to Kyŏngju 慶州 and Sangju 尙州 provinces, and audience usher Yun Kwan 尹瓘 (d. 1111) to Kwangju 廣州, Ch'ungju 忠州, and Ch'ŏngju 淸州, in the same role.

Kich'uk (11th day). The king sent the vice director of punishments Ch'oe Chŏ 崔壽 to Liao with a letter of congratulations on the Day of Heavenly Peace.

Kyŏngin (12th day). The king appointed Ch'oe Sŏk as superintendent of the Civil Personnel Ministry, chief editor of national history, and high grand marshal; Kim Yanggam as high grand marshal; Yu Hong as high minister of works; Ch'oe Saryang as editor of national history; Mun Hwang as administrator of the Palace Secretariat; Yi Chawi as deputy administrator of the Palace Secretariat; Kim Ch'ung'ŭi 金忠義 as director of the Revenue Ministry; Pak Illyang as Hallim academician recipient of edicts; and Yi Ye as Hallim academician.

Kabo (16th day). The king released all those convicted of minor crimes.

Fifth Year of Sŏnjong (1088)

First Month, Spring

Kiyu (1st day). The king canceled the New Year Congratulations.

Muo (10th day). Liao sent the censor-in-chief Yayul Yŏnsu 耶律延壽 as a special envoy bearing an imperial edict.

Second Month

Kabo (17th day). Liao proposed creating a border market on the Amnok riverbank. The king entrusted the matter to the Palace Secretariat vice commissioner Yi An 李顏 (d. 1091), who was sent to Kwiju 龜州 as a commissioner for incense and the Tripitaka (*changgyŏng sohyangsa* 藏經燒香使) with the secret assignment of discussing the implications of the border market [for purposes of defense].

Third Month

Kiyu (2nd day). The king ordered the Secretariat executive Yu Hong and the right recipient of edicts Ko Kyŏng to conduct the Daoist Ch'o ritual at Chŏnsŏng 氈城.[12] This was done to restore the ceremony that had been held there in the past.

Kapcha (17th day). Kim Pup'il 金富弼 and others passed the state examination.

Mujin (21st day). The king appointed Ch'oe Sache as commissioner of the Palace Secretariat.

Fourth Month, Summer

Pyŏngsin (20th day). Due to the drought, the king gathered all his officials and went to the southern outskirts of the capital to conduct ritual prayers for rain. Blaming himself for any lapses in the performance of the six duties 六事, he inquired, "Have political affairs been unstable? Have the people lost their livelihoods? Has the royal palace been too luxurious? Have the consorts made too many requests? Have there been bribes? Have there been too many sycophants?" He ordered a dance with vocal calls for rain, performed by eight young boys and eight young girls. He avoided the main throne hall, reduced the number of side dishes served at meals, forbade music performances, and sat to conduct state affairs without a roof overhead.

---

12. The altar where sacrifices were offered to Heaven. Its location was in present-day Yŏnan, South Hwanghae.

Imin (26th day). The king prayed for rain at the Imperial Ancestral Shrine and the Altar of the Gods of Earth and Grain, and at sites in the mountains and on riverbanks.

Fifth Month

Sinhae (6th day). The Song officials in Mingzhou returned twenty-three men and women from Naju who had been shipwrecked. Yang Pok 楊福 was among them.

Kimi (14th day). Liao sent the acting right cavalier attendant-in-ordinary Ko Tŏksin 高德信 as a response envoy from the Eastern Capital.

Kyeyu (28th day). The king issued an imperial edict.

> Heaven must be reprimanding me for my dimmed virtue. For three months, there has been no rain, which leaves us fearful and apprehensive. In the jails across the country, have there been incorrect judgments imposed on the imprisoned? Let minor criminals who committed petty offenses be pardoned.

Seventh Month, Autumn

The Song officials in Mingzhou returned ten shipwrecked people from T'amna, including Yonghyŏp 用叶.

Ninth Month

The king sent the vice director of imperial stables (*t'aebok sogyŏng* 太僕少卿) Kim Sŏnsŏk 金先錫 (1033–1104) to Liao with a request that the plan to establish a border market on the Amnok River be rescinded. The king's memorial stated:

> This is the third time I raise this issue even though I fear that some may see my obstinacy as a breach of propriety. However, since the entire country desires me to speak, it is impossible to refrain from addressing it again. In the past, when anonymous letters were submitted to the king, all the people somehow knew what was in them. People appealing

injustice in front of the palace loudly beat their drums, and the king could hear everything. None of it was blocked. So if I now stretch out to reach the ears of the extremely just emperor, how can I not give voice to the plaint of my people in another message?

Bowing in reflection, I recall that when the dowager empress Sŭngch'ŏn 承天皇太后[13] oversaw state affairs as regent, it was she who bestowed this fief to us. Like Emperor Shun 舜,[14] we lifted our shields and danced. Then like Yu 禹 attending court,[15] we held up a piece of jade as a loyal vassal. With compliments on our loyalty and integrity, imperial favor was bestowed to us, with the riverside across from Yodong Fortress forming the western boundary of the land we received, and the eastern boundary extending to Kaesasu 蓋斯水, where Chumong crossed the river.[16]

In the twelfth year of T'onghwa (994), we sent the Chŏngwi Ko Yang 高良 to Liao, and he brought back a letter from Emperor Sŏngjong, which stated: "We send this imperial letter to the king of Koryŏ, Wang Ch'i 王治 [King Sŏngjong]. Examining the proposal brought to us by the resident governor of our Eastern Capital So Sonnyŏng, we see that you wanted to mobilize your laborers in the beginning of the ninth month and ordered that the fortress be demolished. This was completed in the first ten days of the tenth month. You have talent that can only be bestowed by Heaven, and with wisdom suitable for this age, you have mastered your work. You have conveyed to us your sincere joy in serving the great as our vassal, and from afar, you have conducted the proper rituals. At an opportune break in the farming season, you gathered your laborers and sought to protect the land against the bandits from the wide plains. Your initial proposal was to build a fortress in a strategic location, and our

---

13. Sŭngch'ŏn (953–1009) was also known as Dowager Empress Chengtian. Named Xiao Yanyan 蕭燕燕, she was the consort of Emperor Kyŏngjong 景宗 and became regent for her son, Emperor Sŏngjong 聖宗 (972–1031), upon Kyŏngjong's death in 982, effectively ruling the Khitan empire until her death in 1009.

14. Legendary emperor (c. 23rd cent. BCE) acknowledged by Confucius to have been a model of virtue, integrity, and filial piety.

15. Yu was one of the four criminals punished by Emperor Shun. The emperor later appointed him as minister of works and then as prime minister. The meeting alluded to here was a gathering of vassals expressing their gratitude before the emperor.

16. Kaesasu is the area in the far northeast where Chumong crossed the Amnok River on a bridge of turtles, according to legend.

government quickly agreed with your plan so that we were aligned in harmony. Indeed, the Jurchen people had already submitted to us and accepted our reforms, so we know they will not dare to violate this agreement. Quickly complete only the repairs to the fortress and promise to forever pursue peace." With such a kind letter, who could ever forget how you have cherished and cared for us?

At that time, our retainer Sŏ Hŭi had jurisdiction over the border area. The resident governor of the Eastern Capital, So Sonnyŏng, had received your order to consult with us and to ensure that both sides of the border were protected. So they apportioned the fortresses that would be built and began to build them. It was for this reason that Ha Kongjin was sent to the border area and appointed the Amnok River ferry manager (*Amnok kudangsa* 鴨綠勾當使). During the day, his duty was to inspect the east side of the river, and he returned to the fortress at night. We relied on you to patrol the river at that time, and the bandits were gradually eliminated. Since no further defenses were needed, the frontier area became peaceful and quiet. Yet, even though the dowager empress's words had been spoken as if just yesterday and before the ink on Emperor Sŏngjong's letter could dry, your officials, in *kabin* (1014), built a bridge over the river, constructed large boats for transport, and put in a road. In *ŭlmyo* (1015), they crossed the border, built a fortress, and massed their troops. In *ŭlmi* (1055), they built a barricade with arrowslits and a station. In *pyŏngsin* (1056), they gave their permission to have the barricade torn down. The emperor's edict, issued at that time, stated: "The remaining matter is trifling and being addressed according to precedent." In *imin* (1062), a trading station 買賣院 was built to the south of the Ŭiju 義州 and Sŏnju region. When we issued a serious warning, your officials demolished what they had built. In *kabin* year (1074), your officials again tried to build an inspection barracks to the north of Chŏngyung Fortress 定戎城.[17] When we protested, they replied that the construction had occurred a long time ago.

For generations, our country has been diligent and loyal, and we have sent tribute every year. We have dispatched envoys several times with messages about these incidents, but your officials have chosen

---

17. Located in the area near present-day Ŭiju.

not to demolish the inspection barracks, the fortress, and the bridge. Indeed, they are still trying to establish a new market on the river today. By doing so, your officials are ignoring the agreement we made with the previous emperor, and disregarding the wholly sincere objections of the little country [Koryŏ]. Still, even though our envoys have had to traverse several thousand *li* on horses and other vehicles, we have ignored our weariness and offered tribute for ninety years without benefit. Many of our people have lamented, and many have become resentful. It was my fate to inherit the merits of my ancestors and with them, to protect the territory beyond our borders. I can only express the agitation these incidents have caused in this memorial. Beyond it, there is confusion: What small profit or future advantage are your officials seeking to gain? The neighboring countries of Chu 楚 and O 吳 each planted melons on their side of the border, and both sides had enough water for their melons, so there was peace. We are earnestly striving to secure the benefits of a Chu or O. Koryŏ's land is so narrow, however, that it is difficult to turn a sleeve when dancing. I have sent petitions several times, but you apparently did not receive them. I stand ashamed at this impasse under Heaven, and I am embarrassed to speak about it among our people. Bowing in supplication, I ask that you seriously consider the concerns of your neighbor country and reject the errors of the officials who hold responsibility for the border region. If we can simply designate fields for farming and dig wells to water them without fear of attack, we will be satisfied with the work we have always done. You must forbid the establishment of the border market and the construction of new buildings, barracks, and fortifications on our side of the border. If you end these disturbances, I will do my utmost to repay your kindness.

Tenth Month, Winter

Chŏngch'uk (5th day). Liao sent the vice minister of imperial sacrifices (*t'aesang sogyŏng* 太常少卿) Chŏng Sŏk 鄭碩 with a letter of congratulations on the king's birthday.

Eleventh Month

Kyehae (21st day). The king gave the name Wang Uk 王昱 (1084–1097) to his eldest son, the prince of Yŏnhwa Palace,[18] along with silverware, rolls of silk and other cloths, grain, a horse saddle and bridle, and slaves.

The king hosted a banquet for the dowager empress at Such'un Palace, attended by the duke of Chosŏn, the duke of Kyerim 鷄林公, and the duke of Sangan 常安公, and by the marquis of Puyŏ 扶餘候 and the marquis of Kŭmgwan 金官候. The banquet did not end until morning.

Imsin (30th day). Kim Sŏnsŏk returned from Liao with an imperial edict.

> You have submitted messages several times to request a halt to the border markets. Upon examination, this is a small matter so how can there be a need to speak in such troubled tones about it? Soon, when it is convenient, we will consult with you further. There has been no decision yet to establish a border market. We are doing everything we can, so be at ease. Let go of your doubts and see our unfathomable will.

Twelfth Month

Kyŏngja (28th day). The king appointed Yi An as director of punishments and senior governmental advisor, and Yi Chain as director of palace administration and vice commissioner of the Palace Secretariat.

This year, a Liao envoy arrived with two thousand sheep, twenty-three chariots, and three horses.

Sixth Year of Sŏnjong (1089)

First Month, Spring

Imsin (1st day). The king canceled the New Year Congratulations.

---

18. Wang Uk became King Hŏnjong in 1094 and reigned for just one year.

Ŭrhae (4th day). The king appropriated grain from the Sinhŭng storehouse 新興倉 for donation to a number of temples in Kaegyŏng where ritual prayers for good fortune were held.

Musul (27th day). The king held the Dispelling Calamities rite in Hoegyŏng Hall for five days.

Second Month

Sinyu (20th day). The king personally offered ritual prayers for good fortune at the Polo Field. He prayed to Heaven and earth, and to the mountain and river gods.

Third Month

Kyŏngin (19th day). The king held the Śūraṃgama-sūtra ritual (nŭngŏm toryang 楞嚴道場)[19] in Kŏndŏk Hall for seven days.

Fourth Month, Summer

Sinch'uk (1st day). There was frost.

Sixth Month

Sinch'uk (2nd day). The king prayed for rain at the Imperial Ancestral Shrine and the seven royal tombs 七陵.

Kyŏngsin (21st day). The king appointed Ch'oe Sache as senior governmental advisor, Pak Illyang as deputy administrator of the Palace Secretariat, Sŏ Chŏng as commissioner of the State Finance Commission, and Kim Sanggi as right scholarly counselor-in-ordinary.

---

19. A recitation of the sutra to repel evil spirits.

Eighth Month, Autumn

Kapchin (7th day). Forty Eastern Jurchens, led by General Submitting to Virtue Sŏhae 西害, were granted an audience and made an offering of horses.

Kyŏngsul (13th day). The Song officials in Mingzhou returned twenty-four shipwrecked survivors, including Yi Kŭnbo 李勤甫.

Kyech'uk (16th day). Repairs to the National Academy were commenced on this day. The king inspected the honor guard and led the procession carrying the tablet of Confucius 文宣王 to the Sunch'ŏn guesthouse for temporary enshrinement.

Pyŏngjin (19th day). The king rendered judgment on capital punishment cases.

Japanese merchants from the Dazaifu 大宰府[20] were granted an audience and made an offering of mercury, pearls, bows and arrows, and swords and knives.

Ninth Month

Ŭrhae (8th day). Liao sent the Yŏngju district surveillance commissioner Yang In 楊璘 with a letter of congratulations on the king's birthday.

Chŏngch'uk (10th day). The king held a banquet for the Liao envoys in Kŏndŏk Hall to celebrate the Day of Heavenly Foundation. He had written the words for a melodic toast to the Khitan dynasty (*ha sŏngchosa* 賀聖朝詞).

> As the cold dew descends, the wind is fierce and the autumn moon is bright. At close to midnight in P'ihyang Hall 披香殿, everything is luminous, and the sound of this song somewhat noisy. If life is a dream, why chase after honor and wealth? Is it not better to sip good wine from a gold cup filled to the brim and share a joyous moment?

---

20. The regional government in Kyushu from the eighth to the twelfth centuries; its name was also written as 太宰府.

Tenth Month, Winter

Kihae (3rd day). Forty people from Song, led by the merchant Yang Zhu 楊註, came with an offering of their native products.

Kiyu (13th day). Fifty-nine people from Song, led by the merchant Xu Cheng 徐成, came with an offering of their native products.

Sinhae (15th day). The king held the three-day recitation of the *Humane Kings Sutra* in Hoegyŏng Hall and fed thirty thousand Buddhist monks.

Muo (22nd day). The king ordered the casting of a thirteen-story golden pagoda for enshrinement in Hoegyŏng Hall, for which he held a dedication ceremony (*kyŏngch'anhoe* 慶讚會).[21]

One hundred twenty-seven people from Song, led by the merchants Li Zhu 李珠, Yang Fu 楊甫, and Yang Jun 楊俊, came with an offering of their native products.

Sinyu (25th day). The dowager empress inaugurated the construction of Kukch'ŏng monastery 國清寺.

Eleventh Month

Chŏngmyo (1st day). There was a solar eclipse.

Twenty-one Eastern Jurchens, led by Chief Kosa, were granted an audience and made an offering of horses.

Twelfth Month

When the new residence of the high minister of works Yu Hong was completed, the king issued an edict bestowing silverware and rolls of silk and ordered the director of imperial stables Yi Chaŭi 李資義 (d. 1095) to provide a saddled horse.

---

21. A Buddhist rite to dedicate a statue, icon, or temple hall.

Seventh Year of Sŏnjong (1090)

First Month, Spring

Chŏngmyo (1st day). The king canceled the New Year Congratulations.
Kich'uk (23rd day). Based on a report from the manager of T'angna, the Foreign Relations Office submitted its own report.

> The ruler of T'angna, the Yugyŏk changgun Kayanging 加良仍, has died. His younger brother [from the same mother] the Paeyung buwi 陪戎副尉[22] Ko Pongnyŏng 高福令 has succeeded him. Following precedent, we should provide the condolence gifts on the accompanying list, and it is appropriate to send them now.

The king approved.
Imjin (26th day). The Hall of Water and Land (*suryuktang* 水陸堂) at Poje monastery was destroyed by fire. Earlier, the Astrological Service administrator Ch'oe Sagyŏm 崔士謙, who was also a Revenue Ministry acting executive (*sŏ hobu nangjung* 攝戶部郎中) and one of the king's favorite officials, had gone to Song to obtain a ritual manual for water and land (*suryuk ŭimun* 水陸儀文) ceremonies. When he returned, he asked the king to build the Hall of Water and Land, but the hall burned down before construction could be completed.

Second Month

Kabin (19th day). Seventeen Eastern Jurchens, led by Commandant Yasa 也沙, were granted an audience and made an offering of horses. The king gave them gifts in accordance with their rank.
Pyŏngjin (21st day). The king appointed Yu Hong as superintendent of military affairs and executive of the Chancellery, Ch'oe Sache as vice director of the Secretariat with a concurrent assignment as Secretariat-Chancellery joint affairs manager, and Yi Chawi as right vice director

---

22. A rank 6b2 title for military officials.

of state affairs, editor of national history, and senior governmental advisor.

Kimi (24th day). Twenty-two Eastern Jurchens, led by Commandant Yoŏnae 裊於乃, were granted an audience and made an offering of horses.

Imsul (27th day). Thirty-four Eastern Jurchens, led by Toktal 禿達, were granted an audience with the court.

Third Month

Kimi (4th day). One hundred fifty merchants from Song, led by Xu Cheng, came with an offering of their native products.

Muja (23rd day). There was thunder and lightning during the night, causing a fire at Sinhŭng storehouse and the halting of required labor at Hŭngwŏn monastery 弘圓寺 and Kukch'ŏng monastery.

Fifth Month, Summer

Pyŏngin (2nd day). The king went to Kŏndŏk Hall to retest the candidates. Yi Kyŏngp'il 李景泌 and others passed the examination. On this occasion, Yi Kyŏngp'il's essay (*chŏngmun* 程文) did not match the proper form, so the authorities involved were criticized.

Sixth Month

Kyŏngja (7th day). The Censorate submitted a petition.

> U Yŏyu 禹汝維, the chief registrar of the Yŏngwŏn Garrison Military Commission (*Yŏngwŏn pyŏngma noksa* 寧遠兵馬錄事), plundered the people in the frontier region, accepted bribes, and created disorder. We request that this case be referred to a Punishments Ministry official (*chŏngwi* 廷尉)[23] for judgment.

---

23. The meaning of *chŏngwi* as a government official responsible for punishments dates to the Han period.

The king approved.

Kapchin (11th day). The king issued a decree.

> There have been several calamities, and the rainy season has passed without rain. Across the country, those sentenced to penal servitude or less for public malfeasance and flogging or less for private malfeasance shall be released. Officials dismissed from office for breaking the law, if found to have received an unfair judgment, shall have their previous position restored.

Seventh Month, Autumn

Kyemi (20th day). The king sent the director of revenue Yi Chaŭi and the vice director of rites Wi Kyejŏng 魏繼廷 as envoys carrying an expression of gratitude and official documents to submit to Song.

Ninth Month

Sinmi (10th day). Liao sent thirty-one officials, led by the Iju district surveillance commissioner Chang Sasŏl 張師說, with a letter of congratulations on the king's birthday.

Kyŏngjin (19th day). The king again held a banquet for the Liao envoys in Kŏndŏk Hall. On this occasion, the three envoys were invited to enter the hall and sit. The relevant authorities remonstrated: "Holding two banquets for the envoys is an event that has not occurred in the past. Having three envoys come into the hall and sit down has never been heard of until now." The king did not accept the remonstrance and said, "The envoys came with a stele inscription from Tianqing monastery 天慶寺 that was personally written by the emperor. Giving it particularly respectful treatment is entirely appropriate."

Muja (27th day). Fifteen Eastern Jurchens, led by General Embracing Transformation Aŏdae 阿於大, were granted an audience and made an offering of horses.

Tenth Month, Winter

Pyŏngo (15th day). The king escorted the dowager empress on a visit to Mount Samgak.

Kyŏngsul (19th day). The king went to Sŭngga Grotto 僧伽窟. He then went to Changŭi monastery 藏義寺.

Kyech'uk (22nd day). The king went to Insu monastery 仁壽寺 and burned incense.

Kabin (23rd day). As the king's procession proceeded along a mountain road, commoners came out to watch. An elderly person aged one hundred as well as three aged eighty or more were granted an audience by the side of the road. The king inquired about their health and gave gifts to each of them.

Muo (27th day). The king went to Sinhyŏl monastery and held the Five Hundred Arhats rite.

Eleventh Month

Sinyu (1st day). The king returned from Mount Samgak and declared an amnesty.

Twelfth Month

Imjin (2nd day). The king prayed for snow to fall.

Kyŏngja (10th day). The king again prayed for snow to fall at a number of shrines 神廟.

Imin (12th day). The king again prayed for snow to fall.

Liao sent the Ikchu district surveillance commissioner Yayul Ich'ing 耶律利稱 as a special envoy bearing an imperial edict.

Song sent a copy of the *Heroic Flowers from a Literary Garden* (*Wenyuan Yinghua* 文苑英華集).[24]

---

24. A large text known as one of the four great books of Song. It was compiled from 982 to 987.

Eighth Year of Sŏnjong (1091)

First Month, Spring

Chŏngmyo (7th day). The king hosted a banquet for a number of officials in Kŏndŏk Hall and gave a horse from the Inner Stables to each of them.

Second Month

Kyech'uk (24th day). Liao sent Choyayŏ 鳥耶呂 as its deputy protocol envoy (*yebin pusa* 禮賓副使) and gratitude response and message envoy from the Eastern Capital (*tonggyŏng chirye hoesasa* 東京持禮回謝使).

Third Month

Pyŏngja (17th day). Forty Eastern Jurchens, led by General Comforting the Frontier Kaedahan, were granted an audience and made an offering of camels and horses.

Fourth Month, Summer

Chŏngmi (18th day). The vice commissioner of the Palace Secretariat Yi Chain died.
Kyech'uk (24th day). The Chancellery executive Chŏng Yusan died. His posthumous name was Loyalty (*chŏngsun* 貞順).

Fifth Month

Kimi (1st day). There was a solar eclipse. Venus was visible during the day and moved across the sky for seventy days.
Ŭlch'uk (7th day). The king prayed for rain at the Altar of the Gods of Earth and Grain. Then he went to Hŭngwang monastery.
Chŏngmyo (9th day). The king prayed for rain at the Imperial Ancestral Shrine and the seven royal tombs.

Sixth Month

Kabo (6th day). The king again prayed for rain at the Altar of the Gods of Earth and Grain.

Chŏngyu (9th day). The king again prayed for rain at the Imperial Ancestral Shrine and at the seven royal tombs.

Kapchin (16th day). The Military and War Temporary Council submitted a petition.

> Last year, when tribesmen invaded Ch'angju 昌州,[25] the chief registrar of the Military Commission An Sŏnjun 安先俊 led his troops on an expedition and camped at the Tŏngyŏng guard post 德寧戍. From there he sent out a detachment under Lieutenant Colonel Ko Maeng 高猛 to pursue and capture the enemy, who were eventually annihilated. At one point, Lieutenant Sunggŏm 崇儉, Sublieutenant Pyŏnhak 邊鶴, and a few others were surrounded by the enemy, but they fought their way out by making a charge, boosting the spirit of all the soldiers. As they have gained much merit by capturing and killing the enemy, please give them official positions and other rewards to encourage them in their future actions.

The king approved.

Pyŏngo (18th day). Yi Chaŭi and others returned from Song and submitted a report.

> The emperor has heard that our country possesses many excellent books. He ordered the commissioner of envoy entertainment to obtain the books, and they wrote a list of the books they wish to have. They gave us the list and said, "Here is what we want. Don't worry if you don't have them all. Copy what you have and send us the copies."
>
> *Baipian Shangshu* 百篇尚書
> *Xunshuang Zhouyi* 荀爽周易, 10 volumes
> Jing Fang's *Commentary on Changes* (Jing Fang Yi 京房易), 10 volumes
> Zheng Kangcheng's *Zhouyi* 鄭康成周易, 9 volumes
> Lu Jizhu's *Zhouyi* 陸績注周易, 14 volumes
> Yu Fanzhu *Zhouyi* 虞翻注周易, 9 volumes

---

25. Present-day Ch'angsŏng-gun, North P'yŏngan.

Records of the Han from the Eastern Library (*Dongguan Hanji* 東觀漢記),[26] 127 volumes

Xie Cheng's *History of the Later Han* (Xie Cheng *Houhanshu* 謝承後漢書), 130 volumes

Han Book of Songs (*Hanshi* 韓詩),[27] 22 volumes

Yezun Maoshi 業遵毛詩, 20 volumes

Lü Chen's *Forest of Characters* (Lü Chen *Zilin* 呂忱字林), 7 volumes

Gu Yupian 古玉篇, 30 volumes

Comprehensive Geography (*Guadizhi* 括地志),[28] 500 volumes

Geographical Records (*Yudizhi* 輿地志),[29] 30 volumes

New Arrangements (*Xinxu* 新序), 3 volumes

Garden of Stories (*Shuoyuan* 說苑), 20 volumes

Liu Xiang's *Seven Records* (Liu Xiang *Qilu* 劉向七錄), 20 volumes

Liu Xin's *Seven Epitomes* (Liu Xin *Qilue* 劉歆七略), 7 volumes

Wang Fangqing yuanting Caomushu 王方慶園亭草木䟽, 27 volumes

Ancient and Modern Records of Proven Formulas (*Gujinlu Yanfang* 古今錄驗方), 50 volumes

Zhang Zhongjing's *Formulas* (Zhang Zhongjing *Fang* 張仲景方), 15 volumes

Yuanbai Changheshi 元白唱和詩

Shenshifang Huangdi Zhenjing 深師方黃帝鍼經, 9 volumes

Jiuxujing 九墟經, 9 volumes

Selections from Classic Formulas (*Xiaopinfang* 小品方), 12 volumes

Taoyinju Xiaoyanfang 陶隱居效驗方, 6 volumes

Shizi 尸子, 20 volumes

Huainanzi 淮南子, 21 volumes

Gongsun Luo's *Selections of Refined Literature* (Gongsun Luo *Wenxuan* 公孫羅文選)

Shuijing 水經, 40 volumes

Yang Hu Laozi 羊祐老子, 2 volumes

Luoshi Laozi 羅什老子, 2 volumes

---

26. This was an official history of the Eastern Han dynasty written in annals-biography style, begun under Emperor Ming (r. 58–76).

27. Abbreviated title of the *Hanshi Waizhuan* 韓詩外傳, transmitted by Han Ying 韓嬰, an early Han scholar from the state of Yan 燕.

28. Written by Li Tai 李泰 and others in 642.

29. Compiled from various sources by Gu Yewang 顧野王 (518–581).

Zhong Hui Laozi 鍾會老子, 2 volumes

Ruan Xiaoxu Qilu 阮孝緒七錄

Sun Sheng's *Chronicle of Jinyang* (Sun Sheng *Jinyangqiu* 孫盛晉陽秋),[30] 33 volumes

Sun Sheng's *Weishi Chunqiu* 孫盛魏氏春秋, 20 volumes

Gan Bao's *Jinji* 干寶晉記, 22 volumes

Spring and Autumn Annals of the Sixteen Kingdoms (*Shiliuguo Chunqiu* 十六國春秋),[31] 102 volumes

Wei Dan's *Houweishu* 魏澹後魏書, 100 volumes

Yu Huan's *Weilue* 魚豢魏略

Liu Fan's *Book of Liang* (Liu Fan *Liangdian* 劉璠梁典), 30 volumes

Wu Junqi's *Chunqiu* 吳均齊春秋, 30 volumes

Yuan Xingchong's *Book of Wei* (Yuan Xingchong *Weidian* 元行冲魏典), 60 volumes

Chen Sun's *Qiji* 沈孫齊紀, 20 volumes

Yang Xiongji 楊雄集, 5 volumes

Ban Guji 班固集, 14 volumes

Cui Yinji 崔駰集, 10 volumes

Annals from the Tomb in the Ji District (*Jizhong Jinian* 汲冢紀年),[32] 14 volumes

Xie Lingyunji 謝靈運集, 20 volumes

Yan Yannianji 顏延年集, 41 volumes

Essence of the Pearls from the Three Religions (*Sanjiao Zhuying* 三教珠英), 1,000 volumes

Kong Huan's *Garden of Literature* (Kong Huan *Wenyuan* 孔逭文苑), 100 volumes

Leiwen 類文, 370 volumes

Lodge of Literature and Forest of Lyrics (*Wenguan Cilin* 文館詞林), 1,000 volumes

Zhu Changtong's *Unrestrained Assertions* (Zhong Changtong *Changyan* 仲長統昌言)

---

30. A history of the Jin 晉 dynasty written by Sun Sheng (302–373) in the Eastern Jin period (317–419).

31. A history of the sixteen states that existed in North China during the Eastern Jin period, written by Cui Hong 崔鴻 in the sixth century.

32. Part of the *Documents from the Tomb in the Ji District* (*Jizhongshu* 汲冢書); the documents were ancient bamboo texts found in the tomb of King Xiang of Wei 魏襄王 (r. 318–296 BCE).

Du Shu's *Discourses on the Body* (Du Shu tilun 杜恕體論)
Zhuge Liangji 諸葛亮集, 24 volumes
Wang Xizhi's *Xiaoxuepian* 王羲之小學篇
Zhou Chu Fengtuji 周處風土紀
Zhang Yi's *Guangya* 張揖廣雅, 4 volumes
Guanxianzhi 管絃志, 4 volumes
Wang Xiangzhuan's *Yinyuezhi* 王詳撰音樂志
Cai Yong's *Yueling zhangju* 蔡邕月令章句, 12 volumes
Xin Dufang zhuan *Yueshu* 信都芳撰樂書, 9 volumes
Gujin yuelu 古今樂錄, 13 volumes
Gong Yang's *Moshou* 公羊墨守, 15 volumes
Gu Liang's *Feiji* 穀梁廢疾, 3 volumes
Liu Shao's *Xiaojing* 孝經劉邵注
Wei Zhao's *Xiaojing* 孝經韋昭注
Zhengzhi 鄭志, 9 volumes
Encomia to the Illustrations for the Erya (Erya Tuzan 爾雅圖贊), 2 volumes
Sancang 三蒼, 3 volumes
Picang 埤蒼, 3 volumes
Wei Hong's *Gongshu* 衛宏宮書
Dictionary of Popular Words (Tongsuwen 通俗文), 2 volumes
General Primer (Fanjiangpian 凡將篇)
Zaixipian 在昔篇
Feilongpian 飛龍篇
Shenghuangzhang 聖皇章
Exhortation to Study (Quanxuepian 勸學篇)
Book on the Mid-dynastic Restoration of the Jin (Jin Zhongxingshu 晉中興書), 80 volumes
Gushikao 古史考, 25 volumes
Notes by Marquis Fu on Things Old and New (Fuhou Gujinzhu 伏侯古今注),[33] 8 volumes
Diagram of the Three Capital Regions (Sanfu Huangtu 三輔黃圖)
Explanatory Notes to Han Officials (Hanguan jiegu 漢官解詁), 3 volumes
Annotated Records of the Three Adjuncts (Sanfu juelu 三輔決錄), 7 volumes

---

33. Written by Fu Wuji 伏無忌 and focusing on imperial titles of the Eastern Han period, celestial patterns, geographical organization, and other topics.

Accounts of Venerable Men and Ancient Affairs of the Yi Division (*Yibu qijiu zhuan* 益部耆舊傳), 14 volumes
Biographies of the Elders of Xiang Yang (*Xiang Yang Qijiuzhuan* 襄陽耆舊傳), 5 volumes
Jikang gaoshizhuan 稽康高士傳, 3 volumes
Xuan Yan's *Chunqiu* 玄晏春秋, 3 volumes
Gan Bao's *Soushenji* 干寶搜神記, 30 volumes
Memorials of Famous Wei Ministers (*Wei Mingchen zou* 魏名臣奏), 31 volumes
Han Mingchenzou 漢名臣奏, 29 volumes
Jinshu qizhi 今書七志, 10 volumes
Generational Records (*Shiben* 世本), 4 volumes
Master Shen (*Shenzi* 申子), 2 volumes
Suichaozi 隋巢子
Hufeizi 胡非子
He Cheng's *Tianxingyuan* 何承天性苑
Gao Shilian Shizuzhi 高士廉氏族志, 100 volumes
Annals of the Thirteen Prefectures (*Shisanzhouzhi* 十三州志), 14 volumes
Gaoli fengsuji 高麗風俗紀
Gaolizhi 高麗志, 7 volumes
Zisizi 子思子, 8 volumes
Gongsun Nizi 公孫尼子
Shenzi 慎子, 10 volumes
Chaoshi Xinshu 晁氏新書, 3 volumes
Fengsu tongyi 風俗通義, 30 volumes
Book of Fang Sheng (*Fan Shengzhishu* 氾勝之書), 3 volumes
Lingxian tu 靈憲圖
Dayanli 大衍曆
Bingshu jieyao 兵書接要, 7 volumes
Sima fa Han tu 司馬法漢圖
Record of Medicinals Gathered by Tong Jun (*Tong Jun Yaolu* 桐君藥錄),[34] 2 volumes
Huangdi Dasu 黃帝大素, 30 volumes
Mingyi bielu 名醫別錄, 3 volumes
Cao Zhiji 曹植集, 30 volumes

---

34. A book on pharmaceutics, attributed to Tong Jun, that discussed the appearance of flowers and leaves.

Collected Works of Sima Xiangru (*Sima Xiangruji* 司馬相如集), 2 volumes
Huantan xinlun 桓譚新論, 10 volumes
Liu Kunji 劉琨集, 15 volumes
Lu Chenji 盧諶集, 21 volumes
Shangong qishi 山公啓事, 3 volumes
Shuji 書集, 30 volumes
Yingqu baiyishi 應璩百一詩, 8 volumes
Gujin shiyuan yinghuaji 古今詩苑英華集, 20 volumes
Grove of Collections (*Jilin* 集林), 20 volumes
Jiranzi 計然子, 15 volumes.

Seventh Month, Autumn

Imsul (5th day). The retired left vice director of state affairs No Tan died. His posthumous name was Upright (*kwanghŏn* 匡獻).

Chŏngch'uk (20th day). The king appointed Kim Sanggi as director of the Revenue Ministry and literary councilor, and Yu Sŏk as deputy administrator of the Palace Secretariat.

Eighth Month

Chŏngmyo. The executive of the Secretariat Ch'oe Saje died.
  The king issued a decree.

  Tian Sheng 田盛 from Song writes letters well. Dong Yang 東養 from Song is knowledgeable in the martial arts. I requested that they stay in Koryŏ, and awarded them rank and additional posts so that others like them can be encouraged to come.

Intercalary Month

Kimi (3rd day). The king avoided the main throne hall, reduced the number of side dishes served at his meals, and authorized the punishments meted to prisoners in red ink.

Kapcha (8th day). The king held the Buddhist Tripitaka ritual in Hoegyŏng Hall and burned incense. He also wrote a poem that demonstrated his adherence to Buddhism.

Ninth Month

Kyŏngin (5th day). The king went to Sangch'un Pavilion and summoned the duke of Kyerim, Wang Hŭi, the duke of Puyŏ, Wang Su, the Chancellery executive Yu Hong, the left vice director of state affairs So T'aebo, the director of military affairs Sŏ Chŏng, the supreme general Wang Kungmo, the Chancellery attendant Ko Kyŏng, and the Hallim academician Son Kwan, as well as others, for a reception with libations. During the reception, he quietly asked them about the situation in the border region.

Kyesa (8th day). Liao sent the Yŏngju district surveillance commissioner Ko Sung 高崇 with a letter of congratulations on the king's birthday.

Eleventh Month, Winter

Pyŏngo (22nd day). The Chancellery executive Yu Hong died.

Kyŏngsul (26th day). The king went to the Altar of the Gods of Earth and Grain and prayed for snow.

Twelfth Month

Kyehae (9th day). The Chancellery executive Yi An died. His posthumous name was Abstention (*yangsin* 襄愼).

Ninth Year of Sŏnjong (1092)

First Month, Spring

Kapsin (1st day). Due to sleet, the king canceled the New Year Congratulations.

Kich'uk (6th day). The retired director of punishments and Palace Secretariat commissioner Pak Yangdan 朴揚旦 died. The king suspended court business for three days.

Chŏngyu (14th day). The king appointed Kim Sanggi as director of the Civil Personnel Ministry and Im Kae as deputy administrator of the Palace Secretariat.

Kyŏngja (17th day). Twenty Eastern Jurchens, led by Arohan, were granted an audience and made an offering of their native products.

Second Month

Kiyu (26th day). A party of Eastern Jurchens, led by General Embracing Transformation Sambin, were granted an audience and made an offering of horses.

The ruler of T'amna, Ŭiin 懿仁, was granted an audience and made an offering of his country's native products. The king promoted him to the rank of Chŏngwŏn changgun 定遠將軍[35] and gave him an official's dress and belt.

Imo (29th day). The king appointed high-level officials, including So T'aebo as senior governmental advisor.

Third Month

Pyŏngjin. In Kaegyŏng, 640 households burned down.

This month, the king grew anxious and weary of state affairs. He felt himself becoming sick and changed his residence to Mundŏk Hall. He ordered the palace physician to prescribe medicines for him to promote health (*yangsŏng pangyak* 養性方藥). Then he suddenly felt something and wrote a long poem in the old style. As he reached the end, he recited, "Even if I question whether the medicine is effective or not, an insignificant life has a beginning, so how can there not be an end? The only

---

35. A rank 5a1 title for military officials.

things worth desiring are doing salutary deeds and worshiping Buddha in the pure land." Although the king was young and in generally good health, these were the words that came to him. The people who were with him were astounded and thought it strange.

Fourth Month, Summer

Ŭlmyo (3rd day). The king appointed his senior governmental advisor So T'aebo as Middle Military commander and provisional superintendent of the Northwestern Frontier District Military Commission (*kwŏn p'an sŏbungmyŏn pyŏngmasa* 權判西北面兵馬事), the Palace Secretariat commissioner Sŏ Chŏng as Middle Military commander and military commissioner of the Northwestern Frontier District, the literary councilor Kim Sanggi as Mobile Headquarters military commissioner and provisional superintendent of the Northeastern Frontier District Military Commission (*kwŏn p'an tongbungmyŏn pyŏngmasa* 權判東北面兵馬事), and the Palace Secretariat deputy administrator Im Kae as military commissioner of the Mobile Headquarters and of the Northeastern Frontier District.

Muo (6th day). The king invested court lady Yi 李 as his Consort.

The king issued a decree bestowing on Wang Pi, the marquis of Kŭmgwan, the additional titles of High Grand Marshal and Director of the Secretariat.

Pyŏngin (14th day). Wang Pi, the Marquis of Kŭmgwan, died.

Mujin (16th day). Liao sent Ko Yanggyŏng 高良慶 as its message envoy from the Eastern Capital.

Sinsa (29th day). The king went to Mundŏk Hall to retest the candidates. Kim Sŏng 金誠 and others passed the examination.

Sixth Month

Kimi (7th day). The king appointed Yu Sŏk as administrator of the Palace Secretariat and Yi Ye as deputy administrator of the Palace Secretariat.

Kyŏngsin (8th day). The king issued an imperial edict.

> Early on, I followed the report of astrologist (*ilgwan* 日官) Ch'oe Sagyŏm and designated Kyŏng Tomb as deficient [for geomantic reasons] and ordered it repaired. Recently, I saw the memorial submitted by the vice director of the Astronomical Observation Institute Hwang Ch'unghyŏn 黃忠現 and others. It says that Ch'oe Sagyŏm made repairs to prevent natural calamities, but the repairs are disturbing the spirit of King Munjong and preventing him from gaining rest. Have the Punishments Ministry arrest Ch'oe Sagyŏm for questioning.

Ŭlch'uk (13th day). The king appointed the literary councilor Kim Sanggi as editor of national history.

Pyŏngin (14th day). The king received the bodhisattva ordination in Kŏndŏk Hall.

Imsin (20th day). The dowager empress held a ten-thousand-day Ch'ŏnt'ae repentance ritual (*yech'ambŏp* 禮懺法)[36] at Kyŏnbul monastery 見佛寺 in Paekchu.

Ŭrhae (23rd day). The king appointed Sŏ Chŏng as senior governmental advisor.

Seventh Month, Autumn

Ŭryu (4th day). The senior governmental advisor Ch'oe Saryang died.

Eighth Month

Ŭlch'uk (14th day). The king appointed Yi Chawi as right vice director of state affairs, provisional administrator of the Chancellery (*kwŏnji munhasŏngsa* 權知門下省事), and commissioner of the Western Capital. Earlier, when Yi

---

36. Repentance rituals for the forgiveness of past sins played a key role in the Tiantai (Ch'ŏnt'ae 天台) revival in the Song. Tiantai monks sought repentance in several ways, using rituals focused on the *Lotus Sutra*, the awakening of great compassion, the Pure Land, and other objects of devotion. In this case, the ritual was likely a Buddhist Assembly of Ten Thousand Days (*Manbulhoe* 萬佛會 or *Manilhoe* 萬日會).

Chawi was a state councilor, he sent a memorial to Song in which the era name was incorrectly written, which Song pointed out by sending it back. Taking responsibility for this, Yi Chawi was dismissed. But after a few months, the king indicated his preference to his favorite officials, and Yi Chawi resumed his position. At the time, people laughed at him.

Mujin (17th day). The king went to the Western Capital.

Kisa (18th day). The king sent Ch'oe Sagyŏm into exile on Sŏnsan island 仙山島.[37]

Ninth Month, Autumn

Imo (2nd day). The dowager empress [Inhye] died at the Western Capital.

Ŭryu (5th day). Liao sent Wang Chŏng 王鼎 with a letter of congratulations on the king's birthday.

Tenth Month, Winter

Pyŏngja (27th day). The king returned from the Western Capital.

Eleventh Month

Kyŏngja (21st day). Venus appeared during the day and crossed the sky.

Twelfth Month

Kyehae (15th day). Twenty Eastern Jurchens, led by Yŏrabul 餘羅弗, were granted an audience and made an offering of their native products.

Imsin (24th day). There was an earthquake.

---

37. Present-day Ch'ŏngsan island.

Tenth Year of Sŏnjong (1093)

First Month, Spring

Kimyo (1st day). The king canceled the New Year Congratulations.

Second Month

Kabin (7th day). The Song sincere envoy (*baoxinshi* 報信使) Huang Zhong 黃仲 came from Mingzhou.

Third Month

Muin (1st day). The king ordered his eldest son, Wang Uk, to live in Such'un Palace. He appointed the deputy administrator of the Palace Secretariat Yu Sŏk and the left grand master of remonstrance Son Kwan as left director and right director of the Crown Prince's Household Management, respectively.

Imo (5th day). The military commissioner of the Northwestern Frontier Circuit submitted a report: "Three northern tribesmen, impressed by our country, came over to submit." The king gave them articles of clothing and land with houses on it.

Fourth Month, Summer

Kiyu (3rd day). The retired Chancellery director Mun Chŏng died.

Kyech'uk (7th day). The king held the Buddhist Tripitaka ritual in Hoegyŏng Hall for six days. He wrote out poems praising the Three Treasures.

Ŭlmyo (9th day). Liao sent the Koju District surveillance commissioner P'ung Haengjong 馮行宗 with the emperor's instructions for the king to return to conducting state affairs even though he was still in mourning.

Fifth Month

Musul (22nd day). The king appointed So T'aebo as executive of the Secretariat, superintendent of the Military Affairs Ministry, and superintendent of the Punishments Ministry; Sŏ Chŏng as left vice director of state affairs and senior governmental advisor; Kim Sanggi as director of civil personnel, editor of national history, and senior governmental advisor; Yu Sŏk as director of rites and senior governmental advisor; Im Kae as director of punishments and commissioner of the Palace Secretariat; and Yi Ye as administrator of the Palace Secretariat and Hallim academician recipient of edicts.

Kyŏngja (24th day). The king founded Hongho monastery 弘護寺 to the east of Kaegyŏng.

Sixth Month

Kapcha (18th day). The king personally conducted the Daoist Ch'o ritual in the Inner Office and prayed for a good harvest.

Seventh Month, Autumn

Kyemi (8th day). The Sŏhae province pacification commissioner (*Sŏhaedo anch'alsa* 西海道按察使) submitted a petition.

> The constabulary (*sungŏmgun* 巡檢軍) at Yŏnp'yŏng island 延平島, under the jurisdiction of the Western Regional Military Command, captured a boat at sea containing twelve people from Song and nineteen people from Wa 倭 [Japan]. They had bows and arrows, swords, armor, mercury, pearls, sulphur, horns made of mother-of-pearl, and other items with them, and it is certain that pirates from the two countries were conspiring to raid our coast. We request permission to send the captured pirates into exile far away and to deliver the weapons and other items to the government office. We also request that awards be given to the soldiers who captured the boat.

The king approved.

Imjin (17th day). The king sent the director of military affairs Hwang Chonggak and the vice director of public works Yu Sin as envoys bearing an expression of gratitude to Song.

Eighth Month

Imsin (27th day). The king commuted the death sentences of criminals across the country and exiled them to offshore islands.

Ninth Month

Chŏngch'uk (2nd day). The king went to the dowager empress Inye's memorial hall to observe the first anniversary of her death (*sosangje* 小祥祭).
Imo (7th day). Liao sent the Yŏngju district surveillance commissioner Tae Kwiin 大歸仁 with a letter of congratulations on the king's birthday.

Twelfth Month

Kapcha (21st day). Liao sent the Anju district surveillance commissioner 安州管內觀察使 Yayul Kwal 耶律括 as a special envoy bearing an imperial edict.

Eleventh Year of Sŏnjong (1094)

First Month, Spring

Kyeyu (1st day). The king canceled the New Year Congratulations.
Imjin (20th day). A comet appeared next to the sun.

Second Month

Pyŏngo (4th day). Due to the frequent occurrence of extraordinary calamities, the king declared an amnesty.

Musin (6th day). When the king made ready to inspect the army, the Censorate remonstrated.

> The army is metal, which can destroy wood.[38] Since it is the height of spring, virtue currently resides in wood, and this vitality can be overturned by inspecting the troops.

The king did not listen.

Third Month

Kapsul (3rd day). The king conducted the ancestral rites in the dowager empress Inye's memorial hall.

Kapsin (13th day). The National Academy chancellor Han Kŏmsam 韓儉三 submitted a memorial requesting permission to retire due to his age. The king approved.

Pyŏngsul (15th day). A party of Eastern Jurchens, led by General Ingu 仍于, were granted an audience made an offering of nine horses.

Chŏnghae (16th day). The king personally conducted the Daoist Ch'o ritual at the Polo Field.

Kabo (23rd day). Chŏng Kŭkkong 鄭克恭 and others passed the state examination.

Summer, Intercalary Fourth Month

Imjin (22nd day). The king became ill.

Kabo (24th day). The senior state councilors, the junior state councilors, and the royal family went to the north gate of Yŏnyŏng Hall to inquire about the king's health.

---

38. Because of its weapons, the military signifies the element of metal, which overcomes wood. The king should not inspect the troops, the memorial argues, because the vitality of the spring would thereby be sapped.

Fifth Month

Imin (2nd day). The king died in the Inner Quarters 內寢 of Yŏn'gyŏng Hall. His body was moved to Sŏndŏk Hall on the same day, where it lay in repose. King Sŏnjong was forty-six and had reigned for eleven years. His posthumous title was Filial Thoughtfulness, and his temple name was Sŏnjong. He was buried east of the city walls. His tomb was named In 仁陵. He received the additional posthumous titles of Generous Benevolence (*kwanin* 寬仁) in the eighteenth year of King Injong (1140) and Revealing Gentleness (*hyŏnsun* 顯順) in the fortieth year of King Kojong (1253).

Yi Chehyŏn's evaluation of the king:

> Poetry is where the striving in the heart goes. What dwells in the heart as a longing is expressed in words as poetry.[39] Looking at King Sŏnjong's poem "Taking Medicine" (*Iyakusi* 餌藥詩),[40] written in Mundŏk Hall, we find it has similarities to Zhao Meng's 趙孟 poem "Seeing the Sun's Shadow" (*Siŭmgaeil* 視蔭愒日).[41] How is this? Although Zhao Meng was a high-ranking official in one of the many states of that time, the nobles ridiculed him when he was reckless with his words. How would this not apply, and even more so, to a king? King Sŏnjong was intelligent and loved to study. He pored over the writings of the sages and never gave way to superficial thoughts. For a sagacious king and his upright officials to reply to each other through poetry is an admirable thing, and when you consider the fervor the Han emperor put into his "Song of the Great Wind" (*Taepungga* 大風歌), how could [Sŏnjong's poem] have been judged inferior? After that, it was scarcely three years before we lost our king. Alas!

---

39. Yi Chehyŏn is quoting the "Great Preface" to the *Book of Songs* 詩經. The translation here is indebted to Hermann-Josef Rollicke's *Die Fährte des Herzens: Die Lehre vom Herzensbestreben (zhi* 志*) im grossen Vorwort zum Shijing* (Berlin: D. Reimer, 1992).

40. *Taking Medicine* (*Iyakusi* 餌藥詩) is recounted in the record for *pyŏngjin* in the third month of the ninth year of Sŏnjong.

41. Zhao Meng 趙孟 (d. 537 BCE) was an aristocrat of Jin 晉 during the Spring and Autumn period (771–476 BCE). The *Zuozhuan*, a commentary on the *Spring and Autumn Annals*, mentions that Zhao Meng, seeing the difference between his morning and evening shadow, became alarmed by the evanescence of life, the subject of his poem.

HŎNJONG

Hŏnjong 獻宗, reigned 1094–1095

Hŏnjong, the Great King of Courteous [Early] Death (*konsang* 恭殤). His given name was Uk 昱. He was the first-born son of King Sŏnjong and his mother was Lady Yi 李, the dowager empress Sasuk 思肅太后. He was born on *ŭlmi* (27th day) in the sixth month of the first year of Sŏnjong (1084). He was very intelligent, and by the age of nine he loved to paint and practice calligraphy. He never forgot anything he had seen or heard.

On *imin* (2nd day) in the fifth month of the eleventh year of Sŏnjong (1094), King Sŏnjong died and Hŏnjong acceded to the throne at Chunggwang Hall in accordance with the late king's regal will.

Accession Year of Hŏnjong (1094)

Fifth Month

Kabin (14th day). King Sŏnjong was buried at In Tomb 仁陵.

Sixth Month

Kyŏngo (1st day). The king's mother was designated the dowager empress.
Kapsin (15th day). The king appointed So T'aebo and Yi Chawi as executives of the Chancellery and supreme pillars of the state, Yu Sŏk as left vice director of state affairs and pillar of the state, Im Kae as senior governmental advisor, Yi Chaŭi as administrator of the Palace Secretariat, and Ch'oe Sach'u 崔思諏 (1036–1115) as left scholarly counselor-in-ordinary and deputy administrator of the Palace Secretariat.
Ŭryu (16th day). King Munjong's consort Lady Kim 金, the lady of Sunghwa Palace 崇化宮主, died.

Muja (19th day). The king went to Sinbong Pavilion and declared a general amnesty.

Sixty-nine people from Song, led by the Dugang Xu You 徐祐, and 194 people from T'angna 乇羅, led by Ko Chŏk 高的, came to offer congratulations on the king's accession to the throne along with their respective native products.

Kihae (30th day). The king gave to the duke of Chosŏn, Wang To, and the duke of Kyerim, Wang Hŭi, the title of High Grand Preceptor; to the duke of Sangan, Wang Su, and the duke of Puyŏ, Wang Su, the title of High Grand Guardian; and to the marquis of Chinhan, Wang Yu, the marquis of Hansan 漢山侯, Wang Yun 王昀, and the marquis of Nangnang 樂浪伯, Wang Yŏng 王瑛, the title of High Minister of Education.

Seventh Month, Autumn

Chŏngmyo (28th day). A party of people from Song led by the Dugang Xu Yi 徐義 came with an offering of their native products.

Eighth Month

Kyŏngo (1st day). The king issued an imperial edict.

> Sŏndŏk Garrison 宣德鎮, under the jurisdiction of Chŏngju, is plagued by locusts, so I command all of my officials to each submit a memorial on the situation.

Kapsul (5th day). Sixty-four people from Song, led by the Dugang Ou Bao 歐保 and Liu Ji 劉及, came.

Eleventh Month, Winter

Imja (14th day). The king gave a banquet at the Polo Field for those who were eighty or older and bestowed assorted goods in accordance with their rank.

Twelfth Month

Liao sent a mission with So Chunyŏl 蕭遵烈 as the memorial service envoy, Yang Chosul 梁祖述 as the deputy memorial service envoy (*ch'ikche pusa* 勅祭副使), So Ch'i 蕭褆 as the consolation envoy, Kwak Inmun 郭人文 as the reporting reinstatement envoy (*kiboksa* 起復使), and others.

Ŭryu (18th day). The memorial service envoy went to the memorial hall to perform the memorial rites for the late king Sŏnjong. The king received the imperial edict and assisted in the rites. The imperial edict stated:

> We miss our former subject the late king, who maintained an upright posture and would have repeatedly received my favor. He has suddenly departed on his endless final journey, but his spirit is not yet distant so great kindness can still reach him. We have sent a selection of ceremonial wines to use in the ancestral rites to give expression to our feeling of loss. We also send the Yŏngju district surveillance commissioner So Chunyŏl and the vice minister of imperial regalia Yang Chosul, who will act as the memorial service envoy and deputy memorial service envoy, respectively. The items we are sending for use in the memorial service are specified in the accompanying list.

The Imperial edict for the ancestral rites stated:

> In our view, the late king's appearance was handsome, and his spirit magnanimous. Happily, he came at a joyful time and he respectfully comported himself in keeping with the splendor of the times. He inherited the great task of his ancestors and continued to rule over a less than civilized land. In a country surrounded by the sea, he was obedient to the old style of dress and was scrupulous in his respect for our court. He truly followed righteousness and was always completely loyal. We would have continued to grant him our favor, but he passed away suddenly. When we heard of his death, we were distressed that we could no longer reward him as we wished. The least we could do was quickly send envoys to raise a cup at his memorial rite, but we think of his beautiful spirit continually and ask that you understand our deep intent.

As soon as the funeral rites were finished, the king returned to the palace. The consolation envoy went to Kŏndŏk Hall to deliver the imperial edict he had brought, which stated:

> Through the memorial submitted to our court, the death of the Koryŏ king is now known to all. Earlier, he had appeared on the edge of the Eastern Sea, and we looked forward to seeing the helpful service he would give us when the sudden report of his death arrived. When we think about it, we realize that he had suffered misfortune at a young age, which was pitiful. But when you consider how appropriately he ceded the throne, your sadness lifts and comes under control, at least a little. When you receive this edict, accept our deep intent.
>
> Now, we have sent the Kwangju defense commissioner (*Kwangju pangŏsa* 廣州防禦使) So Ch'i as our consolation envoy to deliver this edict and gifts of condolence as specified in the accompanying list.

Pyŏngsul (19th day). The reporting reinstatement envoy went to Kŏndŏk Hall to deliver his imperial edict, which stated:

> You have just been compelled to mourn your father and must now carry on the family line. While it may be appropriate that you lie on straw matting placed on the ground to honor and cherish the memory of your father, you must also consider the war-like circumstances your country has been placed in. You should return to conduct court business and preside over state affairs. Although you are preoccupied with posthumous titles, decrees, and gifts, you must try to return to earnest consideration of state affairs. We have sent the minister of imperial entertainments Kwak Inmun with a separate letter of investiture and decree.

The letter of Investiture stated:

> Being devoted to one's parents, it is appropriate that one should be overwhelmed with grief. But being true to one's country, it is also appropriate that one should weigh external forces and begin to pursue measures suited for wartime. In days of yore, Zhao Xiangzi 趙襄子[42] went

---

42. A government minister in the Wu dynasty of the Spring and Autumn period. When the Yue dynasty invaded Wu, Zhao Xiangzi went out on his own to fight, despite not being a military official.

immediately to war because he had been ordered to do so, and Bo Qin 伯禽[43] was entrusted with responsibility because he was talented. We have read the classics and looked at several possibilities, and your country was entrusted to you because we thought you could provide a strong barrier for our imperial household. But your predecessor died, due to Heaven's indifference, and in the wake of his death, it is fitting that rule over the territory has passed to you. Mindful of auspicious days to come, we have advised you to end your mourning, and in consultation with others, we now inform you of the special favor we will grant.

You, Wang Uk, having become the king of Koryŏ, are the son who has received happiness and fortune, including the many talents that make you exceptional. You were born from the energy of the seven constellations, and from early on, you were endowed with wisdom. You also received the quality of wood, the element that gives you your benevolence. When you were young, your outstanding abilities were recognized by all, and you inherited the country at the height of your development. But after watching your father wasting away, you were heartbroken when the news came of his death. Overwhelmed with grief, you consented to suffer for three years the suppression of your own true feelings while bearing the responsibility of ruling over the uncivilized country of Koryŏ without vacating your position for even a single day. We have therefore made a point of issuing this order for you to stop wearing mourning dress. We are also bestowing lofty status on you and elevating your rank and giving you new fiefs. Having inherited your country, you must now begin to repay the hopes of so many people.

Ah! If you think about your ancestors who subordinated themselves to our court, they clearly swore fealty under Mount Tai 泰山 and became model vassals of the Eastern Sea. They respected the emperor and defended the people with magnanimity. They gave assistance to their children and bequeathed everything to their descendants. Looking at the past eight generations, you can see that they enjoyed great prosperity and thus were granted investiture. They also respected the dying injunctions of their great ancestor and thought for a long time about his lofty and ambitious plans. But needing to be diligent and frugal, they pursued correct policies and faithfully protected the people. Remember their lessons and you too will be careful and restrained.

---

43. Bo Qin, the son of the duke of Zhou, became king of Lu (Lu Jun 魯君).

We bestow on you the titles of Cavalry General-in-Chief (*p'yogi tae-janggun* 驃騎大將軍), Acting Grand Marshal, Director of the Secretariat, Supreme Pillar of the State, and King of Koryŏ with a fief of seven thousand households and an actual fief of seven hundred households. The relevant authorities will select a date and follow the appropriate procedures to issue the order of investiture.

Hŏnjong First Year (1095)

First Month, Spring

Musul (1st day). The king canceled the New Year Congratulations.

A comet appeared next to the sun.

Since the king was young, he did not yet know how to cultivate his mind or reflect on himself. Beyond summoning three or four palace physicians to inquire about medical writings, he did little more than practice writing and painting.

Kyŏngsul (13th day). The king appointed Wang Kungmo as provisional superintendent of the Military Affairs Ministry.

Second Month

Kyŏngjin (14th day). The king went to Pongŭn monastery to hold the Lantern Festival.

Kapsin (18th day). Twenty-eight Eastern Jurchens, led by General Embracing Transformation Sora, were granted an audience and made an offering of horses.

Chŏnghae (21st day). Forty-eight Eastern Jurchens, led by General Supporting the State Tumun 豆門, were granted an audience and made an offering of horses. The king granted them a personal audience and went to Sŏnchŏng Hall, where he ordered the royal attendant Ch'oe Hongsa 崔弘嗣 (1043–1122) to question the Jurchens about conditions on the frontier. Then he gave them food and drink, an official's dress and belt, and hemp cloth and silk.

Sinmyo (25th day). Thirty-one merchants from Song arrived, led by Huang Chong 黃冲 and Hyejin 惠珍, a monk of the Chaŭn (Ch. Ci'en) 慈恩 school. The king ordered the royal attendant Mun Ik 文翼 to prepare a carriage with a canopy to welcome Hyejin and to have him stay at Poje monastery. Hyejin was persistent in stating, "I wish to visit a sacred cave on Mount P'ot'arak 普陁落山,[44] and that is why I have come. Please let me go to see it." The court discussed his request but in the end denied it.

Third Month

Sinch'uk (6th day). The duke of Sangan, Wang Su, died.

Fourth Month, Summer

Kimyo (14th day). Yu Chin 兪進 and others passed the state examination.

Fifth Month

Pyŏngsin (2nd day). The dowager empress went to Hyŏnhwa monastery to observe the first anniversary of King Sŏnjong's death with a memorial service.

Kiyu (15th day). The king appointed Yu Sŏk as superintendent of the State Finance Commission, Yi Ye as director of the Ministry of Punishments and literary councilor, Yi Chaŭi as commissioner of the Palace Secretariat, and Son Kwang as administrator of the Palace Secretariat and Hallim academician recipient of edicts.

Kyech'uk (19th day). Ko Su 高遂, the Eastern Capital's response envoy, came from Liaodong. He brought large amounts of twill damask and brocade and colored thread, offering them in his private capacity. The king went to Kŏndŏk Hall to see him personally and after asking the royal attendants

---

44. There was a cave associated with the bodhisattva Avalokiteśvara at Naksan monastery on Mount P'ot'arak 普陁落山, located in present-day Yangyang-gun, Kangwŏn.

to discover whether the resident governor of the Eastern Capital was doing well or not, bestowed food and drink and articles of clothing.

Sixth Month

Kimyo (15th day). The king received the *pratimokṣa* vows 木叉[45] in Kŏndŏk Hall.

Seventh Month, Autumn

Musul (5th day). Koryŏ began using the Liao era name of Such'ang 壽昌.
Pyŏngo (13th day). A ritual offering of food and drink was presented at the Imperial Ancestral Shrine.

Although the king was in mourning, he did not fail to perform the proper rituals, such as the Rites to Heaven, the Rites for the Earth Gods, the ancestral worship at the Imperial Ancestral Shrine, and the Rites to the Gods of Earth and Grain.
Kyech'uk (20th day). Eighty people from T'angna 乇羅, led by Ko Mul 高勿, were granted an audience and made an offering of their native products.
Kyŏngsin day. Yi Chaŭi was discovered to be plotting rebellion and was executed.
Kyehae (30th day). The king appointed So T'aebo as provisional superintendent of the Civil Personnel Ministry (*kwŏnp'an ibusa* 權判吏部事), and Wang Kungmo as provisional superintendent of the Military Affairs Ministry (*kwŏnp'an pyŏngbusa* 權判兵部事).

Eighth Month

Kapcha (1st day). The king appointed Hwang Chungbo 黃仲寶 as right vice director of state affairs.

---

45. Buddhist vows to refrain from immoral actions, including murder, theft, slander, lewdness, and intoxication.

Ŭlch'uk (2nd day). The king appointed his uncle Wang Hŭi, the duke of Kyerim, as director of the Secretariat. All the officials lined up at his house to offer their congratulations.

Kapsul (11th day). Sixty-two merchants from Song, led by Chen Yi 陳義 and Huang Yi 黃宜, came with an offering of their native products.

Kyemi (20th day). The king appointed Son Kwan as commissioner of the Security Council (*ch'umirwŏnsa* 樞密院使), and Ch'oe Sach'u as director of the Civil Personnel Ministry and administrator of the Security Council (*chi ch'umirwŏnsa* 知樞密院事).

Kapsin (21st day). The king ordered the pagoda at Hwangyong monastery in the Eastern Capital to be repaired.

Ninth Month

Ŭlmi (3rd day). The king appointed So T'aebo as superintendent of the Civil Personnel Ministry (*p'an ibusa* 判吏部事) and high minister of education with the rank of T'ŭkchin; Kim Sanggi and Yu Sŏk as vice directors of the Secretariat with concurrent assignments as Secretariat-Chancellery joint affairs managers; Im Kae as superintendent of the Revenue Ministry (*p'an hobusa* 判戶部事), left vice director of state affairs, and high minister of works; Wang Kungmo as superintendent of the Military Affairs Ministry, right vice director of state affairs, senior governmental advisor, and pillar of the state; and Hwang Chonggak as deputy administrator of the Security Council (*tongchi ch'umirwŏnsa* 同知樞密院事).

Pyŏngsin (4th day). Yi Chaŭi's confederate Kim Tŏkch'ung 金德忠, a Military Affairs assistant executive (*pyŏngbu wŏnoerang* 兵部員外郎), was exiled to a faraway place.

Musul (6th day). The king issued an imperial edict.

> Earlier, powerful traitors plotted rebellion and were executed. This was due to the increased power of the generals and the state councilors. Although the rebellion was crushed, I need to constantly examine my conscience and seek perfection. All those who were injustly imprisoned

shall be freed. Across the country, those guilty of petty crimes who pay their bail with copper shall be pardoned.

Kyŏngja (8th day). The king appointed Kim Sŏnsŏk as director of the Ministry of Punishments, and Wang Kungmo as superintendent of the Military and War Council (*p'an to pyŏngmasa* 判都兵馬事).

Tenth Month, Winter

Kisa (7th day). The king issued a decree.

> In undeservedly coming to the throne, I inherited the unfinished work of my late father, the former king. I am still young, and because my body is frail and weak, I have not been able to uphold the authority of the state, disappointing everyone's expectation. As a result, disloyal officials have repeatedly interfered with the Inner Quarters, and traitorous conspiracies are being hatched in the houses of the powerful. All these things are due to my shortcomings, and I have thought constantly about the difficulties of being a ruler. My uncle the Duke of Kyerim is rightfully the next in the line of succession, and I will cede the throne to him and retire to a detached palace to live out my remaining days.

The king ordered Kim Tŏkcho 金德鈞 and the other royal attendants to welcome Wang Hŭi, the duke of Kyerim, to his new residence. Then the king abdicated and retired to a detached palace.

On *kapchin* (19th day) in the second intercalary month of the second year of King Sukchong's reign (1097), King Hŏnjong died at Hŭngsŏng Palace 興盛宮. King Hŏnjong was fourteen and reigned for one year. His posthumous title was Embracing [Early] Death (*hoesang* 懷殤). He was buried east of the city, and his tomb was named Ŭn 隱陵. When King Yejong 睿宗 acceded to the throne (1105), King Hŏnjong's posthumous title was changed to Courteous [Early] Death, and his temple name was changed to Hŏnjong. In the fortieth year of King Kojong's reign (1253), King Hŏnjong was given the additional posthumous title of Righteous Comparison (*chŏngbi* 定比). Yi Chehyŏn's evaluation of the king:

The reason King Yu 禹 the Great handed the throne to his son was that he was concerned about his descendants. Even if an unborn child is installed as the new king [upon his father the previous king's death], the court remains stable because the order of succession has been established. The three sons of King Hyŏnjong passed the kingship from brother down to brother. But when King Sunjong became king, he died from deep grief and had no heirs, so the throne was passed on to King Sŏnjong. When King Sŏnjong died, he had the crown prince for an heir. This was King Hŏnjong. The people used to a brotherly succession said, 'King Sŏnjong had five younger brothers, but still he installed his young son as king!' This was correct, but they acted as if it were wrong. How shallow their thinking! If you cannot obtain a royal family like the Duke of Zhou's or vassals like the marquis of Bolu 博陸[46] who can be entrusted with carrying on the task of governance, then the fate of the country will come under threat and fall into jeopardy. If later generations should encounter misfortune and the throne must be given to a newborn infant, take this as a warning about what must be guarded against.[47]

---

46. This was Hou Guang 藿光 (d. 68 BCE), who was famous for deposing Prince Liu He 昭帝 and installing Emperor Xuan 宣帝 because of his belief in the importance of having a competent ruler take the throne.

47. In this passage, Yi Chehyŏn supports the idea of intergenerational succession. But in the event that a young child is given the throne, there must be strong supporters in the government who can assist in providing competent rule.

APPENDIX

Weights and Measures

Weights and measures varied over time, across regions, and according to the object being measured. Although exact values for the Koryŏ dynasty are unknown, estimates using imperial units of measurement can be provided to assist readers in gauging the quantities represented in the *Koryŏsa*.

Length

ch'i 치/*ch'on* 촌 (寸)	1.19 inches
cha 자/*ch'ŏk* 척 (尺)	11.9 inches
po 步	6 feet
li/ri/i 리 (里)	0.24 mile
p'il 필 (匹)	Bolt (of cloth), approx. 40 feet
chang 장 (丈)	10 *ch'ŏk* (119 inches)
kan 칸 (間)	The space between the pillars of a building, ranging from 8 to 10 *ch'ŏk*

Area

kyŏl 결 (結)	Based on fertility, ranging from 2.25 to 9 acres
chŏngbo 정보 (町步)	2.45 acres

Weight

nyang 냥 (兩)	0.75 ounce
kŭn 근 (斤)	1.2 pounds
kwan 관 (貫)	8.3 pounds

Volume (dry measure)

sŭng 승 (升)	3.2 pints
tu 두 (斗)	4 gallons
sŏk 석 (石)	40 gallons
kak 각 (角)	8 to 10 gallons (depending on the commodity)

CONTRIBUTORS

John B. Duncan is professor emeritus at the University of California, Los Angeles. He received his PhD in Korean history from the University of Washington in 1988 and has taught in the Department of Asian Languages and Cultures at UCLA since 1989. His primary research interests are in the late Koryŏ and early Chosŏn periods, with some work on the Open Ports period of 1876–1910. He is the author of *The Origins of the Chosŏn Dynasty* and edited or co-edited *Rethinking Confucianism: Past and Present in China, Japan, Korea, and Vietnam*; *Reform and Modernization in the Taehan Empire*; and *The Institutional Basis of Civil Governance in the Chosŏn Dynasty*.

Howard Kahm is an associate professor at Underwood International College of Yonsei University. He received his PhD from the Department of Asian Languages and Cultures at the University of California, Los Angeles, in 2012, and his BA from Williams College in 1997. He has written several articles on Korean social and economic history.

Kim Yunjung is a researcher at the Seoul Historiography Institute, a public research institution. She received her PhD from the Department of History at Yonsei University in 2017. Her research focuses on the self-identity of Koreans in the middle ages, approached through the medium of material culture. She has written or co-authored several articles and publications on Koryŏ and Chosŏn.

Dennis Lee is a specialist in artificial intelligence/natural language processing, focusing on machine translation. He received his PhD from the Department of Asian Languages and Cultures at the University of California, Los Angeles, and was a postdoctoral fellow at Harvard University and an assistant professor at Yonsei University. Currently, he is an independent researcher in the field of context-coded machine translation. He has written several articles about early Korean-Japanese relations and has been translating premodern classical Chinese texts since 2006.

Lee Jong-rok is a researcher at the Center for Korean History of Korea University. He received his PhD from the Department of Korean History at Korea University in 2022 and has written several articles on ancient Korea and Koguryŏ.

Joseph Jeong-il Lee is a research fellow at the Northeast Asian History Foundation. He received his PhD from the Department of Asian Languages and Cultures at the University of California, Los Angeles, in 2007, specializing in the geopolitics and international relations of premodern East Asia, especially between the fifteenth and seventeenth centuries. He is a member of the editorial boards of the *Journal of Northeast Asian History* and the *International Journal of Korean History*. He has written several articles about Korean-Chinese relations in the sixteenth and seventeenth centuries, particularly during the East Asian War of 1592–1598, and is engaged in translating the diplomatic documents exchanged between Chosŏn and Ming from 1593 to 1608.

Lee Joung Hoon is a lecturer at the Seoul University of Science and Technology. She received her PhD from the Department of History at Yonsei University, specializing in premodern and Koryŏ history. She has written several articles on Koryŏ and a monograph titled *Koryŏ chŏn'gi chŏngch'i chedo yŏn'gu* [The political system in the early Koryŏ dynasty] (2007).

Sinwoo Lee is an associate professor at California State University, Chico. She received her MA from Yonsei University and her PhD from the University of California, Los Angeles; she was a postdoctoral fellow in Korean studies at the University of Pennsylvania in 2018–2019. Her research focuses on the urban history of Korea from the late nineteenth to early twentieth centuries.

Park Jongki is professor emeritus in the Department of Korean History at Kookmin University. He received his PhD from the Department of Korean History at Seoul National University and has written numerous books and articles on Koryŏ and premodern Korean history, including *Saero ssŭn obaeknyŏn Koryŏsa* [Five hundred years of Koryŏ history] (3rd ed., 2020) and *Koryŏsa ŭi chaepalgyŏn* [Rediscovering Koryŏ history] (2015).

Sheen Joohyun is a research professor at the Institute for Global Korean Studies of Yonsei University, Mirae Campus. He received his PhD from the Department of History at Pennsylvania State University, and he studies the intellectual history surrounding the publication and dissemination of Chinese Christian texts during the seventeenth and eighteenth centuries. He has written several articles on the Jesuit mission to East Asia.

Aeri Shin teaches scientific writing as an invited professor at the Korea Advanced Institute of Science and Technology. She finished her coursework toward a PhD in Korean history at Harvard University, where she received an MA in regional studies–East Asia after completing her BA in religion and Sanskrit studies at Columbia University.

Edward J. Shultz is professor emeritus at the University of Hawai'i at Mānoa. He first went to Korea as a Peace Corps volunteer upon his graduation from Union College in New York in 1966. After receiving his PhD from the University of Hawai'i in 1976, he taught at the University of Hawai'i and at several universities in Korea until he retired. His major area of research is the history of Koryŏ, with a special interest in social, institutional, and political history.

INDEX

Accommodations Service, director of, 57
An Minbo, 130, 143
Anbyŏn district, 18
Anju, 145
Astrological Service, 19, 60, 64, 218; administrator of, 64, 248, 293; superintendent of, 220; executive of, 19, 72
Astronomical Observation Institute: superintendent of, 220; vice director of, 307
Audience Ceremonies, commissioner of, 10
Audience Ceremonies and Presentations: commissioner of, 246, 277; recipients of edicts in the office, 160
audience usher, 28, 162, 246, 283

Capital Garrison Division: lieutenant colonel of, 68; supreme general of, 44
Capital Gate Division, executive captain of, 213
Capital Marketplace Office, 95
Capital Security Division, supreme general of, 106
Censorate, 11, 35, 52, 69, 72, 73, 76, 77, 82, 106, 108, 109, 144, 170, 180, 207, 274, 294, 312; administrator of, 156, 163, 195, 230; general censor of, 14, 20, 128, 130, 156, 165, 178, 190, 220, 227, 249, 251, 261, 277, 28;3 superintendent of, 38, 89, 158; vice director of, 7, 12, 15, 20, 101, 139, 157, 162, 188, 194, 222, 249, 251, 277, 280

Ch'ae Ch'unghyŏn, 10, 87
Ch'ae Ch'ungsun, 16
Chancellery, 19, 74, 122, 124, 125, 159; administrator of, 307; attendant of, 20, 227, 304; director of, 24, 27, 33, 49, 54, 63, 68, 69, 73, 75, 79, 84, 86, 92, 121, 127, 139, 142, 162, 166, 167, 177, 184, 210, 217, 225, 264, 270, 271, 272; executive of, 27, 73, 92, 108, 262, 273, 278, 293, 297, 304, 314; vice director of, 8, 14, 15, 49, 112, 143, 162, 251, 279
Chang Chŏng, 103, 106
Chang Kŭngmaeng, 75
Changdan county, 183
Ch'angju, 206, 298
Changju, 57, 114
Changyang prefecture, 88
Changyŏn county, 76
Chi Maeng, 41, 121, 127, 144
Ch'idam station, 102, 115
Chin Chamgo, 188, 220
Chin Hyŏnsŏk, 14, 20, 30, 35
Chinju, 130, 283
Chinmyŏngp'o, 92
Cho island, 187, 188
Cho Ong, 68, 88
Cho P'ae, 11
Chŏ Wŏnbin, 188, 221
Ch'oe Chean, 7, 14, 23, 49, 63, 68, 69
Ch'oe Ch'iwŏn, 216
Ch'oe Chongp'il, 123, 124
Ch'oe Ch'ung, 7, 29, 43, 49, 68, 73, 75, 84, 87, 92, 121,189, 270
Ch'oe Hang, 184
Ch'oe Hongsa, 273, 319
Ch'oe Pokkyu, 79
Ch'oe Posŏng, 68, 88, 105

331

332 INDEX

Ch'oe Sach'u, 314, 322
Ch'oe Sagyŏm, 293, 307, 308
Ch'oe Sahun, 228, 249
Ch'oe Sahyŏn, 246, 249
Ch'oe Saje, 245, 249, 303
Ch'oe Sang, 130, 145, 161, 179, 186
Ch'oe Saryang, 222, 273, 279, 280, 281, 283, 307
Ch'oe Sayŏl, 272, 277, 283
Ch'oe Sŏk, 96, 157, 217, 220, 227, 243, 244, 253, 272, 277, 278, 279, 280, 281, 283
Ch'oe Sŏngjŏl, 102, 125
Ch'oe Suk, 139, 272
Ch'oe Sungmang, 76, 96
Ch'oe Wŏnjun, 67, 143, 159
Ch'oe Yŏnha, 25, 26, 35, 65, 87
Ch'oe Yubu, 161, 195, 205
Ch'oe Yugil, 215, 217, 219, 220, 226
Ch'oe Yusŏn, 76, 100, 104, 123, 160, 162, 185, 195, 210, 217, 271
Ch'oja island, 94
Chŏllyŏng, 110
Ch'ŏnan district, 252
Chŏng Chang, 52
Chŏng Inji, 5, 66, 134, 200, 260
Chŏng Kŏl, 87, 89, 92, 98
Chŏng Paegŏl, 7, 239
Chŏng Yusan, 190, 191, 195, 205, 206, 215, 217, 219, 226, 243, 297
Chŏngbyŏn Garrison, 68, 94
Chŏnghae county, 226
Chŏngjong, 5, 66, 71, 77, 83, 150, 153, 155, 270
Ch'ŏngju, 130, 283
Chŏngju, 11, 57, 100, 160, 209, 211, 234, 315
Ch'ŏngsaek Garrison, 44
Chŏngyung Fortress, 287
Chŏngyung Garrison, 222
Chŏnju, 130, 283
Ch'ŏnmyŏng, 116
Chŏnsŏng, 284
Ch'ungju, 130, 150, 283
Civil Personnel Ministry, 11, 64, 71, 79, 80, 88, 122, 139; administrator of, 156, 244; assistant executive of, 35;
director of, 7, 14, 73, 219, 231, 234, 244, 276, 305, 310, 322; executive of, 249; superintendent of, 49, 121, 162, 185, 272, 277, 283, 321, 322; vice director of, 245
commissioner for incense and the Tripitaka, 284
consolation and pacification commissioner, 130
Construction and Maintenance Directorate: director of, 186; vice director of, 122, 179
county governor, 76, 79
crown prince: administrator of the readers-in-waiting for, 145; advisor to, 217, 219, 245; companion of, 162, 193; grand guardian of, 227, 245; grand preceptor to, 184, 196 junior guardian of the crown prince, 121, 219, 227, 234; junior preceptor to, 217; proclaimer to, 161
Crown Prince's Household Management: director of, 88, 309; vice director of, 219

defense commissioner, 36, 71, 99, 122, 317
deputy recipient of edicts, 157, 192, 199, 222, 246, 251
dowager empresses. See indivdiual names of empressesdowager queen. See Yongsin (dowager queen)
drafter of imperial edicts and proclamations, 7, 207, 257

Eastern Capital, 12, 18, 20, 121, 130, 212, 216, 283; deputy resident governor of, 45, 168, 282
Eastern Frontier, military commissioner of, 187, 188, 212
Eastern Frontier Circuit: military commissioner of, 6, 30, 114, 160, 211; Military Field Office, 46; vice military commissioners of, 30, 128
eminent grand guardian, 281
eminent grand marshal, 167

eminent grand mentor to the crown prince, 281
eminent grand preceptor, 105, 271, 281
eminent grand preceptor to the crown prince, 281
eminent minister of education, 102
eminent minister of works, 162, 224, 239, 281
eminent vice director of imperial regalia, 125
empress. See Sasuk (empress)
Envoy Escort Division, grand general of, 97, 157
executive captain, 213

Food Service, 51
Foreign Relations Court, 170
Foreign Relations Office, 45, 123, 245, 247, 293; assistant executive of, 197; director of, 89, 163, 219, 273; vice director of the Foreign Relations Office, 282

Gracious Consort (hyebi), 8, 20
Gracious Consort (yŏbi), 27, 36
grand general, 41, 90
grand general guarding imperial tombs, 153
grand guardian, 49, 271, 315
grand marshal, 14, 73, 101, 106, 112, 156, 166, 239, 270, 271, 283, 306
grand master admonisher, 162
grand master of remonstrance, 14, 20, 143, 163, 165, 168, 179, 190, 191, 192, 193, 194, 195, 216, 219, 227, 309
grand mentor, 92, 197
grand preceptor, 7, 23, 87, 184, 189, 196, 225, 239, 257, 258, 260, 270, 315

Ha Churyŏ, 104, 189
Ha Hŭnghyu, 41, 74, 154
Ha Kongjin, 287
Haeju, 145
Haerin, 132, 147, 185
Hallim Academy, 109, 214, 261; attendant in the, 142; Hallim academician, 100, 105, 158, 160, 192, 195, 205, 219, 283, 304, 310; Hallim academician lecturer-in-waiting, 49; Hallim academician recipient of edicts, 14, 44, 92, 249, 283, 310, 320; superintendent of, 162
Han Kongsŏ, 144, 145, 161
Han Yŏnjo, 14
Hangma Garrison, 161
Hoegyo station, 281
Hogyŏng. See Western Capital
Hong Ki, 166, 227
Hong Pin, 41, 43
Hong Tŏgwi, 77, 163, 188, 195
Hong Tŏksŏng, 219
Hongju, 130, 226
Hongwŏn county, 250
Hŏnjong, 289, 309, 318
Hŭnghae prefecture, 264
Hŭnghwa Garrison, 9
Hwang Chonggak, 273, 282, 311, 322
Hwang Churyang, 7, 23, 29, 49
Hwang Hangji, 31, 162
Hwan'ga county, 171
Hwangbo Yŏn, 97, 121
Hwangbo Yŏng, 12, 20, 43, 49, 73, 79
Hwangbo Yuŭi, 8, 15, 49, 65
Hwangju, 13, 126, 134
Hyŏnjong, 5, 65, 66, 74, 103, 104, 255, 264, 324

Im Chonghan, 13, 30
Im Chongil, 139, 145, 158, 161, 167
Im Hŭiyŏl, 187, 188
Im Kae, 249, 269, 277, 280, 305, 306, 310, 314, 322
Im Yugan, 20, 34, 70
Imdo county, 89
Imjin county, 68, 169
Imperial Archives, 61, 128, 150, 152, 153, 166; collator in, 103, 157, 160; director of, 89, 212, 219, 276; vice director of, 193, 199
Imperial Army, grand general of, 97
imperial diary keeper, 152

Imperial Manufactories Directorate: director of, 58; superintendent of, 159; vice director of, 165
Imperial Medicine Directorate, vice director of, 80
Imperial Music Office, executive of, 58
imperial recorder, 7, 14, 238
Imperial Regalia Court: assistant executive of, 77, 92; director of, 14, 64, 188, 249, 272, 282; superintendent of, 44
Imperial Secretariat, 36, 64, 287; director of, 5, 7, 23, 46, 66, 87, 121, 160; executive of, 43, 47, 73, 92, 121; drafter of, 10, 12, 145; vice director of, 8, 23, 144
Imperial Secretariat–Chancellery, 30, 45, 96, 97, 149, 158; joint affairs manager, 8, 14, 15, 23, 49, 143, 144
Imperial Stables Court, 171; director of, 166, 181, 189, 214, 292; vice director of, 285
Ingnyŏng county, 165
Injong, 65, 255, 258, 313
investigating censors, 11, 77, 190
Inye (dowager empress), 256, 311, 312

Kaegyŏng, 8, 9, 63, 103, 126, 142, 180, 194, 224, 290, 305, 310
Kaesŏng district, 182
Kang Kamch'an, 184
Kang Sŭngyŏng, 19
Kang Wŏn'gwang, 157, 188, 194, 196
Kanghwa county, 182
Kim Che, 196, 201, 202, 204, 219, 226, 228, 234, 245
Kim Chŏngjun, 7, 35, 50, 89, 108, 121, 143, 151
Kim Ch'ungch'an, 7
Kim Ch'unggan, 102
Kim Haenggong, 10
Kim Haenggyŏng, 160, 185, 195, 226, 279
Kim Hwasung, 98, 158
Kim Hyŏn, 7, 11, 104, 144, 156, 159
Kim Ka, 10
Kim Maeng, 184

Kim Sanggi, 192, 220, 269, 276, 290, 303, 305, 306, 310, 322
Kim Sŏnsŏk, 285, 289, 323
Kim Tan, 99, 128
Kim Tŏkpu, 193, 200, 251
Kim Ŭijin, 76, 156, 162, 185, 194
Kim Wŏnch'ung, 20, 27, 39, 73, 89, 92, 270
Kim Wŏnhwang, 139, 158, 162, 163
Kim Wŏnjŏng, 89, 101, 105, 114, 121, 127, 144, 156, 162, 166
Kim Yakchin, 130, 194, 216, 219, 220, 227, 253
Kim Yang, 161, 182, 200, 220
Kim Yanggam, 192, 194, 195, 214, 220, 226, 228, 244, 245, 253, 262, 273, 278, 279, 280, 283
Kim Yangji, 113, 162, 179
Kim Yŏnggi, 7, 12, 20, 51, 57, 73, 106
Ko Kyŏng, 251, 277, 284, 304
Ko Yŏl, 43, 58, 74, 127
Ko Yu, 134, 193
Kojong, 65, 255, 258, 313, 323
Koman island, 226
Kongju, 130
Kŭmgyo station, 145
Kŭmju, 20, 91, 125, 132
Kŭmyang county, 90
Kwak Sin, 7, 20
Kwangju, 18, 130, 140, 141, 172, 182, 283
Kwiju, 24, 98, 283
Kyŏngju. See Eastern Capital
Kyŏngju, 214
Kyŏrŭng, 75

Law and Regulation Council, 13
left granary, adjunct inspectors of, 180
lieutenant, 205, 298
lieutenant colonel, 98, 110, 209, 298
literary councilor, 303, 306, 307, 320
local administrative leader, 129

major, 58, 68
matron for housekeeping, 270
mentor to the crown prince, 161

INDEX 335

Military Affairs Ministry, 42, 170;
assistant executive of, 96, 283,
322; director of, 10, 11, 19, 20, 58,
93, 158, 163, 168, 182, 185, 195,
222, 228, 243, 244, 248, 272,
282, 304, 311; executive of, 130;
superintendent of, 185, 197, 217,
226, 244, 293, 310, 319, 321, 322;
vice director of, 76, 191, 193, 200,
205, 206, 269
Military and War Council, 46, 71,
92, 120, 145, 161, 170, 232, 298;
superintendent of, 323
Military Commission of the
Northeastern Frontier Circuit,
administrator of, 280
Military Recruitment Office, 43
Milsŏng, 20
Min Ch'angsu, 130, 200, 215
minister of education, 49, 75, 87, 112,
126, 156, 163, 195, 199, 271, 315,
322
minister of works, 23, 41, 74, 87, 121,
127, 156, 173, 195, 226, 251, 271,
283, 292, 322
Mun Chŏng, 193, 200, 219, 226, 227,
243, 244, 251, 309
Mun Han, 76, 272
Mun Hwang, 222, 228, 273, 280, 281,
283
Mun Samyŏng, 15
Mun Yangnyŏl, 92, 94, 188
Munjong, 7, 23, 64, 65, 66, 256, 257,
259, 260, 263, 265, 267, 268, 269,
271, 307
Munju, 108

Na Min, 280, 306, 341, 346
Naju, 130, 283, 285
Nanwŏn, 147, 178
National Academy, 159, 291, chancellor
of, 205, 250, 312
national history: chief editor of, 217,
283; compilers of, 37; editor of, 23,
49, 248, 279, 283, 294, 307, 310
Naval Administration Office of the
Southeastern Province, 280

Naval Administration Office of the
Southeastern Sea, 91, 156, 213
Naval Administration Office of
Wŏnhŭng Garrison, 212
No In, 157, 195, 206, 220, 226
No Tan, 178, 214, 216, 219, 227, 228,
247, 249, 273, 303
Northeastern Frontier Circuit: royal
commissioner of warehouse
inspection for, 87, 169; vice
military commissioner of, 193, 194
Northeastern Frontier District: chief
military commissioner of, 91;
military commissioner of, 31,
50, 51, 89, 94, 99, 171, 211, 213,
234, 275, 280, 306; military
commissioner of the Mobile
Headquarters of, 167; vice military
commissioner of, 76, 98, 163, 165,
166, 186, 188, 191, 200, 205, 250
Northeastern Frontier District Military
Commission: administrator of,
71, 189; chief registrar of, 92;
superintendent of 220, 306
Northern Frontier Circuit, military
commissioner of, 6;
Northwestern Frontier Circuit: military
commissioner of, 22, 24, 30, 44,
71, 168, 280, 309; vice military
commissioner of, 30, 193, 194
Northwestern Frontier District:
military commissioner of 99,
114, 208, 109, 306; vice military
commissioner of, 71, 76, 165, 190,
191, 200
Northwestern Frontier District
Military Commission:
administrator of, 163, 166,
179, 186, 188, 205, 244, 250;
superintendent of, 220, 306

Ongjin county, 20
Onsu prefecture, 252

P'ach'ŏn county, 24, 93
pacification commissioner, 169, 310
Paekchu, 307

Paengnyŏng Garrison, 95
Pak Chongdo, 76, 99
Pak Ch'ungsuk, 22
Pak Illyang, 222, 239, 246, 283, 290
Pak Sŏnggŏl, 80, 91, 108, 112, 121, 167, 264
Pak Yangdan, 189, 305
Pak Yangmyŏng 20
Pak Yuin, 44, 73
Pakchu, 24
Palace Administration: assistant executive of, 130, 152, 217; director of 7, 31, 206, 289; executive of, 7; vice director of, 25, 179, 220, 272, 282
palace censor, 7, 11, 30, 76, 102, 165, 190, 192, 218, 251
palace recipient of edicts, 160
Palace Revenues Court: director of, 97; vice director of, 30, 168, 186, 189, 225
Palace Secretariat, 18, 122; administrator of, 19, 38, 89, 123, 157, 161, 162, 219, 226, 228, 231, 249, 273, 283, 306, 309, 314, 320; commissioners of, 7, 12, 14, 20, 23, 38, 39, 70, 76, 89, 92, 98, 114, 158, 162, 163, 228, 239, 249, 273, 284, 305, 306, 309, 320; deputy administrator of, 87, 89, 105, 139, 186, 219, 226, 243, 283, 289, 290, 303, 305, 306, 309, 314; superintendent of, 245; vice commissioner of, 47, 217, 283, 289, 297
P'alchoŭm Pugok, 233
P'arŭm island, 67
P'oju Fortress, 114, 121
Pongju, 88, 172
Pongsŏng county, 126, 252
proofreader, 142
Public Works Ministry, 40, 108; assistant executive of, 152; director of, 7, 30, 38, 74, 88, 104, 122, 139, 154, 159, 166, 200, 219, 220, 224, 228, 249, 269, 275; executive of, 67; vice director of, 38, 39, 123, 143, 222, 311

Punishments Ministry, 20, 27, 47, 76, 159, 239, 269, 307, assistant executive of, 130; director of, 7, 38, 44, 51, 104, 121, 158, 206, 215, 219, 222, 274, 289, 305, 310, 320, 323; superintendent of, 92, 185, 195, 205, 228, 310; vice director of, 71, 165, 188, 217, 283
P'yŏnghae prefecture, 170
P'yŏngju, 248
P'yŏngni station, 206
P'yŏngno Garrison, 105, 168, 209

recipient of edicts, 20, 35, 50, 102, 199, 243, 246, 284
rectifier of omissions, 190, 192, 220, 227, 246, 276
regional military command, 6, 70, 109
regional military commissioner, 231
reminder, 7, 11, 43, 106, 134, 157, 220, 221, 227, 257
resident governor of the Eastern Capital, 149
resident governor of the Western Capital, 128
Revenue Ministry, 10, 172, 239, 322; administrator of branch office, 350; assistant executive of, 237; director of, 7, 80, 88, 104, 110, 121, 123, 158, 159, 166, 215, 219, 222, 228, 239, 244, 269, 272, 283, 295, 303; executive of, 31, 246, 293; superintendent of, 49, 279; vice director of, 34, 143, 194, 200, 228, 272
right granary, adjunct inspectors of, 180
Rites Ministry, 8, 107, 140, 200, assistant executive of, 153; director of, 7, 76, 87, 98, 104, 179, 219, 226, 239, 245, 247, 310; executive of, 130, 245; superintendent of, 49, 160, 215, 226; vice director of, 163, 216, 228, 239, 269, 270, 273, 295
royal commissioner of warehouse inspection, 169
Royal Guard Division: grand general of, 97; supreme general of, 105

Royal Land Office, 153
royal preceptor, 75, 132, 147, 178

Saengyang station, 110
Sakchu, 24, 133
Samch'ŏk county, 14, 104
Sangju, 18, 130, 283
Sasuk (empress), 314
scholarly counselor-in-ordinary, 7, 14, 30, 34, 35, 104, 159, 162, 185, 216, 220, 226, 249, 252, 290, 314
secretarial attendant and receptionist, 98, 99
Secretariat, 134, 139, 142, 160; director of, 160, 175, 184, 189, 239, 257, 258, 260, 270, 271, 306, 319, 322; executive of, 167, 201, 243, 253, 262, 273, 278, 284, 303, 310; vice director of, 162, 197, 219, 253, 293, 322
Secretariat drafter, 214
Secretariat–Chancellery, 147, 148; joint affairs manager of, 162, 176, 197, 219, 253, 279, 293, 322
Security Council: administrator of, 322; commissioner of, 322; deputy administrator of, 322
senior governmental advisor, 7, 15, 23, 29, 43, 73, 108, 121, 127, 144, 159, 161, 162, 170, 184, 195, 217, 219, 226, 234, 244, 246, 248, 262, 273, 279, 289, 290, 294, 305, 306, 307, 310, 314, 322
Sin Su, 188, 220
Sinhŭng storehouse, 290
Slave Bureau, assistant executive of, 152, 218
Sŏ Chŏng, 179, 290, 304, 306, 307, 310
Sŏ Kyŏngŭi, 77
Sŏ Nul, 24, 43, 46
So T'aebo, 274, 276, 304, 305, 306, 310, 314, 321, 322
Sŏ Tan, 98, 99
Sŏgok county, 55
Son Kwan, 190, 304, 309, 320, 322
Sŏndŏk Garrison, 315
Song Tŏgyŏn, 250, 251

Sŏngjong, 286
Sŏngju, 165
Sŏnjong, 90 127, 181, 224, 257, 258, 260, 314, 316, 320, 324
Sŏnju, 11, 287
Sŏnsan island, 308
Southern Capital, 189
State Affairs Department: director of, 105, 106, 173, 239, 260; eminent director of state affairs, 163, 195; executive of, 20; office chief of, 10, 20, 27, 37, 166, 190, 191, 192, 194, 195, 219, 273; vice director of, 9, 11, 14, 16, 23, 37, 38, 43, 53, 57, 62, 68, 73, 74, 75, 88, 89, 90, 96, 102, 103, 105, 112, 121, 127, 139, 144, 145, 146, 158, 159, 161, 162, 179, 189, 191, 195, 200, 216, 217, 219, 220, 249, 251, 253, 273, 282, 293, 303, 304, 307, 310, 314, 321, 322
State Finance Commission, 101, 165; commissioner of, 11, 290; superintendent of, 167, 320; vice commissioner of, 71, 76
state preceptor, 75, 147, 185
subcolonel, 58
Suju, 182
Sukchong, 114, 173, 224, 271, 304, 315, 322, 323
Sunjong, 80 111, 119, 138, 177, 255, 256, 260, 261, 263, 264, 265, 266, 269, 270, 324
supervising secretary, 10, 12, 69, 113, 199
supreme general, 68, 110, 154, 304

Tae Yŏllim, 10
Taegu county, 192
T'aejo, 26, 41, 42, 46, 65, 116, 122, 124, 125, 272, 278
T'aeju, 24
T'amna, 6, 21, 56, 91, 107, 134, 149, 163, 164, 166, 186, 232, 238, 285, 305
T'angna. See T'amna
Tea Ritual Office, 80
Tŏkchong, 5, 6, 21, 31, 65, 122, 255, 274

Tŏksu county, 127
Tongjin guard post, 14
Tongju, 182
T'osan county, 83
Towŏn, 182

U Wŏllyŏng, 227
Ŭich'ŏn, 178, 268
Ŭiju, 287
Ŭn Chŏng, 153, 199
Unam county, 89
Unhŭng granary, 180; adjunct inspectors of, 180

vice commissioner for pacification, 96
vice defense commissioner, 71
vice director of imperial regalia, 250, 272, 282

Wang Ch'ongji, 38, 76, 87, 108, 112, 142, 156, 162, 184, 239, 271
Wang Chŭng. *See* Sŏnjong
Wang Hu. *See* Ŭich'ŏn
Wang Hŭi. *See* Sukchong
Wang Hŭm. *See* Tŏkchong
Wang Hun. *See* Sunjong
Wang Hwi. *See* Munjong
Wang Hyu. *See* Sunjong
Wang Ibo, 30, 110, 143, 167
Wang Kado, 65
Wang Kae, 106, 164
Wang Ki. *See* Sŏnjong
Wang Ki, 7, 23, 87, 160, 191
Wang Kungmo, 272, 304, 319, 321, 322, 323
Wang Musung, 102, 139, 158, 161, 167, 185, 197, 198
Wang Ong. *See* Sukchong
Wang Pi, 224, 271, 306
Wang Sŏ. *See* Munjong
Wang Sŏk, 222, 244, 253, 262, 273, 278
Wang Su, 195, 214, 239, 271, 304, 315, 320
Wang To, 163, 224, 271, 315
Wang Uk. *See* Hŏnjong
Wang Ŭm, 224, 271, 275
Wang Un. *See* Sŏnjong

Wang Yu, 271, 315
Water Control Court, director of, 71, 79, 88, 181, 280
Weaponry Directorate: executive of, 126; vice director of, 19
Western Capital, 6, 22, 43, 70, 109, 110, 111, 128, 142, 143, 154, 211, 231, 243, 247, 275, 276, 280, 282, 308; administrator of, 282; commissioner of, 15, 23, 110, 162, 167, 216, 226, 279, 307; deputy resident governor of, 35, 168, 282,
Western Regional Military Command, 100, 109, 182, 310; commander in, 151
Wi Chŏng, 41, 88
Wi Kyejŏng, 276, 295
Wiwŏn Garrison, 24
Wŏn T'aejin, 14
Wŏn Yŏng, 30, 38
Wŏnhŭng Garrison, 57
Wŏnhye (dowager empress), 66

Yang Chin, 37
Yang island, 67
Yang Kam, 87, 93
Yang Sillin, 152, 227, 251
Yang Taech'un, 30, 71
Yangju, 182
Yejong, 323
Yi An, 283, 289, 304
Yi Chain, 249, 261, 269, 276, 289, 297
Yi Chakch'ung, 7, 14, 20, 29, 49
Yi Chaŭi, 292, 295, 298, 314, 320, 321, 322
Yi Chawi, 222, 245, 251, 273, 280, 281, 283, 293, 307, 308, 314
Yi Chayŏn, 12, 38, 47, 73, 87, 92, 101, 108, 113, 121, 127, 142, 271
Yi Chehyŏn, 65, 255, 258, 313, 324
Yi Chingmang, 186, 191, 205, 216, 217, 246
Yi Chŏng, 185, 216, 219, 220, 225
Yi Chŏnggong, 153, 156, 192, 219, 222, 248, 251, 253, 262, 272
Yi Ch'onghyŏn, 181, 200
Yi Chujwa, 14, 38

Yi Chun, 140, 220
Yi Hoe, 11, 38, 57
Yi Hwang, 166
Yi Injŏng, 39, 63, 71, 89, 102
Yi Kong, 11, 16
Yi Sŏk, 205, 224
Yi Sŏnggong, 31
Yi Sŏngmi, 152, 212
Yi Suhwa, 10, 76, 96
Yi T'aeksŏng, 88
Yi Tan, 8, 80
Yi Tanggam, 219, 225
Yi Tŭngno, 123, 165
Yi Ŭi, 243, 245, 249, 252
Yi Ŭngbo, 14, 68, 73
Yi Ye, 270, 283, 306, 310, 320
Yi Yŏnggan, 37, 49, 104, 105
Yi Yubaek, 87, 88
Yi Yuch'ung, 139, 157, 158, 162, 167, 170, 195, 198, 201
Yi Yudo, 11
Yi Yujŏk, 130, 152, 161, 165
Yi Yuryang, 44
Yŏl island, 94
Yŏlsan county, 47, 93, 94
Yŏm Han, 212, 243, 244, 248
Yŏmju, 145
Yŏngam prefecture, 149
Yŏngdŏk Garrison, 10
Yŏnggwang prefecture, 223
Yŏngju (region), 249
Yongju, 108
Yongmun granary, adjunct inspectors of, 180
Yongsin (dowager queen), 82
Yŏngwŏn Garrison, 60
Yŏnp'yŏng island, 310
Yŏnsŏng prefecture, 88
Yu Ch'am, 44, 149
Yu Ch'ang, 7, 38, 39
Yu Chingp'il, 15, 23, 36, 47
Yu Chisŏng, 7
Yu Hong, 199, 206, 217, 219, 231, 239, 240, 241, 242, 245, 249, 262, 273, 278, 280, 283, 284, 292, 293, 304
Yu Kŭmp'il, 122
Yu Kyo, 10, 58
Yu Paegin, 37
Yu Pang, 18, 27
Yu Sin, 282, 311
Yu So, 14, 27
Yu Sŏk, 275, 282, 303, 306, 309, 310, 314, 320, 322
Yu Tŭkso, 72, 220
Yu Un, 7